A History of The Foster's Oval

A History of The Foster's Oval

NICK YAPP

PELHAM BOOKS
Stephen Greene Press

PELHAM BOOKS/Stephen Greene Press

Published by the Penguin Group
27 Wrights Lane, London W8 5TZ, England
Viking Penguin Inc., 40 West 23rd Street, New York, New York 10010, USA
The Stephen Greene Press Inc., 15 Muzzey Street, Lexington, Massachusetts 02173, USA
Penguin Books Australia Ltd, Ringwood, Victoria, Australia
Penguin Books Canada Ltd, 2801 John Street, Markham, Ontario, Canada L3R 1B4
Penguin Books (NZ) Ltd, 182–190 Wairau Road, Auckland 10, New Zealand

Penguin Books Ltd, Registered Offices: Harmondsworth, Middlesex, England

First published 1990

Typeset in Linotron 10/12½pt Concorde by
Goodfellow & Egan Ltd, Cambridge
Printed and bound in Great Britain by
Butler and Tanner Ltd, Frome, Somerset

A CIP catalogue record for this book is available from the British Library.

ISBN 0 7207 1925 9

Contents

PART THREE

Foreword

by Michael Reynolds,
Foster's Executive Director of Public Affairs

Foster's sponsorship of that venerable old cricket ground, The Foster's Oval, while at first sight a very radical and revolutionary arrangement, is in fact a completely natural association between a company with very strong links with cricket and an institution that desperately needed support.

In the last 10 years the realities and implications of an organisation like The Oval trying single-handedly to maintain its ageing fabric in the face of stringent financial constraints, became ever more apparent.

And the threat was clear: that The Oval would be lost, even as a county ground.

That couldn't be allowed to happen. All the history of the first UK Test Match in 1880, Surrey's great traditions and successes, Sir Len Hutton's 364 in 1938 and a host of other great sporting occasions was a heritage worth retaining.

At the same time, Foster's had a tradition of heavy involvement in cricket – both in Britain and Australia – so what could be more natural than bringing the two together?

The result was funds for the redevelopment of the west side of the ground with the construction of a new stand and a multi-purpose sports centre to be named after Ken Barrington, as well as the renovation and maintenance of existing stands and buildings.

But the most important result of all was that the future of The Foster's Oval was now secure.

In this fine book, Nick Yapp chronicles all the history and heritage of one of the world's most famous sporting venues, from its beginnings, through almost 150 years of glory and excitement – but, fortunately, not to its end.

The Foster's Oval and Surrey County Cricket Club can now look forward to the future with confidence – and here's to the next 150 years!

Preface

by Bob Willis

My first memory of The Foster's Oval, as it is now known, came during one of the most famous Tests at the ground. It was 1968, and England's supporters and players were desperately hoping that the ground would dry out sufficiently quickly so that Derek Underwood could weave his deadly magic on the Australians. The rest, as they say, is history. Except that a shy, gangling lad had turned up for a lift to go and play his first game for Surrey Seconds that day.

Kenny Barrington, who was still an England player, invited me into the England dressing-room and also for a bite to eat with them at lunchtime. It was a typically kind gesture from Kenny and we were great friends after that until his untimely death in 1981. How fitting that The Foster's Oval will soon have a memorial to this great man of Surrey cricket.

The Oval saw my first-class début in 1969 – against Scotland. Hardly a memorable encounter, but it was good enough for me. I made friendships there in those early days that will last a lifetime, with men like Jim Cumbes, Dudley Owen-Thomas, Geoff Howarth and Robin Jackman. In fact, there are so many great names from Surrey cricket who have been of invaluable help to me.

Arthur McIntyre, that fine wicket-keeper, was the first to spot my potential and he picked me for Surrey Schools against Surrey Colts. Alec Bedser was always a fount of commonsense and advice as England selector and it was John Edrich who was directly responsible for getting me on my first England tour in 1970/71. John knew I could bowl fast, even though I was erratic, and for him that was enough. The Oval and its great names have been good to me.

Now that I am retired, busily convincing myself that there are no current players as good as in my day (now where have I heard that before?), I am in a better position to appreciate the need to maintain traditions in cricket. What a tragic loss The Oval would have been. After all, it was the ground where the legend of The Ashes was born.

Thanks to the generous support of Foster's, the future of The Oval is assured and as we move into the brave new world of the Foster's Oval, there is no doubt in my mind that those traditional elements that have made it such a world-class cricket ground will live on.

Acknowledgements

Everyone to whom I turned has been extremely helpful in the preparation of this book. At the Surrey County Record Office in Kingston-on-Thames, the staff always had the right documents available at the right time, and carted the enormous Minute Books of the SCCC to and fro uncomplainingly. At the Oval, my every wish (save that of actually being allowed to play for Surrey) was met, and I should like especially to thank Derek Newton, David Seward, Mark Newton, Peter Large, Harry Brind, Steve and Andrew Howes, and Bill Norman for their time, patience, information and expertise. I should also like to thank Ian Scott-Browne and Geoffrey Howard for their valuable contribution in reading the typescript.

And I shall be forever grateful to my agent, Patricia Robertson, and my publisher, Roger Houghton, for conjuring up what has been the most enjoyable piece of work I've ever had to do.

The author and the publishers gratefully acknowledge the assistance of Foster's and of The Surrey County Cricket Club in the researching and the writing of this book.

Sweet Kennington Oval, I'd stand without rest
From eleven to seven, and think myself blest
In the rear of the crowd to get peeps at the crease,
While the popular bats make a hundred apiece.

CRICKETY CRICKET – DOUGLAS MOFFAT 1897

A History of The Foster's Oval

PART 1

21st July 1955. In the distance, the hills of Camberwell. © *Hulton-Deutsch Collection*

Chapter One

'. . . A Parcel of Ground In A Certain Oval . . .'

If you cycle from the Hobbs gates at Foster's Oval, in any direction, you go a fair way before your leg muscles are really tested. To the west, the first slope is to be found at Vauxhall Bridge – other than that you may proceed to Hyde Park before dropping a gear; to the east, the first hill is to be found at Camberwell; and, to the north, you may cross the river at Waterloo Bridge and proceed beyond Euston to Camden Town before the pedalling gets tough. Only to the south, going towards Clapham Common, is there any problem, and that not for a mile or more.

Kennington is flat. It is said that, in the days long before there was such a thing as cricket, it was part of a wide bay that extended from the hills of Camberwell in the east to the hills of Clapham in the west. Certainly, it was part of the wide Thames basin. As that river narrowed, people settled on its fertile shores. The Romans are believed to have drained the land, and they built a road that passed through Kennington on its way to Canterbury. In Saxon times, the area was dominated by one Brixi, 'a Saxon proprietor in these parts', according to J. Allen's *History of Lambeth*, published in 1826. Brixi gave his name to Brixton, just up the road from Kennington, but Kennington meant, originally, King's Town, and antiquarians and historians tell us that there was for many hundreds of years a royal residence less than half a mile from the present Oval.

In 1016, Canute sailed up the Thames in an attempt to capture London and, to avoid fortifications near London Bridge, widened a ditch running south of the river and thereby ingeniously sailed through Newington Butts (it probably took him less time than it does today by car) and on to Kennington, passing very near the Oval. Hardicanute lived and died not far away. In the Domesday Book, Kennington is called 'Chenintune', and Teodoric the Goldsmith held it of King Edward the Confessor for five hides. It was worth three pounds.

The old manor house of Kennington is supposed to have stood a little east of the Wandsworth Road, and the demesne lands of the manor changed hands, or, more accurately, changed families, many times. Some families failed to produce heirs, and the land reverted to the Crown. Other families behaved less than wisely in political terms, and the land was forfeited to the Crown. In 1337, on the eve of the Hundred Years' War, when cricket was 'cricce', a rough game played in rough fields by rough monks, Edward III granted the manors of Kennington and Vauxhall, then tiny settlements to the south west of London, to Edward, Earl of Chester and Duke of Cornwall, commonly known as the Black Prince. Geoffrey Chaucer was made Clerk of Works to the Manor of Kennington in 1389, for which, with several other charges, he received two shillings a day.

The old palace was pulled down by Henry VIII to supply material for the completion and adaptation of Whitehall shortly after Wolsey's disgrace in 1530, but the land has been owned by the Duchy of Cornwall ever since, and the most famous part has, for nearly a hundred and fifty years, been the most lovable, if not the most beautiful, of cricket grounds.

Early in the seventeenth century, a survey was made of the Manor of Kennington. What is now the Oval, was part of a close, or enclosure, of some 38 acres, bounded by Kennington Common, Vauxhall Creek and other enclosures belonging to John Groome, Edward Carpenter and William Cockerman. The site of the Oval itself was leased successively to Richard Salter, Mrs Marie Coxe and George Coxe. By 1667, the lessees were John Morrice and Robert Clayton, who built a brick wall on or near the site of the present Oval, against which to grow fruit. The soil must have been good. William Malcolm, who had a sub-lease from the Clayton family in the middle of the eighteenth century, was required to pay not only money rent, but to provide 'one hundred of Asparagus in the month of January every Year', which must have required extremely good husbandry.

It was not the most salubrious of neighbourhoods. Nearby was Spring Gardens, a place of entertainment, where Samuel Pepys was shocked by the behaviour of certain young blades. Kennington Common was the site of public executions, including some of the Jacobite rebels in 1745; St Marks Church was built on the very spot where the gallows stood. It was also an area much frequented by itinerant preachers, who, we are told by Allen, 'received a lively welcome' from what may well have been the ancestors of the lively Oval crowds of the 1920s and 1930s.

Under an Act of Parliament of 1622 (21 Jas 1 c29 private), leases of the Duchy of Cornwall lands could be granted for a maximum of three lives or 31 years, but one family maintained their interest in the Oval site from 1661 until 1834. This was the Clayton family. In 1776, Sir William Clayton obtained an Act of Parliament to enable him to grant building leases of a considerable area of Kennington, and it was about this time that the distinctive 'oval' shaped piece of land was formed when Clayton built a roadway round it.

The tenement was subsequently divided, like Gaul, into three. In Hodskinson and Middleton's Survey of the Manor in 1785, there is a plan of the Oval showing it to be divided further, into six plots, with a pond where the West Terraces now stand, and all part of the demesne of William Clayton. The Claytons were an important family – Clayton Street, which runs from roughly deep long on if the bowling is at the Pavilion end, was named after them. They were not, however, local, but came from Harleyford in Buckinghamshire (hence the Harleyford Road – long off to deep third man with the bowling at the Pavilion End), and in 1785, the land itself was occupied by James and George Middleton, who were market gardeners and nurserymen.

In the Surrey Record Office at Kingston-on-Thames, there is what must have been a second lease to the Middletons, dated 29th June 1790. Reference is made to an earlier lease of 1777 by which Clayton had reserved to his own use 'a certain Blank piece or parcel of Ground intended to be left void in a certain Oval'. It is the earliest reference to an 'Oval'. By the lease of 1790, Clayton leased for sixty four and a half years 'all that piece or parcel of land situate lying and being in Kennington aforesaid and called the Oval containing by estimation 10 acres and a quarter of an acre . . . together with the dwelling houses and other buildings thereon erected'. The rent was fifty one pounds per annum of 'lawful money of Great Britain', possibly a great deal easier to come by than one hundred of Asparagus.

Under the terms of the lease, the Mitchelsons were to build a brick dwelling house of the first, second or third rate of building, as per the Act of 1773, which was to be inspected by Charles Alexander Craig of Scotland Yard in the County of Middlesex. The dwelling house was to be 'fronting or opposite the street intended to be made leading from the said Oval towards Kennington Common', which means on the south, or Pavilion, side. The Mitchelsons were also to insure this building. For their part, the lessors were to make a forty foot wide road from the north end of the Oval (now known as the Vauxhall End) to the 'high road to Westminster Bridge Road', and another road from the south end to the 'highway leading to Clapham'. The Oval itself was to be enclosed with 'open iron or wood palisade fence or live growing hedge'.

There were also trade restrictions: the 'piece or parcel of land' was not to be used for the purposes of 'Melting Tallow Chandler Soap Boiler Distiller Sugar baker Brewer Public house Smith or Butcher or Keeping Slaughterhouse Furnace or Cooks or Oil Shop or use any Forge or oil or other noisome or offensive trade'. Nothing was said about a cricket ground.

The area developed. In 1816, Vauxhall Bridge was opened and Harleyford Road and Camberwell New Street were built. A Turnpike Map of the early nineteenth century shows turnpikes to the north and south of the Oval, in Harleyford Road, Harleyford Street and Camberwell New Road. There was little housing development before this, and market gardening and dairy farming were both very profitable. Allen's *History of Lambeth* contains the following description of the area: 'These schools (the Parochial Schools for the Kennington District) are on the left hand side of the road, going from Vauxhall to Camberwell; and adjoining the Oval, a beautiful nursery ground of an oval form, from whence it takes its name, the owner of which, a Mr Mitchelson, lately died of an advanced age of nearly one hundred years, and who from his very long proprietorship here, was a sort of living chronicle of the former state of the neighbourhood. The spot is particularly delightful, the sides of the road, for some distance, being formed by this nursery ground, and a fine plantation laid out to resemble a park; as also a half dozen or more charming little villas. The whole of this ground, and beyond, from South Lambeth to Vauxhall and Kennington Lane, formed the park of Sir Noel Caren (sometimes referred to as 'Caron'), the Dutch Ambassador.' Allen goes on to say that the neighbouring Kennington Common, now Kennington Park, during the summer season 'is much frequented by cricketers, for whom ample accommodation is made by the landlord of the Horn Tavern'. More, much more of them later.

The Times first mentions Kennington Oval on 18th May 1818. It is not a happy report, dwelling as it does on the aftermath of a flooding of the creek that ran alongside the Oval. 'Yesterday, about 3 o'clock, the body of another man was found drowned in the creek near Kennington Oval, within a hundred yards of the place where the body of Mr Tinkler, late landlord of the 'White Horse', Brixton Hill, was found. The body was carried to the 'Clayton Arms' in Clayton Street, where the other body lay, and was shortly afterwards recognised to be a porter in the employ of a shopkeeper in the neighbourhood, who, it is supposed, was drowned in the creek as he was returning home to his employer with a truck full of empty bottles. The truck was found next morning shattered to pieces and all the bottles broken. Amongst the many sufferers from the flood, we have to notice Mr Perry, the brewer, Mr Fenton, a brickmaker, and Mr Martin, a market gardener, who has lost to the amount of £100, all his garden being flooded.' 'Mr Martin' was a local resident, who lived at the corner of Bowling Green Street, and who was a well known 'fighting man' of the time, by which was meant a pugilist rather than a brawler.

On 31st August 1826, the remainder of the term of the Clayton lease was assigned by the trustees and executors of the late James Mitchelson to the Rev. William Otter, minister of St Mark's, Lambeth, the Oval's parish church. The rent was still £51 per year, but £1299.13s.11d. was paid for the stock and crops of 'that Messuage or Tenement situate standing and being in the Oval at Kennington in the parish of St Mark's Lambeth in the County of Surrey . . . commonly called or known by the name of the Oval.'

The Mitchelsons had obviously fulfilled their responsibility to enclose the Oval, for, in a counterpart lease of 1827, there is a clause to paint the iron fence in 'oil'. The land was now part nursery ground and part pasture, and the rent had been increased to £130 per annum. On the south (Pavilion) side of the Oval was a messuage or tenement (i.e. a dwelling) ' . . . together with a garden in front of the said messuage and now enclosed by two hedges . . .' The dwelling house was occupied by Elisa Pryce, widow.

The Clayton interest in the property lapsed in 1834, and on 8th January 1835, William Otter was granted a head lease of the property by the Duchy for 99 years. The church of which he was minister was, indeed still is, a fine, imposing building. The reason why Otter purchased the lease of the Oval was to provide a site for a similarly imposing minister's house, and, by developing the rest of the site, to provide an endowment for the living.

Otter's plans were laid before the Prince's Council of the Duchy. One of the members of the Council, Lord Bexley, proposed a 'General Idea of Improvement'. Bexley's idea was to 'Inclose an Oval of an Acre or an Acre and a half in the Centre, and plant it with Lime Trees, to form an open Grove, with Gravel Walks round and across it, under the Trees'. It would have been a semi-formal pleasure garden, but a Gravel Walk makes a poor wicket: hard for a fast bowler to get any sort of lift, and of little encouragement to a spin bowler, so it is as well that Lord Bexley's scheme came to naught. The remainder of the Oval site would have been divided into 21 lots, one for the minister's house and the remainder for cottage villas, 'of a general similarity, tho' not exact uniformity of appearance'. Negotiations over the minister's house lapsed, and the plan was forgotten.

The Rev. Otter was, therefore, left with the lease and a nursery ground that was proving unprofitable. The following year, he petitioned the Duchy with a request for a building lease. 'The market gardens in the immediate vicinity of London have gradually declined in value'. Reasons for this are not clear: it may be that the development of the railway system was already beginning to affect the use of land, by bringing produce to the capital quickly and freshly from land where it could be far more cheaply grown. It is also possible that market gardening was simply less profitable relatively when compared with the financial gains that could be made by developing the land. In any event, opinion in the Duchy was divided. James Bailey, the surveyor, was against the idea, advising that the value of the surrounding property would be greatly decreased if the Oval was developed. The Oval afforded 'not only the advantage of a large, open space, for the free circulation of air; but also, a pleasant and agreeable object . . . to look upon'.

Bailey had other plans for the site. He proposed a road running across the Oval from south east to north west (long off to deep third man with the bowling from the pavilion end), flanked by six pairs of houses. Round the Oval 'ring road' were to be other pairs of houses facing outwards. The debate continued over the next four years. A road was to be built running from north east to south west. More pairs of houses were to be built. Otter died, but negotiations continued with his Trustees. And then, in 1845, came the formation of the Surrey County Cricket Club and its betrothal to the Oval. Before discussing the wedding and the marriage, however, it may be appropriate to examine the suitor's background.

The earliest known reference to cricket in Surrey is in a document relating to a dispute over a plot of land in Guildford in 1598 and chronicled in Russell's *History of Guildford*, 'Anno 40 Eliz 1598 John Derrick, Gent, one of the Queen's Majesties Coroners of the County of Surrey aged 59 saith this land before mentioned let to John Parrish Innholder deceased that he knew it for fifty years or more. It lay waste and was used and occupied by the inhabitants of Guildford to saw timber in and for Sawpits and for makinge of frames of timber for the said inhabitants. When he was a scholler of the Free School of Guildford he and several of his fellows did run and play here at Crickett and other plaies and also that the same was used for baiting of bears in the said time until the said John Parrish did inclose the said Parcell of land.' By 1700, Surrey cricket had moved appreciably nearer to London. The *'Post Boy'* of March of that year contained the following advertisement:

> 'These are to inform Gentlemen or others, who delight in cricket-playing, that a Match at Cricket, of 10 Gentlemen on each side, will be played on Clapham Common, near Fox Hall, on Easter Monday next, for £10 a head a game, (five being defign'd) and £20 the odd one.'

At the same time, cricket was being played on both Walworth and Kennington Commons. By the middle of the eighteenth century, Frederick Louis, Prince of Wales, was taking an interested and active part in Surrey cricket. It is said that he even selected the Surrey eleven, but in 1751, he was killed by a blow from a cricket ball. During the next twenty years, cricket was certainly played in Richmond, Kingston, Croydon, Chertsey and elsewhere in Surrey, and, by the turn of the century, a county identity seems to have emerged. There was a county eleven in the first three decades of the nineteenth century (it included Tom Hayward's grandfather) but it ceased to exist in 1830.

The direct predecessor of the Surrey Club was the Montpelier Club, formed in 1840, who played on the grounds of the Bee Hive Tavern in Walworth. In 1844, they lost this ground when it was purchased and required for building. The Treasurer of the Montpelier Club was Mr William Baker, who had a more famous friend in cricketing circles, William Ward, M.P. for the City of London and a director of the Bank of England. Most significantly, Ward was the man who, some twenty years earlier, had bought Thomas Lord's interest in that other London cricket ground for £5000, and had thereby saved it from building development which would have limited the playing area to far less than the present 'square'. Ward was himself a great cricketer: his 278 for the Marlybone Club against Norfolk at Lords in 1820 remained the record score on that ground until Percy Holmes made 315 not out for Yorkshire against Middlesex in 1925.

Baker and Ward approached the Otter Trustees. In March 1845, the Trustees duly reported to the Duchy that they were 'desirous of letting it (the Oval) to a Gentleman who proposes to convert it into a Subscription Cricket Ground'. The new lessee was to be William Houghton of Brixton Hill, President of the Montpelier Club, and the dowry was to be a rent of one hundred and twenty pounds per annum, with another £20 in taxes, for a lease of 31 years.

Conversion of the Oval from market garden to cricket ground was rapid. The lease was signed on 10th March 1845. The first cricket match appears to have

In the days when the Mitchelsons grew their vegetables on the Oval. Cricket on Kennington Common, about 1840. © *Hulton-Deutsch Collection*

been played in May. In the intervening two months, the land had to be cleared and laid with ten thousand turfs, the contract going to Mr M. Turtle of 6, Clapham Road (opposite St Mark's Church) and costing £300. The turfs came from Tooting Common. There is some difference of opinion as to the state of the land. Most sources agree that there was some kind of farmhouse in front and slightly to the east of the present Pavilion. In *Surrey Cricket*, by Lord Alvestone and C.W. Alcock, respectively President and Secretary of Surrey CCC at the turn of the century, mention is made of the remains or foundations of an old wall. Alverstone and Alcock quote Allen's *History of Lambeth*: 'Caron House, a noble residence with a large park adjoining, built by Sir Noel Caron, the Dutch Ambassador to the Court of England for twenty-eight years in the reign of Elizabeth and James I . . . had a large park for deer which extended to

Vauxhall and Kennington. A great part of the walls surrounding this park still exist, particularly one piece across Kennington Oval'. Other authorities make no mention of this wall, but there was work enough to be done. Documents relating to the Kennington Demesne describe the land as being 'in a most ruinous condition and from the effluvium arising from decayed vegetables a nuisance and a source of ill-health'.

Meanwhile, great strides were being taken in the formation of the Surrey Club. For some time, the problem of setting up such a club had been the absence of a suitable ground, but on 30th August 1845, a second meeting took place at the Horns Tavern, which was reported in detail in the *Sunday Times*.

'FORMATION OF A SURREY CLUB'

. . . that obstacle (lack of ground) was now, however, happily removed by the appropriation of the Kennington Oval to the purposes of cricket (cheers). A finer ground than the Oval would make in another year it would be impossible to find (Hear, hear). It was indeed admitted by all who had seen it to be in every respect worthy, as well as fitted for, the occupation of a county club. No sooner had he mentioned that there was such a ground, coupled with the fact that it was accessible by omnibus or by steam from all parts of the metropolis, in about a twenty minutes' ride, and that he thought there was, consequently, a good opportunity for the formation of the long talked-of "county club" than Mr Ponsonby instantly expressed his desire and readiness to assist in the work (cheers). The first public step towards the attainment of the sought-for end had been the match which had just terminated (Gentlemen of the County of Surrey v Players of the County of Surrey) . . . After a variety of other toasts had been proposed by the Chairman, amongst which were "Mr Felix and the Bat" – "Mr Denison and Slow Bowling" – and "Success to Mr Houghton and his new ground", the parties separated.'

Two months later, on 19th October 1845, there was a further meeting at the Horns Tavern, 'for the purpose of receiving a communication from the committee of the newly formed "county" club . . .' In the early part of the afternoon, prior to the meeting, about twenty five of the members had assembled on the Oval and 'had a hit'. 'The ground was in very beautiful order'. The meeting ended in good spirits: 'Mr Denison, at the request of many gentlemen, sang a song entitled "The Fine Old English Cricketer" written by F.T. Finch Esq. of the Blackheath Club'. The song ran to eight verses and eight choruses.

The Officers of the Club were W. Strahan, Esq. of Ashurst, Dorking (President), the Hon. F. Ponsonby (Vice President), William Houghton, Esq. (Treasurer), and William Denison, Esq. (Honorary Secretary). In March 1846, the officers and the committee approved a circular to be sent to potential members:

SIR,

The County of Surrey for many years held a high position in the "Cricket" world, and was distinguished for having vanquished the most powerful "Elevens" which could be brought against its own by the other Counties of England. The ordinary casualties of life, however, as time progressed, tended to a severance of that strength, which in respect to a "County's" play, must be concentrated and in reference to the support and maintenance of the "Noble Game" must be held together.

To restore the "County" to its former role in a Cricketing sense, the "Surrey Club" has been founded.

The objects of the Committee will be to seek out, and bring together, the "Cricketing" talent, which for several years has been spread about the County to play Matches of importance, not only upon their own ground, (the Oval, Kennington), but in different parts of Surrey, and to engage the best Bowlers the County will afford, to be in attendance at the "Oval" for the practice of the Members of the Club.

I am requested therefore by the Committee, to solicit your aid and support in the undertaking, and to add that they will be happy to receive your authority to propose you as a member of the "Surrey Club".

I have the honour to remain,

Sir,

Your obedient servant,

WILLIAM DENISON, Hon. Sec.

Denison has been described as the father of daily newspaper cricket reporting. He was a freelance writer and a very hard worker – he claimed that he existed on an average of less than four hours' sleep a night. In the late 1830s and the 1840s, he was responsible for many of the cricket reports in *The Times*, and from 1843 to 1846, he compiled his own cricket annual. He occasionally played for Surrey, but was strongly opposed to the adoption of round-arm bowling, considering it inaccurate, unscientific, 'throwing, pure and simple', and dangerous. He died in 1856, at the age of fifty five.

Despite the good wishes of the Surrey Club and the toasts pledged to his success, Houghton's connection with the Oval was not a happy one. He was a chemist by trade, and, perhaps not surprisingly, his interest in the Oval, and its rotting vegetation, waned almost from the moment he became lessee. The turfs were laid, but the fortunes of the Montpelier Club began to decline. The ground itself was a popular venue, but Houghton got into financial difficulties. Further, in June 1847, at a meeting of the Surrey Club at the Oval, it was stated that several complaints had been made (following a wet day) as to the state of the ground. As late as 1854 there was some discussion as to whether to dissolve the Club.

The future of the Oval was by no means assured.

Chapter Two

'... Some of the Best Wickets in the World ...'

In the next thirty years (1850 to 1880), the modern game of cricket was established. It was a period that saw the creation of a County Championship, the imposition of the Rule of Law from the MCC at Lords, the emergence of overarm bowling, great improvements in batting technique, and the budding and flowering of William Gilbert Grace.

The very names of the players suggest two sides of a watershed. When the North played the South on 17th July 1850, the scorecard listed Caffyn, Felix, Mynn, John Lillywhite; the Lords Bathurst, Burghley and Guernsey; Parr, Clarke and John Wisden, who, that memorable day, clean bowled ten of the South in their second innings. 'Young Wisden,' recorded *The Times*, 'will be found to have taken vast liberties for he dispersed 10 of the wickets ... And so the South were vanquished in one innings by 19 runs.' The very language of the report seems archaic: '... vanquished in one innings for 19 runs' means, in modern translation, 'lost by an innings and 19 runs'. It was an age of top-hatted cricketers, of mighty men who took off their jackets and rolled up their sleeves to play – there was no need of a dressing-room.

Twenty nine years later, on 3rd and 4th June 1879, the same two teams reveal a new generation of cricketers: Hornby, Ulyett, Arthur Shrewsbury, Alfred Shaw, Lord Harris, and, of course, W.G. himself – not a top hat to be seen. We have averages, County Champions, statistics, tours, and, the following year, we have the first ever Test Match on English soil, between England and Australia at Kennington Oval.

As far as the Surrey County Cricket Club and the Oval were concerned, however, these were not easy years. A start had been made, a Club had been formed, and George Brockwell and William Martingell had been engaged as professional bowlers. Martingell, a former shoemaker and gamekeeper, was a bowler of unusual excellence, according to contemporaries, 'with a strong curl from leg.' On 29th April 1846, Denison reported that four boys had been engaged to attend on each practice day for the members' benefit; that the Committee had also ordered a catapulter for use of the members; that the requisite number of stumps had been ordered of Page of Kennington; and that as there was no ballmaker in Surrey, they had given directions for an equal number of balls to be purchased of Duke and Dark.

Four early Surrey cricketers. From the left: T. Sherman, Julius Caesar, W. Caffyn and
T. Lockyer. Coloured lithograph after J. C. Anderson, 1852.

Cricket was most decidedly under way, but the Club's tenure of the ground
was by no means secure, and Houghton, who held the lease, can hardly be said
to have had his heart in cricket. There were frequent disagreements and ructions
between Houghton and the Club (of which he was Treasurer), many of them
concerning other uses of the Oval. Houghton was a poor financial manager, and
it wasn't long before he was in pecuniary difficulties. He hoped to make money
from the sale of refreshments at the Oval, but his licence to do so had to be
renewed annually. Meanwhile, he staged walking matches of 'far from good
class', poultry shows and other events 'certainly not calculated to improve the
character of the ground'.

Then, as so often since, the Club was fortunate to have an ally in the Duchy of
Cornwall. The Duchy had an interest in the entire neighbourhood, and stepped
in to prevent some of Houghton's more ambitious and less desirable pro-
motions. In 1851, he was refused permission to stage a walking match and other
amusements. The Easter Poultry Show of 1852 was prohibited. Houghton's
application for a refreshment licence in March 1853 was rejected. The situation
was, however, a complicated one. The character of the neighbourhood was
being preserved, but Houghton's finances weren't, and, to some extent, on them
depended the future of the Surrey Club.

Worse, a threat to the continued use of the Oval as a cricket ground now came
from within the Duchy of Cornwall itself. In 1851, a Bill was being prepared by
the solicitor to the Duchy to enable the Duchy to build two 'half crescents' over
its area. The then Prince of Wales (later Edward VII) was only ten years old, a
minor, and Albert, Prince Consort, was acting on the young prince's behalf.

With a surprising appreciation of the sacredness of cricket for a man of German origin, Albert stayed the hand of the Duchy's solicitor. The Bill was not promoted, 'so that London has good reason to be grateful to him (Albert) that it did not lose one of the few spaces it has for the purposes of recreation'.

John Burrup, Secretary at the Oval from 1848 to 1855. *From the Oval Collection.*

By this time, John Burrup had succeeded William Denison as Honorary Secretary, and he began to put pressure on Houghton, persuading the Committee to pass a resolution declaring that no further matches should be played at the Oval, the first appearance of boycott at the ground. To hammer home the point, the Committee leased another ground, near Coldharbour Lane, Brixton, scarcely a mile away. With the Duchy refusing permission to hold other entertainments and the Surrey Club refusing to play cricket at the Oval, Houghton bowed to the inevitable and gave up the lease. On 25th November 1854, a new lease, for 21 years or three lives, was assigned by Sir William Dannielle of Eastbourne, bart., and others, executors of the Rt. Revd. William Otter, Bishop of Chichester, to Henry Mortimer of the Stock Exchange, Esq., Charles Hoare of the Brewery, East Smithfield, and Alexander Marshall of Broadwater, Godalming, Esq.

Hoare was the new Treasurer of the Surrey Club: Marshall and Mortimer were prominent members. The lease described the property as '... that piece or parcel of ground formerly Nursery or Garden Ground called the Oval in Kennington ... with two dwelling houses converted into one messuage, and offices, sheds and other buildings'.

The ground soon became one of the popular places of resort, and 'a Saturday afternoon at the Oval' one of the best-known pleasures of London life, but the facilities for cricket were primitive. The Reverend T.O. Reay, writing fifty years later, described the Oval in 1852: 'The Surrey Club had not even a pavilion in which to dress or undress ... a few forms at the side of the field gave a limited accommodation to the cricket-seers, while a frequently re-iterated cry of "Orders, gentlemen, orders!" went round the ground from the throats of itinerant pot-boys.' The earliest picture we have of cricket at the Oval is an engraving by C. Rosenberg, published in 1848. Clearly depicted is St Marks Church, to the left of a solid looking messuage as we look at the picture – the old dwelling houses converted into a pavilion. Next to the pavilion is a wooden structure that was used as a players' room, and adjoining that is a small building used by Fred Lillywhite for the sale of scorecards and *Fred's Guide*.

Lillywhite pioneered scorecards on English cricket grounds, and even took a printing press and scoring tent with him during the first English tour of the USA and Canada in 1859. William Caffyn, in his autobiography *Seventy-one Not Out* has described what a great nuisance it was: 'It was a most complicated arrangement, and took a lot of carting about, and he was always complaining

The Oval in 1849.
© *Hulton-Deutsch Collection*

that the railway porters did not stow it away properly, until at last George Parr (the Captain) lost all patience and in pretty plain language consigned both Fred and his tent to an unmentionable region . . .'. Back to the Oval in 1848 – there is a ring of spectators, but no accommodation for them, and, at deep square leg (the engraving shows bowling from the Vauxhall end) a small tent used by the scorers. On the other side of the Harleyford Road are St Marks Vicarage and a 'residence of Mr Copeland', a fine looking villa, and there is an abundance of trees, that neither Albert nor the Prince of Wales were later able to save.

The bowler is bowling to a six-three field (slip, two gullies, wicket-keeper standing up, short third man, cover, wide mid-off, backward short leg, long leg and mid-on), and has his left hand slightly raised, as though about to adjust the field. The wicket is pitched, as now, Pavilion to Vauxhall end, though some early sources have suggested that, in the early days, wickets were pitched across the ground. Two Surrey players of around 1850 (William Caffyn and G.R. Bennett) asserted otherwise.

But there is, again, a quaintly old fashioned look about the game in progress in Rosenberg's engraving. There are still top hats for umpires and one or two of the players, though many favour what Sir Neville Cardus has described as 'Bill Sykes caps'. The whole scene appears very static, almost like some table-top game of cricket. It is difficult to imagine these men sprinting round the boundary, diving for a slip catch, running a sharp single. Order, civility, dignity and equilibrium control the game and every action in it. It is, after all, 1848 – the year of revolutions throughout Europe, when empires shook and kings tottered off their thrones, and the firebrands of liberty and nationalism blazed from the Atlantic to the Baltic. It was an age of demand and demonstration, of massive petitions and marches by the Chartists and others in England. Given such a volatile and dangerous state of affairs throughout Europe, it is hardly surprising that no bowler was permitted to raise the arm above the shoulder.

Although most bowlers were round arm, there were still plenty of underarm bowlers to be seen in the 1850s and 1860s, and umpires of the day were content to permit the exercise of both skills. This settled and satisfactory state of affairs was about to be challenged, and the impetus for change came from the Oval.

In late August 1862, Surrey played All England. The match was described by *The Times* as 'not only one of the most extraordinary matches ever chronicled in the history of cricket, but the most extraordinary'. There was nothing unusual about the result, a draw. All England batted first and made 503, up to then the highest score ever recorded. T. Hayward, uncle of a later and greater T. Hayward, made 117: 'a magnificent innings . . . gained in a masterly manner . . . The fielding of Surrey was excellent, and no fault could be found with the bowling, beyond it not being equal to the splendid batting it had to contend against'. Thus it took All England the best part of two days to make their record breaking score, and Surrey began their first innings shortly before six o'clock on the second day.

The 'Old' Surrey Eleven outside the old Surrey tent. © *From the Oval Collection*

The opening bowlers for All England were Mr V.E. Walker and Edgar Willsher, the latter having made 54 in the All England innings, and having been described by Caffyn as 'the most difficult of bowlers I . . . ever met'. But Willsher was to stamp his identity on the match in a far more dramatic way. In the words of *The Times*: ' . . . we regret to state after a four had been scored off Willsher for a "no ball", called by the umpire, John Lillywhite, and called so successively for four or five balls following, a "sensation" scene took place. Willsher threw the ball indignantly on the ground and left the field, followed soon after by the rest of the eleven, and all play was put to an end for the evening'.

The "sensation" scene was short lived. As soon as the confrontation between Willsher and Lillywhite began, the Surrey Club held a committee meeting in the pavilion. It was not an easy matter to resolve. There is no doubt that several bowlers had been steadily raising their arms above the shoulder, and that Law X – the law forbidding such action – was under threat and that the MCC's resistance to this threat had proved inadequate. It is also certain that most umpires had been turning a blind eye to overarm bowling. Willsher had a reputation for getting his arm higher than most, but Lillywhite was at pains to point out to the Surrey Committee that it was not the high action that he objected to, but that he considered Willsher had been "throwing". Lillywhite had acted according to his honest conviction, and stated that he intended to continue to do so. The Surrey Committee had a problem on their hands, and, like many committees before and since, decided that, whatever else happened, the game must go on. Lillywhite felt obliged to resign from his post in the match, and another umpire was appointed. Willsher apologised for leaving the ground and the match recommenced the following morning.

The matter of "high bowling" did not, however, rest there. The problem now passed to the MCC, and highlighted the unsatisfactory state of affairs at Lords. The headquarters of cricket had been in decline for some time. It had no professional cricketers, poor facilities, an inadequate pavilion and no decent pitch. In all this it compared badly with the Oval. It had also failed to establish its authority over the game. Law X had been flouted again and again. Willsher was not disciplined for his sensation at the Oval. Some of the counties began calling for a Cricket Parliament to take over the running of the game. On 10th June 1864, a meeting was held by the MCC in the Tennis Court adjoining the Lords ground – shades of the French Revolution – to discuss Law X. The Committee was bitterly divided over the issue of whether or not to permit overarm bowling. Mr R.A. Fitzgerald, Honorary Secretary of the MCC, was opposed to "high bowling", on the basis that overarm bowling was less skilful than round arm bowling, or underarm bowling, and that this was shown to be so by the large scores made off it. This ingenious argument chose to overlook that the record score of the All England XI had recently been made against roundarm bowling. The Honourable Frederick Ponsonby, a leading member of the Surrey Club and the MCC, and a man of whom we shall hear more, took a far more pragmatic view. Umpires couldn't be expected to rule on whether a bowler's arm was high or not without offending or upsetting one side or the other. For the sake of peace on the cricket field, Ponsonby supported overarm bowling. This sensible, if naive and less than morally water-tight argument won the day by 27 votes to 20 'amid much cheering'. The days of roundarm and underarm bowling were numbered.

It is possible that one of the reasons why Fitzgerald disapproved of what had happened at the Oval was that he disapproved of the Oval itself. In his view it was too large, and the innings played there were 'too big', games there lasted too long and time wasn't strictly kept at Kennington. Most of all, the 'great southern champions (Surrey) were too prodigal of their "largesses", and too elated by success to distinguish the right recipients of their bounty'.

The MCC at Lords wrestled with the bowling dilemma, and Fitzgerald tried to come to terms with his distaste. They had other problems to deal with – how to codify the laws and bring effective centralised control to the game. Meanwhile, further developments were taking place at the Oval. The Surrey Club was prospering. Marshall, Mortimer and Hoare proved able lessees, and member-ship of the Club grew. In 1855, William Burrup had succeeded his twin brother

John as Honorary Secretary, a post he held for the next seventeen years. The little pavilion became inadequate, and in 1858, the Club applied to the Duchy of Cornwall for permission to build a larger one.

The old Pavilion. Note the scoreboard. © *Hulton-Deutsch Collection*

The architect selected by the Club for this project was Richard Roberts, one of the longest serving members of the Club, and someone who could bring his own experiences of the shortcomings of the old building to the planning requirements of the new. Originally, the new pavilion was intended to stand opposite the end of Clayton Street, but the residents protested, and Roberts's pavilion was built at the south-east end of the ground. It consisted principally of a large club-room, with better dressing- and changing-room facilities for the players behind it. In 1861, Surrey pioneered the covered scorebox and telegraph board, and they were the first club to give 'talent sovereigns' to a player at the end of his innings, if he was a batsman, or at the end of the opponents' innings if he was a bowler. The spectators and supporters among the general public, who were already gaining a reputation for occasional bursts of rowdyism, were less well served. Nothing was done for them. They still stood in a ring round the ground, as depicted by Rosenberg, with no seats, no stands, no covering, no embankments. And yet they continued to turn up in ever increasing numbers.

For Surrey, cricket was going from strength to strength. The new pavilion was adorned with a marble slab commemorating the great deeds of the season of 1853, when Surrey were unbeaten, gaining victories over Sussex, Nottinghamshire, and England, among others. The slab is still to be seen in the present Pavilion, at the top of the first flight of stairs from the Members' Entrance, in the hallway outside the Long Room. There, carved for eternity, we hope, are the details. It honours a team effort – there is no invidious mention of any one cricketer. And yet Surrey undoubtedly had its outstanding players at this time. Perhaps the most famous, certainly the longest lived, was William Caffyn, who was ninety-one years old when he died at Reigate in Surrey in August 1919.

Caffyn was an all-rounder with career aggregates of 8768 runs and 1343 wickets. He also scored the first ever century for Surrey, in 1858, against England at the Oval. As a batsman he preferred the better tended and altogether more reliable wicket at the Oval to the rough old patch at Lords. (In 1859, Surrey – and other counties – refused to play at Lords as the wicket was so bad. Nothing like that has ever happened at the Oval.) He was an excellent cutter of the ball, like many small, compact players, and, although he had a very different physique, there appears to have been something of the Botham in him. Dowson, a contemporary of Caffyn's in the Surrey XI, stated: 'Curiously enough we were always glad when he had a good innings, as the more runs he made the better he bowled', and Herbert C. Troughton, another contemporary, wrote: 'He was rather impetuous and was apt to get himself out by adopting hitting tactics before he got set'. He was also a great favourite with the crowd at the Oval, and was nicknamed "the Surrey Pet". Caffyn's obituary in *Wisden* was rather doubtful of his bowling prowess, as was the Hon G.G. Lyttelton, but he took a great many wickets, and, again like Botham, 'he seemed to love bowling, and when he did not go on first, his joy, when he was put on was unmistakable'. He had an easy and graceful delivery, could bowl round or over the wicket, and could be deadly on a pitch that gave him help. Even after Law X was changed, Caffyn remained a round arm medium fast bowler, naggingly accurate, containing rival batsmen on the true Oval pitches in a career that lasted from 1849 to 1863, when he settled temporarily in Australia, and from 1872 to 1874. He was a brilliant fielder, and a member of the first ever party of cricketers to leave England, on their tour of Canada and the USA in 1859. He must be the only first class cricketer to have a personal best analysis on the Hoboken ground, where he took 16 wickets for 24 runs against a United States XXII. The team photograph, which may well have been taken in the United States, shows Caffyn sitting in the front row, his right hand holding the handle of a bat, his left hand resting on his knee. They are a motley looking bunch, wearing a variety of coloured shirts, some striped, some spotted, and a mixture of ties and neckerchiefs – not a crowd to bump into on a dark night.

Surrey were well represented on that tour: Julius Caesar, Tom Lockyer (the wicket-keeper), and H.H. Stephenson, set sail on 7th September with eight other professionals. Tom Lockyer, like Caffyn, was a great favourite with the Oval crowd. He was a particularly good 'taker' on the leg side, and could stand up to some of the fastest bowlers of his day. He was also a hard and powerful hitter. Julius Caesar remains perhaps one of the best known of the Surrey XI of the 1850s and 1860s, by virtue of what W.C. Fields might have described as his "euphonious appellation". He was another small man, 'very fierce with his bat, and quick of eye and feet'. He also had a reputation as a practical joker, though contemporaries (or at least near contemporaries) assert that his 'quips and gibes, boisterous and personal at times . . . (were) mostly good-tempered withal, and taken in good part'. 'Mostly' suggests that some of the merry gibes and quips, however, had more sting to them: sadly, details of such have not survived. From the earliest days at the Oval, right up to the 1870s, the players' dressing room, as opposed to that of the gentlemen, was at the top of a flight of steps leading to a balcony attached to the old Surrey tavern. Local ale may well have had a part to play in some of the merriment.

H.H. Stephenson was captain of the first ever team to go to Australia, a man who was 'in his prime, a great batsman, a most difficult bowler, and an accomplished wicket-keeper'. He was a great supporter of the reciprocal tours by English and Australian teams and a very popular cricketer.

Through the hard work of the MCC and the county committees, a structure was being built in the 1850s and 1860s that still shapes most of the first-class game today. Cricket matches on the leading grounds were already divided into three categories: inter-county games that counted towards the championship, first-class representative games (North v South, Gentlemen v Players, Surrey v All England), and minor or other matches. The Oval was home to matches in all three categories. It was, and still is, of course, the venue for almost all Surrey first-class games: an occasional game was played at Godalming in the early days, but the Guildford Cricket Week wasn't introduced until July 1938. But the Oval also staged many representative games (Gentlemen of the South v Players of the South, Surrey v The World), and, for one-day matches, the ground was leased by a variety of Surrey schools, the Royal Engineers, the Law Society, the Clergy of Southwark and the London Meat Traders Association.

The Oval was a busy place. In October 1861, ten of the players selected to tour Australia mustered at the Surrey Tavern, and from there journeyed by cab to the Great Northern Railway headquarters at King's Cross, for the first leg of the journey, to Liverpool. Several members of the Surrey Club took places in the train, 'determined', says *The Times*, 'to accompany them to Liverpool', whence the team took passage in Brunel's famous *Great Britain*. There is a photograph of the party in the MCC collection. Mallam, the Manager, is staring into the distance, wearing a vast top hat and looking a little like John Wilkes Booth, the young actor who was still three years away from his most famous role at the Ford Theatre, Washington DC. Caffyn holds a cricket ball in his right hand.

Stephenson, with luxuriant dark beard and moustache, is staring straight at the camera. The touring party are all dressed in whites, and have a uniformity that was missing from the group that toured the USA and Canada two years earlier.

Seven years later, in 1868, came the first tour of Britain by Australian cricketers, the 'Aboriginal Black Australians' as they were called. It was in many ways an extraordinary concept. As a race, the Aborigines had been treated abominably in their homeland. Diseases brought out by white settlers had decimated tribal groups, others had been deprived of their land, persecuted, shot, and had had their traditional way of life destroyed by European farming methods. And yet, in the Harrow-Edenhope area of western Victoria, they had taken to cricket, and the tour had been organised by a group of the more sensitive and intelligent whites, led by Tom Hamilton.

They came to London as something of a curiosity – 'many and confused were the ideas generally entertained respecting these Aboriginals', reported *The Times* – and played their first match of the tour at the Oval on 25th and 26th May 1868, travelling up by train from West Malling in Kent on a day of bright sunshine. On the first day, 7000 spectators turned up at the Oval, a gate exceeded today only by a Test match or the sadly rare event of Surrey reaching the semi-finals of one of the Knock-Out competitions. The match was a great success. Of the press only *The Times* was less than satisfied, and the promoters and William Burrup, the Surrey Secretary, were well pleased. The game ran the full two days and was followed by a third day of sports. Altogether some 20,000 people attended the Oval, and paid over £600 for admittance. Surrey's share of the gate was £150. After all expenses had been paid, the syndicate promoting the tour were left with over £300 profit. The Aborigines played two more fixtures at the Oval: a one-day game in September, which was drawn, and their final match of the tour in October, when Surrey won by nine wickets. After this game, the entire Aborigine team was entertained at dinner by the Surrey Club.

Four years earlier, a very young man who was to prove an even greater draw to the South London crowds played his first match at the Oval. He was William Gilbert Grace, later 'The Doctor' or plain 'W.G.', and, later still, the 'G.O.M.'. Grace was not a Surrey man: he learnt his cricket in the fields and orchards of his native Gloucestershire. But he had a great affection for the Oval, which served him well as an arena for his immense talent. He is regarded by most writers on cricket as the person who, by virtue of his own ability, produced the modern game. 'Grace's skill as a batsman,' wrote Cardus in *The Great Victorians*, 'may be said to have orchestrated the simple folk-song of the game; his personality placed it on the country's stage.' Eye-witnesses considered him the greatest batsman of the age. Grace considered himself the greatest bowler, and, in his more agile youth, he was an outstanding fielder. Searching through contemporary scorecards, early editions of *Wisden* and memoirs of Victorian cricketers, the impression is that Grace burst upon the scene, the complete artist from the first time he took guard. In his second season of cricket, at the age of seventeen, he was selected to play for the Gentlemen against the Players at both Lords and the Oval. A year later, in 1865, he established himself as the best batsman in England with two wonderful innings at the Oval. He scored 224 not out for England v Surrey (his first hundred in first class cricket, and at that time a record for the ground), and 173 not out for the Gentlemen of the South v Players of the South, following that with 8 wickets for 10 runs in the same match. In those days there were no sixes, and even fours were hard to come by on what was the largest playing area in the country. Grace was eighteen, and a superb athlete. The story has been told many times of how he missed the third day of the England v Surrey match to attend an Athletics meeting at Crystal Palace, where he won the 440 yards hurdles.

From then on, the Oval was one of his favourite and most successful grounds. In 1890, he wrote 'A Review of the Game' for the *English Illustrated Magazine*: 'At the Oval you get some of the best wickets in the world, and some batsmen prefer it to Lords. It is not so fast for one reason, although, for myself, I still prefer a fast wicket as long as the ball comes true. The soil is undoubtedly different from that at Lords, for very rarely do you get the sticky and unplayable wicket'. On the fine Oval wicket, Grace played his last first-class match, in 1906, at the age of fifty eight, for the Gentlemen of England v Surrey. He scored 15 (in two hours at the crease) and 25, and bowled two overs for 5 runs without taking a wicket. It was an Easter game, played in bitterly cold weather and snow fell on the first day.

For all his alleged irascibility, perhaps because of it, he was loved by the Oval crowd, who flocked to see him in numbers too many for comfort. The Surrey Club had become almost too successful; certain matches pulled vast crowds, more turnstiles had to be installed, and Richard Roberts's Pavilion was outgrown within a generation. It was time for further developments to take place.

Cricket has never been a highly profitable game financially in England. Even when their team was riding high in the 1860s, the Surrey Club were having occasional difficulties in balancing their books. This is, sadly, a theme to which we have constantly to return. But there is something unnecessarily impish about the gods of cricket. The moment Surrey, flushed with success, renewed their lease and having decided to embark on improvements at the Oval having received the necessary permission from the Duchy of Cornwall, the Surrey XI hit a bad patch. The crowds, *mirabile dictu*, remained enthusiastic, loyal, appreciative, though they may have lacked some of the refinement of the punters at St John's Wood. Almost entirely male, though there were 'several ladies . . . in carriages and on horseback' when Surrey played the Aborigines, the crowd at the Oval was composed of soldiers, porters, labourers, postal workers, sailors, clerks, and a great many of those humble men of private means who have always found time to spend a day or two in the bleachers on the gasholder side.

18th July 1906. W. G. Grace, at the age of 58, leaves the field after scoring 74 in his final appearance from the Gentlemen v Players.

'The Oval has a strong hold upon the non-aristocratic class,' wrote Charles Box, in an essay entitled 'The English Game of Cricket', published in *The Field* in 1877. 'Its associations are adapted to their means in general, and its position to their time and convenience in particular. Their conditions of enjoyment are not trammelled, and their native instincts are allowed fuller play than would be considered quite in keeping at some loftier institutions. Here a boisterous shout with its echo is not regarded as a breach of etiquette, and a little homely badinage is not construed into vulgarity. As a rule, the visitors to this locality know something of the game, and can, therefore, applaud the right man and the right act at the right time . . .'

In May 1873, work was being planned on the Pavilion. A little more income had been generated by allowing local and national firms to post advertisements on boards round the ground. Those who took up this offer were entitled to free entrance. In 1874, the Otter Trustees put the remainder of the leasehold interest up for auction, and it was bought by the Surrey Club for £2800. To give them time to raise this money, Surrey were given a thirty one year lease. The lease included a clause limiting the uses to which the Oval could be put: 'no game of sport other than the games of Cricket, Baseball, Football, Tennis, Fives and Racquets and Amateur Athletic Sports shall be played'. There were to be no more of Houghton's Poultry Shows, but, perhaps understandably, there was some trouble with the groundsman, Street. In September 1874, at a Committee meeting, 'the state of the ground being considered unsatisfactory, the Secretary was requested, after providing the necessary assistance, to inform Street that unless the condition of the ground be altered materially during the recess and to the satisfaction of the Committee, they will be compelled to place the management of the ground in other hands'. Poor Street, that same year the same Committee had decided to allow Rugby Union Internationals to take place at the Oval, not the best winter treatment for a cricket ground.

On 8th May 1875, Marshall, Ponsonby and Mortimer leased the Tavern for seven years to Frederick Trotman of Regents Park, Middlesex. The annual rent was £250, and the Tavern was to be insured for £4000. The following year, part of the north end of the Oval was leased to William Michael Adams of 20 Bridge Row, City of London, gent., as a covered and open air roller skating rink. The hope was that profits resulting from this would enable the Committee 'further to extend their operations' in the furtherance of cricket, and that it would 'enlarge their sphere of utility as purveyors of athletic amusements for South London'. In 1876, it was resolved that a stand should be erected for the comfort of at least some of the patrons of the Oval, and that the press-box be moved to accommodate this. By 1878, Trotman, lessee of the Tavern, had a rival in another part of the ground, when a Mr Tunewall was allowed to set up a refreshment bar at each side of the ground. That same summer, steps were taken 'with regard to the improvement of the ground in the purchases of sheep, loam, etc.' And in May 1879, Ponsonby and others leased the tavern 'called the Surrey

Club House' to Octavius Edward Cooper and Charles Peter Matthews, 'trading as Ind Coope and Co., of Burton on Trent'. Finally, in 1880 itself, a circle of embankments round the ground was completed using earth excavated for the enclosure of the Vauxhall Creek, that same creek in which the unfortunate porter was drowned in May 1818.

These improvements were timely. The Oval was only months away from staging the first ever Test Match in England.

Chapter Three

England v Australia, September 1880

In 1880, events in South Africa were stumbling towards the First Boer war, George Newnes began publication of his weekly *Tit-Bits*, Thomas Hardy wrote *The Trumpet Major*, and the Rev. William Booth adopted a new name for his evangelical missionary workers – The Salvation Army. Gladstone was Prime Minister, but it was in many ways the zenith of British Imperialism: the stage management of Disraeli had only recently added 'Empress of India' to Victoria's billing. Daily, the newspapers carried details of British troops preparing for battle, or of battles themselves, or of lists of casualties in some far-flung corner of the great Empire. It is hardly surprising that to *Wisden*, *The Times*, *The Morning Post* and to most journals, the Australians were 'the Colonials' or 'the Colonists', though perhaps the MCC member who assumed in 1878 that all Australians were 'niggers' was a little out of touch. Not for long: two minutes later he met Spofforth.

Two English teams had already toured Australia. In March 1877, Australia had beaten England by 45 runs at Melbourne, in a match where Charlie Bannerman made 165, the only first-class century of his career. Surrey provided two members of the England team – Henry Jupp and James Southerton. A third Surrey member of the touring party, the wicket-keeper, Pooley, was languishing in New Zealand. He was never given another chance to play for England. The team was not the strongest England could muster, being composed of professionals only. A second Test was played a fortnight later, again at Melbourne, which England won by 4 wickets, largely thanks to innings of 52 and 63 by George Ulyett. Spofforth made his debut for Australia, but performed only moderately well, taking 4 wickets for 111 runs in the match. The game was virtually won by Yorkshire rather than England, since Yorkshire players scored 329 out of England's cumulative 356.

In January 1879, a third Test took place at the Melbourne Cricket Ground. Australia won by ten wickets, and F.R. Spofforth had match figures of 13 for 110, including the first ever Test hat-trick. On this occasion the English team was composed almost entirely of amateurs, if not gentlemen, and was originally billed as the 'Gentlemen of England, with Ulyett and Emmett'. Something of the

J. Blackman   T. Horan   G. H. Bailey.   D. W. Gregory.   J. Conway.   A. Bannerman.   C. Bannerman.   W. L. Murdoch.
F. R. Spofforth.   F. Allan.   W. Midwinter.   T. W. Garrett.   H. F. Boyle.

The Australian team, 1878. 'Not until Monday, May 27th, 1878 did the English public take any interest in Australian cricket.' – A. G. Steel. *From the MCC Collection*

pedigree of the team may be gauged from the fact that it was skippered by the Fourth Lord Harris (2 and 4, and 0 for 14), and included The Mackinnon of MacKinnon, 35th Chief of the Clan Mackinnon (0 and 5, did not bowl). Both these worthy gentlemen were cleaned bowled by Spofforth in both their innings.

The previous year, a party of Australians, including Bannerman and Spofforth had toured England. They were badly mauled by the Gentlemen of England (not including Harris and MacKinnon) at Prince's Ground in June, but had the better of a drawn match against the Players of England at the same ground in September. Their only other defeat was at the beginning of the tour, when a strong Notts side beat them by an innings in weather that was wickedly cold. The Australians beat a strong MCC side at Lords in a remarkably low scoring game. MCC made 33 and 19, Spofforth took 6 for 4 and 4 for 16, and Boyle 3 for 14 and 6 for 3. The match was over in four and a half hours. In the words of Sir Pelham Warner: 'The match created a sensation'. *Punch* celebrated the Australian victory in verse:

> The Australians came down like a wolf on the fold:
> The Marylebone cracks for a trifle were bowled;
> Our Grace before dinner was very soon done,
> And Grace after dinner did not get a run.

Wisden, in a lengthy description of the game, recorded that 'a stream of at least 1000 men rushed frantically up to the pavilion, in front of which they clustered and lustily shouted, "Well done, Australia!" "Bravo, Spofforth!" "Boyle, Boyle!", the members of the MCC keenly joining in the applause of that "maddened crowd" who shouted themselves hoarse before they left to scatter far and wide that evening the news how in one day the Australians had so easily defeated one of the strongest MCC elevens that had ever played for the famous old club.

On 2nd and 3rd September 1878, the Australians played Eleven English Professionals at the Oval, in a match that suffered from some poor organisation. The Surrey Club had placed the Oval at the disposal of the Australians, who were to make all the arrangements for the match, meeting the expenses but taking the profits. *Wisden* gave a diplomatic account of all this: '... owing to some very much debated, but never clearly explained, misunderstanding as to remuneration, many of the very best professionals of England did not play. It is impossible to give space in this little book to a full, and, consequently, fair expression of the published Why's and Wherefore's of this little misunderstanding, and so the compiler passes it by with the expression of regret that it ever occurred, and with a further regret that it was not amicably arranged.'

And so to 1880 and the 6th, 7th and 8th of September. The Australians had had a highly successful tour, being beaten only twice, but no arrangements had been made to play a Test until Alcock, the Surrey Secretary, offered the Oval as a venue. The Australians cancelled their game against Sussex – it is not recorded what the Sussex Committee thought about that – and Alcock and the Surrey Committee invited the cream of England's cricket to take part. At that time, the Committee of the ground where a representative match was to be played acted as selectors. The team, in batting order, was E.M. and W.G. Grace, Lucas, Barnes, Lord Harris, Penn, A.G. Steel, Hon A. Lyttelton, G.F. Grace, Shaw and Morley. *The Times* described this team as 'probably the strongest combination that has ever entered a cricket field'. Of the three professionals, Barnes was a hard-hitting batsman, Shaw and Morley were highly respected bowlers. Lyttelton was a wicket-keeper and useful batsman. Lucas was regarded by *The Morning Post* as 'the second best contemporary batsman' – no prizes for guessing who was the best. Steel was an all-rounder, according to Sir Pelham Warner 'there have been few greater all-round cricketers' (and he wrote that in 1945), and the Graces were, of course, regarded as capable of winning any match on their own. It was a strong team, though a little 'southern' in character, and *The Manchester Guardian* certainly had reservations about it: 'At the first glance the team may seem to be a really "representative" one, but strong as it is there can be no doubt that it would have been immensely improved had Mr Hornby, the famous Lancashire amateur, and George Ulyett, the crack batsman of Yorkshire, a fine bowler and a splendid "fielder", been included in it.' In fact, both Hornby and Ulyett had turned down invitations from the Surrey Committee.

THE AUSTRALIAN ELEVEN, 1880.

G. E. PALMER.   W. H. MOULE.   G. J. BONNOR.   G. ALEXANDER.   T. U. GROUBE.
R. SPOFFORTH.   H. F. BOYLE.   W. L. MURDOCH.   P. S. M'DONNELL.   A. C. BANNERMAN.
A. H. JARVIS.   J. SLIGHT.   J. M BLACKHAM.

Spofforth (injured) and Jarvis were the two players omitted from the Australian team at the first Test match in England. © *Hulton-Deutsch Collection*

The Australian team consisted of A.C. Bannerman, Murdoch (Captain), Groube, McDonnell, Slight, Blackham, Bonnor, Boyle, Palmer (thought by some to be as good a bowler as Spofforth), Alexander and Moule. It was a strong side if a little untried – seven were making their Test Match debut – but it was without Spofforth. Late in August, in a match against Eighteen of Scarborough and District, he had received a blow on his right hand while batting, the result of what *The Times* referred to as 'some questionable bowling'. It must have been a tough game: it was one of the few defeats the Australians suffered on their tour, and it kept Spofforth out of cricket for three weeks. Looking back, with the knowledge of what was to happen at the Oval in 1882, it is hard not to regard Spofforth's injury as critical to the outcome of the 1880 Test, though the Eighteen of Scarborough might well have disagreed, for the injury did not take place till the final innings of a match that the Australians lost by 90 runs.

For much of the season it appeared doubtful that any Test would take place. There was an unpleasant legacy of England's last tour of Australia. The special correspondent of *The Manchester Guardian* wrote: 'The treatment which an English Eleven received in Australia induced a hostile feeling against the Colonial team, and in addition to this feeling there was the knowledge that the Australian Eleven had come over here on a purely commercial speculation. Their object was to make money, and they have followed out this programme with the utmost pertinacity and success . . . Lord Harris, who had the best right to complain at the treatment he and his team had received in Australia, waved all objections on that score, and his Lordship was selected as the captain of the English Eleven . . .'

They may have been seeking to make money on their tour, but the Australians had also been playing fine cricket. British players tended to suggest that this was mainly against inferior teams, and for some months 'very general regret' had been expressed in cricketing circles 'at the apparent certainty that Spofforth and his companions would return to Australia without having been met in fair fight by an Eleven really representing the cricketing strength of the mother country . . . It was therefore very gratifying to find that at the eleventh hour the difficulties in the way of a match of such importance had been overcome'. Both Lord Harris and C.W. Alcock, the Surrey Secretary, had worked hard to achieve this.

The umpires for the Test of 1880 were H.H. Stephenson of Surrey and Bob Thoms of Middlesex, both regulars at the Oval. Thoms began his career at a time when Fuller Pilch was the best batsman in England, and he had a fine reputation as an umpire, and was the subject of an article in *Cricket* in 1885: 'So universal, indeed, has been his popularity of late years that when the first match between England and Australia was arranged at the Oval in 1880, he was selected . . . to umpire, as high a testimony to his efficiency as could be given. No better proof of his impartiality can be adduced . . . than the readiness with which his appointment has always been received by the Australian teams, who, not as a rule tolerant in the matter of umpiring, have always shown a marked sense of Thoms's capabilities behind the sticks.'

The Oval was not looking its best for the occasion, and facilities were poor. There was immense interest in the game – a large number of spectators were present when the gates opened at eight on the morning of 6th September – and reports vary as to just how big the crowd was. *The Manchester Guardian* reckoned that in the course of the day 'there could not have been less than 30,000 spectators'; *Wisden* thought just over 20,000 which seems the more likely figure based on match receipts. However many there were, 'the prepara-

R. A. Thoms (1826–1903), a popular and trusted umpire, who stood in the first Test match in England.

tions for their accommodation were miserably inadequate' and many thousands of the visitors never saw a ball bowled during the day. They crowded the grandstand (the new covered stand with seats for 1200 spectators), climbed on the fences and into the trees, and on to the roofs of the permanent buildings on the ground. They endeavoured 'from the precarious elevation of piles of brick, broken chairs, old sofas, or dilapidated boxes, to gain some knowledge of what was passing in the roped arena'. Thousands more promenaded outside, never catching a glimpse of the play, but satisfying their curiosity on the 'scraps of information that were doled out to them by the more fortunate'. *The Morning Post* thought 'the people behaved on the whole conspicuously well, though as is always the case at big matches, some insisted upon remaining inside the ropes . . . The applause was generous but judicious, liberal but discriminating'.

England won the toss and decided to bat on what was described as a perfect wicket, 'in favour of heavy scoring'. On the first day the weather was dull, but the light was good except for the last hour of play. At 11.30 precisely, Murdoch led out his team and a 'warm compliment was paid to the Colonials'. The Champion, yet another sobriquet for W.G. Grace, and his brother, Dr E.M. Grace, 'were received with cordial applause as they appeared at the wicket'. The Australian opening bowlers were Boyle and Palmer. Palmer was a steady fast medium bowler, but lacked the skill and penetrative venom of Spofforth. On this particular wicket, Boyle, without Spofforth as his partner, was unable to produce the destructive power he had unleashed against the MCC at Lords in 1878.

Murdoch set what would hardly be thought of today as an attacking field. Palmer bowled to a slip, point, mid off, cover, short mid on, extra mid on, long on, long leg and extra long on. Boyle's field was similar. They gave the Graces little trouble, E.M. batted 'carefully and well' (he drove and cut Palmer for two 4s in the first over), and 'after a few minutes had elapsed it became apparent to all who were familiar with "W.G.'s" playing that he was in his very best form and bent on making a heavy score'. Nevertheless, with the first ball of the third over, Palmer nearly yorked him. Dr E.M. Grace played with 'unusual care, and refused to be tempted out of his ground by the most cunning devices of the bowlers'. The score mounted steadily, at a run a minute, and when it reached 41, Murdoch took Boyle off and replaced him with Alexander. The Graces continued to score – 'the Champion's play was magnificent, and showed that he possessed in undiminished excellence, the complete mastery of the bat which has earned him that proud title'. His drives were especially 'a treat to witness' – always hard and along the ground. He appeared in no difficulties whatsoever, though a piece of sharp fielding by Palmer nearly ran him out.

Murdoch made another bowling change, bringing Bannerman on in place of Palmer. Bannerman then missed a sharp chance for a caught and bowled when E.M. Grace had scored 25 and the total was 70. 'Dr E.M. Grace then showed his appreciation of the escape by driving Bannerman twice for 4', but it wasn't an expensive miss. The same batsman gave Alexander an easy catch at cover. (91 for 1). W.G. was now joined by Lucas, who was a free and graceful player. 'His extraordinary power of getting "on the top" of the ball, and his quickness and dexterity in stopping "shooters" served as powerful reminders of Daft and Caffyn in their best days.'

At five to one, the hundred came up at better than a run a minute. At eight minutes to two, the score reached 150, and at two o'clock, 'when the Australians retired to recruit their energies at the luncheon table', the score was 167 – Grace 82, Lucas 41. In those days, the lunch interval lasted from two o'clock to a quarter to three. It then took Grace and Lucas only twenty five more minutes to reach 200, but 'a few minutes after this . . . Mr Lucas had the misfortune to play a ball hard on to his left foot, and it rebounded from thence on to his wicket, dislodging the bail'. Bannerman was the lucky bowler. (211 for 2). This brought Barnes, 'the hope of Nottinghamshire', to the wicket. He showed 'some excellent cricket until he unfortunately put a ball on to his wicket'. Reports in British newspapers were full of 'unfortunately', 'misfortune', 'bad luck', especially where English cricketers were concerned. There was seldom any question of bad judgement, stupidity or lack of skill.

Lord Harris joined Grace, but, with the score at 281, the Champion's 'bails were removed by a plain-looking ball from Palmer'. W.G. had scored 152 (twelve 4s) and had given only one difficult chance (dropped by Alexander at long-off from the bowling of Bannerman) in four hours. It was reckoned to be his best innings for two years. He was now 32 years old and in the prime of his career.

The ordeal was not over for the Australians. Penn and Lord Harris both batted well, Harris taking nine off one over from Alexander – a more considerable feat than first appears when we remember that in those days an over consisted of only four balls. It took exactly two hours from the lunch interval for the score to reach 300 (150 in 120 minutes), but the Australian fielding showed 'no signs of deterioration'. With the score at 322, Bannerman, whose bowling *The Morning Post* regarded as 'fairly good . . . by no means terrifying', bowled Penn for 23. In slight rain, Steel came in to bat, and he and Harris put on 82, repeatedly driving the ball to the boundary. Some reporters felt the wicket was playing 'somewhat treacherously', but the rain probably made life more difficult for bowlers and fielders. Lord Harris was then easily caught by Bonnor off Alexander for 52, and Mr Steel hesitating somewhat at a ball from Groube, drove the ball too high and was finely caught by Boyle'. (410 for 7).

It was still raining, which can't have been much fun for the watchers on the roofs and in the trees, the light was now decidedly bad, and there was little time before close of play. These were not the most welcoming conditions for the next batsman, Mr G.F. Grace, 'whose inclusion in the Eleven had been objected to by many'. He failed to score, being caught by Bannerman off Moule. (410 for 8).

On the second day, the weather was glorious 'with everything that is necessary to exhibit the national game in its highest perfection'. There was another large crowd: 19,863 passing through the turnstiles. 'This enormous crowd,' reported *The Morning Post*, 'behaved with the utmost good humour, and kept admirable order.' The expectation was for an England victory. Chances of a draw were described as remote. 'Play was resumed with commendable punctuality at five minutes past eleven.' England batted for a further twenty minutes, scoring only ten more runs and losing their last two wickets – Shaw bowled Moule without scoring, and Morley was run out for 2. Lyttelton was left with 11 not out.

And so, at twenty to twelve, the Australian openers, Bannerman and Murdoch, came to the wicket, to face the bowling of Morley from the Pavilion end, and Steel from the Vauxhall end. The English field was no more attacking than that of the Australians – point (E.M.G), short mid off (W.G.), cover (Lucas), mid on (Barnes), third man (Harris), extra mid off (Penn), short leg

(Steel), mid on (G.F. Grace), and slip (Shaw). The wicket played very fast and true, and this 'materially diminished the effectiveness of Mr Steel's bowling'. At first Morley (left arm, medium fast) was very erratic, but Murdoch was out of touch. After several uneasy overs, he 'placed the ball' in the hands of Barnes at mid wicket (28 for 1, of which Bannerman had made 26). Morley now began to find line and length and bowled Bannerman with an unplayable ball (39 for 2). Groube lost his off stump to a 'swift breaking ball' from Steel, Slight was caught off Morley, and Blackham was caught and bowled off a skier in the same over. (84 for 5). McDonnell had dug in, but, after he had made 27, he was easily caught by Barnes at mid on, again off Morley. Bonner, described as the tallest cricketer in the world, 'showed a desire to hit'. Shaw, 'being of an accommodating disposition, sent down a ball of the necessary "length"'. But Bonner got underneath it, the ball went 'higher than a kite', so high, reputedly, that the batsmen had turned for their third run before G.F. Grace made a well-judged catch on the boundary. For once in the game he had done something right, and he was rewarded by a 'ringing cheer'.

Palmer was bowled by Morley, W.G. made a smart catch at slip to get rid of Alexander off Steel's bowling, and, at lunch, the Australians were 126 for 9. The bowling had been tight, but the English fielding had not matched the Australian, and several chances had been missed. It must, nevertheless, have been a happy luncheon for the English team, and, although there was a stubborn little last wicket stand, the Australian innings ended not long after the interval, when W.G., in his second over, had Moule caught by Morley. Boyle was left with 36 not out, and the total was 149. Morley finished with 5 for 56.

The follow-on was 'a matter of course', and it wasn't long before bets were being made that the match would be over in two days. Australia's second innings began disastrously. Murdoch changed the batting order, opening with Bannerman and Boyle. Bannerman attacked from the start, but, when he had made only 8, he hit Shaw to leg and Lucas, 'running a considerable distance, secured the ball amidst uproarious applause' from his local crowd. (8 for 1). Murdoch came in, 'just in time to see Boyle cleverly run out' (13 for 2) and Groube caught at slip by Shaw off Morley without scoring (14 for 3, facing arrears of 271).

McDonnell joined Murdoch and they 'fairly collared' the bowling, forcing Harris to make one bowling change after another while they added 83 runs. The crowd were appreciative of the fight, 'Melbourne or Sydney could hardly have been more enthusiastic'. The hitting was hard and clean, some of the best of the match. The English fielding was good, and *The Manchester Guardian* felt the game was 'played to perfection all round'. The stand was eventually broken by W.G., who trapped McDonnell l.b.w. for 43. Slight was soon splendidly caught by Lord Harris from a hard and lofty hit (101 for 5), and this brought the 'Herculean' frame of Bonnor to the wicket. Harris rang the bowling changes – Lucas, Barnes, W.G., Steel, Morley – but Murdoch (79 overnight) and Bonnor

(13) held out. Even so, it was a hopeless position: they were still 101 runs behind England, and had only four wickets left. The papers helpfully commented that, although the Australians never knew when they were beaten, this time they were beaten.

The first Test in England. His Lordship in hot pursuit. © *Hulton-Deutsch Collection*

But, the next day, the papers were suitably generous in their appreciation of the great fight put up by the Australians. *The Manchester Guardian* reported that 'the third day's play in the great match between England and Australia will long be remembered for the extraordinary change that came over the game, and the magnificent stand made by the Australian captain'. *The Times* recorded that Mr Murdoch battled 'in a manner simply perfect . . . The second innings of Australia for 327 runs surprised everyone, as a single-innings defeat seemed inevitable. Surprises are so general in cricket that many people were afraid that this characteristic of the game would be most unpleasantly exemplified.'

Play resumed shortly after eleven o'clock on Wednesday 8th September, Murdoch and Bonnor resuming their innings to the bowling of Morley and Steel. The weather was dull, and there was a much smaller crowd (only 3751 paid at the turnstiles), in anticipation of an early victory for England. The wicket, admittedly, favoured batting. Steel was able to get very little turn, but he got one past Bonnor's bat (181 for 7), and soon after took a return catch from Palmer (187 for 8). With two wickets left, Australia were still 84 runs behind, but Murdoch was there yet. Again Harris rang the bowling changes, trying Steel, W.G., Shaw, Lucas, Morley and Penn. Alexander dug in and stayed while Murdoch got his century. The longer the fight went on, the more it seemed Australia might avoid an innings defeat, the more the crowd applauded. Morley changed ends – he even changed sides, bowling round the wicket. Eventually, with the score at 239, Morley found the edge of Alexander's bat and he was caught at slip by Shaw. 32 runs were needed to make England bat again.

'It was then generally agreed that the match was over, but the event falsified the prediction . . . Of the Australian team it may be said that there is no "tail".' Moule, the last man in, supported Murdoch wonderfully. The pair added 88 for the last wicket, of which Moule's share was 34. 'Change after change of bowling was resorted to, but curiously, it never seemed to occur to Lord Harris to put on either G.F. or E.M. Grace. Surely the former had a better claim than Mr Penn or Mr Lucas, and the effect of the Doctor's (E.M.'s) lobs might have worked a surprising effect on the game.'

At seven minutes past one, the Australians saved the innings defeat, having scored 90 in almost even time, and at two o'clock Murdoch equalled W.G.'s record score of Monday. The innings lasted into the afternoon session, and it must have occurred to Lord Harris that there would come a point where the time factor had to be considered. More bowling changes – Barnes was tried. The crowd began to laugh at England's discomfiture, 'twas ever thus at the Oval. But, not long after the lunch interval, the innings came to an end. Barnes knocked Moule's off stump out of the ground. Murdoch had gone in first wicket down with the score at 8, and remained not out 153 out of Australia's 327.

England needed only 57 to win, an 'apparently easy task', but 'in accomplishing it, the run of ill luck and bad play combined was so persistent that the hearts of their backers almost failed them for fear'. Boyle and Palmer bowled unchanged, and the Australian fielding was a revelation. Nothing like it had been seen before, each man backing up, long off and long on moving briskly in even when the ball was played carefully back to the bowler. Harris sent in Lyttelton and the luckless G.F. Grace as openers, and poor G.F. promptly gained his pair, this time bowled by Palmer (2 for 1). It was to be his second and last innings in a Test match, a sorry career record that can hardly have been equalled and can never be surpassed.

Lucas joined Lyttelton, made two runs and was then caught at the wicket by Blackham off Palmer. The same bowler then yorked Lyttelton (22 for 3). At the other end, Penn was batting steadily, and Barnes now cut Palmer for four. Two runs later he gave a simple catch to Moule at mid on off the bowling of Boyle. E.M. strode out to save the Grace's family honour, but was bowled second ball by Boyle (31 for 5, twenty six still needed).

The spectators cheered when W.G. appeared. With the score at 45, Bonnor dropped Penn at slip. It was a hard chance, but the outcome of the game may have hung on it. Slowly, carefully, Grace and Penn nudged England to 52, and Grace then cut Palmer for 4 to level the scores. The Champion then pushed a single off the next ball to give England victory, the winning hit coming at a quarter past four. 'Thus, amid the greatest excitement, a victory was declared for England by five wickets. Lord Harris then came to the front of the Pavilion, and, amid cheers, said that he was pleased with the manner in which the game had been conducted throughout. Since this was the end of the tour, he asked the crowd to wish the Colonists a safe voyage home. Loud calls were then made for Murdoch and W.G. There were many indications that the sporting spirit prevailed.'

The following morning, *The Morning Post* commented on this. 'Now that England and Australia have met and fought so good a battle, there seems no reason why the hatchet should not be buried for ever, and the memories of old grievances fade away before newer and more happy thoughts, which this match engenders, and if this reconciliation takes place – however informally – the public will have to thank Lord Harris, without whose co-operation the match could not have come off, the Committee of the Surrey Club, who with their Secretary worked untiringly to make the affair a success, and also in some degree our consistent advocacy of the playing of such a match.' There was no false modesty about *The Post*, and no mention of Surrey's 'miserably inadequate preparations'.

But the match had been a success, in cricketing and financial terms, conducted throughout, according to *The Sportsman*, 'in the most pleasant and liberal spirit . . . and productive of the best all round cricket that has ever been seen . . . from first to last the reception of the Colonials was most hearty and sportsmanlike.' The total receipts at the gate were divided equally between the Surrey Club and the Australians, the latter receiving about £1400 as their share. The expenses were borne by Surrey.

It was a triumph in many ways, of organisation, of cricket, of burying-the-hatchet. But, less than a fortnight later, there came tragedy. G.F. Grace, who was 29 years old, died at a hotel in Basingstoke. He had had a cold during the Oval Test, but had gone on to play in a match in Gloucestershire – South of England v Stroud – making 44 in his last innings. At home, he complained of illness, but began his journey to London, stopping off in Basingstoke. While there, he was 'confined to his hotel by inflammation of the lungs'. A few days later, he died. *The Times* wrote warmly of him: 'his manly and straightforward conduct and genial manners won him not only popularity, but the esteem of hosts and friends'.

And he made a great catch on the boundary in the first Test ever played in England.

Chapter Four

Great Matches 1845 to 1880

Thirty five years is a long time in any sort of history, including cricket. Only a handful of cricketers have had careers spanning such a period: Grace; Hirst and Close of Yorkshire; 'Plum' Warner and J.T. Hearne of Middlesex; and Lord Harris, who kept going until 1911, playing for Kent at the age of sixty. Looking back from the present (1989) to 1954, there is to be seen a different age – no one-day cricket; English cricketers still legitimately playing in and against South Africa; Hutton, Compton, Edrich, Evans, Bailey, Laker, Lock and Statham still in the Test side; Pakistan's first official Test; no sponsorship; no names on the lapels of players' shirts; no Sunday cricket – and a strong determination that there never should be such a thing; and only fourteen Test matches in the year, compared with over thirty nowadays, to say nothing of one-day Internationals.

A similar gulf existed between 1845 and 1880. At the beginning of this period, the almanacs and annuals recorded the deeds of Alfred Mynn and Fuller Pilch, of William Clarke and Joseph Guy. There were no pads, bats were made from a single piece of wood, and it was illegal to sweep or roll the pitch between innings. Only Sussex, Nottinghamshire and Surrey existed as county sides, in terms of present first-class status. There was no distinction between first-class and minor counties until 1864, when a County Championship was first introduced, to be contested between Cambridgeshire, Hampshire, Kent, Middlesex, Nottinghamshire, Surrey, Sussex and Yorkshire.

In 1845, bowling was either underarm or round arm, and cricketers from any part of the country played for whichever team would hire them. By 1880, overarm bowling had long been legalised, and rules governing playing qualifications for counties had been agreed. In 1845, there were no scoreboards, no scorecards, no *Wisden*, no Tests, and no tours (although an attempt had been made in 1789 by the Duke of Leeds to take a party of cricketers to Paris, at the invitation of the British Ambassador to France, but, understandably, the tour was cancelled – it was not an auspicious date for noblemen to visit Paris). In 1845, there were striped shirts and all manner of hats – boaters, billycocks, toppers and flat 'ats. W.L. Murdoch's team, that questioned the establishment order of things almost as much as Darwin, Freud and Marx were doing elsewhere, wore whites, and matching blazers and caps, and, in photographs, appear models of uniform decorum.

But in 1845, there was the Oval, a brand new cricket ground for the Montpelier Club, late of the Bee Hive Ground, Walworth. There is a dispute over who first played at the Oval. From certain records, it would appear that the first match ever was that between W. Fould's XI and W. Houghton's XI, on 13th May 1845. The first game involving the Montpelier Club was that against Clapton, on 17th July. Although there was no *Wisden* at that time, full details were listed in *Lillywhite's Cricket Scores and Biographies of Celebrated Cricketers:*

CLAPTON

Anthony Gibson Esq	run out	2
T Craven Esq	c Coltson b Garland	9
C Gordon Esq	b Garland	9
E Cooper Esq	b Gardner	18
John Walker Esq	c Peto b Lewis	8
A K George Esq	b Gardner	1
W H Davies	c David b Gardner	13
W Nicholson	b Lewis	28
S Lancaster	b Garland	12
G Bode	c Garland b Lewis	5
G Trust	not out	4
	Byes 11 Wides 23	34
		143

MONTPELIER

H Gardner Esq	c Walker b Craven	23
J Grove Esq	run out	0
J Spenceby Esq	run out	31
C Coltson Esq	hit wicket b Craven	11
C Whything Esq	not out	1
	Byes 4 Wides 7 Noes 2	13
		79

Match unfinished
Mr Coltson got all his runs by singles

'This is, it is believed, the first match that ever took place on Kennington Oval. The extent of the ground is 10 acres, and, as the name implies, oval in shape . . . during the winter of 1844–5 it was arranged that the Montpelier Club should remove to the Oval, and the Club very generously gave a large sum of money from their funds to enable the new proprietor make the new ground good for cricket by laying down with turf about 4 acres in the centre . . .'

At least five other matches were played at the Oval that summer. Montpelier played Lingfield, and Islington Albion (twice); the Gentlemen of Surrey took on the Players of Surrey, the former team including Felix and William Denison; and 'A Surrey XI So Called' played against Mitcham. All these games were unfinished, and the highest total was 150 by the Players of Surrey. The first definite result at the Oval was on 26th May 1846, when the MCC beat Surrey by 48 runs, thanks largely to the bowling of W. Hillyer, who took 14 wickets for the MCC.

A variety of clubs and teams played at the Oval; the South London Club, Montpelier, I Zingari, the Blues, the House of Commons. And there were clubs from all over the south east of England and the far flung suburbs of London, who came as visitors: Putney, Banstead, Clapton, Islington, Chatham, Sevenoaks Vine, Blackheath, Southgate. The mighty Alfred Mynn made his first appearance at the Oval on 11th June 1846, playing for Mitcham against Surrey Club. He made one of the first 50s on the ground, and a fortnight later was back, playing for Kent against Surrey.

The first of several tied matches at the Oval occurred on the 1st, 2nd and 3rd July 1847, when Surrey played Kent. Surrey batted first and made 112 (J.M. Lee Esq 40, N. Felix Esq 46 not out). Hillyer took six wickets and Mynn four. Kent then made 127 (W. Pilch 24, F. Pilch 29). Mynn, all six foot and twenty stone of him, was understandably run out for 6. In their second innings, the Surrey tail wagged – Lee made 20, Felix 25, Hoare 26, D. Hayward (going in at number nine) 24, Chester (at number ten) 36. 'Kent made it a tie in their second innings with only seven wickets down,' reported Lillywhite, 'but the last three, Whittaker, Martin and Belton failed to make the winning run.'

On the 22nd, 23rd and 24th July 1847, the MCC beat Surrey in a game that was remarkable as it was the first instance at the Oval of a side following on and winning. Surrey made 197, a good score in those days – Felix 42, Hoare 38, Hillyer took 5 wickets. The MCC made only 91, but in their second innings more than doubled this, being all out for 216. Surrey, needing 111, the dreaded 'Nelson' to win, were all out for 101, Hillyer taking another six wickets. Fred Lillywhite's *Cricket Scores and Biographies* was delighted: 'the MCC followed their innings and won the match!!! This is the only match ever played in which the side having to follow its innings, being 100 runs behind, did yet win the match. The rule was first made in 1835 and continued till 15th May 1854, when the MCC settled that the 100 should be reduced to 80 for two or three-day matches, and 60 for a one-day affair. After that, several times has a side followed and won.'

An early low point in Surrey's lost fortunes at the Oval was on 16th and 17th August 1847, when Clapton beat Surrey by an innings and 81 runs. Two days later, a novelty match was played: Slow Bowlers of the Surrey Club v Fast Bowlers of the Surrey Club. Slows scored 114 and 85, of which 20 were extras, the one advantage that the Slow Bowlers might expect. The Fast Bowlers scored 153 and 46 for 3 wickets. Novelty matches were often held. They attracted followers who might not otherwise be tempted to go to a game of cricket, and they enabled the same players to turn out in a variety of guises. In 1850, Right-Handed Surrey Club beat Left-Handed Surrey Club by an innings and 66 runs. The match was played 'for the benefit of Sherman, Lockyer, Brockwell and Taylor, bowlers to the Surrey Club' (Lockyer was not yet regarded as a specialist wicket keeper). In 1858, England played Eighteen Veterans, who included Martingell and Mynn. As late as 1874, a novelty match was arranged for Gentlemen of England Who Had Not Been Educated At The Universities v Gentlemen of England Who Had Been Educated At The Universities (Past and Present).

Sherman was a neat looking cricketer and a fine all-rounder. A series of games were played between the Gentlemen of the Surrey Club and County and the Players. The Gentlemen seemed determined that the odds should be in their favour, for they played as Sixteen in July 1849, and Twenty in September 1849, both times against only eleven Players. In the second of these matches, Sherman took 10 wickets in the first innings of the Gentlemen and 11 in the second. He also top scored in both the Players' innings, with 32 not out and 36. Two years later, in a flurry of undiplomatic cricket, the Players beat the Gentlemen of Surrey by 263 runs. Sherman came very close to being the first person to score a century at the Oval, on 9th September 1850, when he made 93 for the Players of South v Sixteen Gentlemen of South.

There were still dozens of matches played at that time where one or both teams exceeded eleven players. In July 1853, an England Eleven played Twenty two of I Zingari at the Oval. I Zingari included its quota of aristocrats, including the Earl of Leicester, Viscount Dupplin, and Lord Guernsey. 'This match was played for Thomas Beagley's benefit. Tremendously muddy and dirty and very heavy rain, but I Zingari continued in the field. The result of this match (unfinished) showed the utter inequality of a contest between Eleven and Twenty Two when the latter can field as well as bowl. Generally the England Elevens find themselves opposed to twenty twos most of whom do more harm than good in the field, and drop catches innumerably . . .' Thomas Beagley was an old Hampshire cricketer. The two teams played another benefit for him later in the season, as this first game was ruined by rain.

The first appearance of Julius Caesar at the Oval was in August 1848, when he played for Godalming against the Surrey Club. The Surrey Club gave up this match – '509 runs in this match, and only 26 wickets got,' recorded Lillywhite. The following year, Julius Caesar joined Surrey, as did two other early heroes, Tom Lockyer and William Caffyn. In the following three seasons (1849–1851), the County was unbeaten. 'Lovers of the noble game soon began to flock round the standard of Surrey, and success in the tented field added greatly to its prosperity.'

In 1848, Fourteen of Surrey beat England by 8 wickets, in a game where England took 508 balls to score 77 runs in their second innings. Batting was a slow and on the whole defensive art in those days. Newspaper reports praised the 'defence' of many batsmen, without considering the effect such technique might have on the game, the spectators, or the outcome of the match.

In 1857, two fixtures were held at the Oval for the first time. On 25th and 26th June, Rugby played Marlborough as Lord's was unavailable. The two schools met twice more at the Oval, in 1863 and 1867. The other innovation was Gentlemen v Players, a fixture that proved very popular and was an annual event at the Oval as well as Lord's. A strong Players side, including Caesar, Caffyn, John Lillywhite, Parr, Wisden and Lockyer, beat the Gentlemen by 10 wickets. Four of the Walker brothers of Southgate and Middlesex played for the Gentlemen.

1857 was a good year for Surrey, who lost only one game, at Manchester by three runs, and the following year they were undefeated, with victories over Kent and Sussex, Cambridgeshire, Notts, England, and the North of England. Membership doubled in three years, and the Committee began to look round for matches 'of still greater attraction'. In the same year came at long last the first century at the Oval, and the first team score of over 300. Playing for Surrey Club, F.P. Miller Esq. scored 135 not out against Westbourne Club (Lord's) with Grundy. Haygarth had now taken over from Fred Lillywhite as compiler of the *Cricket Scores and Biographies*, and he added a surly footnote to this match: 'The Westbourne was a minor club meeting at Lords.' Despite this, Miller's was a great achievement. Anyone who has inspected and handled a bat of that vintage will appreciate the strength and grit that must have been needed to play such an innings, and the amount of Sloan's liniment that needed to be applied afterwards.

John and William Burrup, writing in Lillywhite's *Cricket Scores*, described Surrey's performance in 1859, 1860 and 1861 as 'honourably maintaining her position, winning very uphill matches, where the odds have been considerably against her, including, for the first time, single-handed against England; at the same time losing others which seemed an easy task' – plus ça change . . .

Occasionally in cricket, a match goes down in history as belonging to one player: Laker's Test at Old Trafford in 1956, Fowler's Match at Lords in July 1910, Jessop's Test at the Oval in 1902. In terms of a remarkable all-round performance, the match between Surrey and England in 1859, on 21st, 22nd and 23rd July, may accurately be described as Walker's Match. Vyell Edward Walker was twenty two years old when he played the game of his life, for England against Surrey. He scored 20 not out and 108, and, with his lob bowling, took all ten wickets in Surrey's first innings and another four in the second.

By 1862, Surrey were strong enough to take on All England in a three-day game played on 25th, 26th and 27th August. All England batted first, and got off to a good start, J. Grundy, a professional, scoring 95. Surrey used several bowlers: Caffyn, Humphrey, Mr Miller, Griffith, Stephenson – even the wicket-keeper, Lockyer, was tried. By close of play on the first day, however, All England were in a strong position: 3 for 244, with Carpenter 61 not out and Hayward 28 not out.

On the second day, runs continued to come at a steady pace. Eventually, Carpenter was caught and bowled by Stephenson for 95, but Hayward went on to make 117 before he was bowled by Lockyer. Both Carpenter and Hayward received talent money from the Surrey Club on their return to the pavilion. Hayward was out with the score at 402 for 5. Anderson was joined by the Hon C.G. Lyttelton, and together they put on 43 before Lyttelton was caught at the wicket by Griffith off the bowling of the Surrey captain, Miller. It was accepted practice at that time to change wicket-keepers during the course of an innings, specialist techniques developed later in the century. All but the last two batsmen, Mr V.E. Walker and Biddulph, made a few, and the innings closed at 503, which was then the largest score ever recorded in cricket.

It had taken All England the best part of two days to amass that score, however, and it was almost six o'clock on the second day before Surrey began their first innings, Mortlock and Humphrey facing the bowling of Walker and Willsher. Humphrey was out with the score at 4, Mr Burbridge strode to the wicket, and then came the sensation described in Chapter 2. Willsher was no balled five times in a row by John Lillywhite, the umpire, and the game was abandoned for the rest of the day, with the Surrey score at 15 for 1. Eventually the match was ruined by rain, and ended in a draw, Surrey making 154 for 6 in their second innings.

Mention has already been made of the first ever tour by a party of Australian cricketers to Britain in 1868. The first match of that tour was Eleven Aboriginal Black Australians v Eleven Gentlemen of Surrey Club, held at the Oval on 25th and 26th May.

One of the men most responsible for organising the tour of the Aborigines was Charles Lawrence, an ex-Surrey player who had gone on the first tour of Australia in 1861, and had settled there, becoming the proprietor of a hotel. Lawrence was a friend of another Surrey cricketer, H.H. Stephenson, and had maintained his links with the Surrey Club. Added to that, it was William Burrup, the Surrey Secretary who had assisted the departure of Stephenson's party to Australia, seven years earlier, arranging Lawrence's life insurance, organising the farewell dinner at the Bridgehouse Hotel, London Bridge (run by the family of Julius Caesar), and travelling to Liverpool to see the party embark.

When Lawrence returned to London in the spring of 1868 to captain the Aboriginal team, he attended the Surrey Cricket Club Dinner, and arrangements were made for the first match of the Aborigines tour to be played at the Oval. The Aborigines were based at West Malling, in Kent, and there is evidence that they practised hard for their opening match. The opening day was a fine one, and the visitors travelled by train from Kent. A great deal of publicity surrounded them at this stage of their tour, and a great deal of curiosity followed them. People wanted to know how they spoke, how they behaved, and what they looked like. *The Times* devoted most of the space in its report of the first day's play to these matters: 'Their hair and beards are long and wiry; their skins vary in shades of blackness, and most of them have broadly-expanded nostrils, but they are all of the true Australian type . . . In order that the lookers-on might be able to recognize each man, a sash differing in colour was affixed to his shirt.' *Sporting Life* sought to reassure its readers: 'They are the first Australian natives who have visited this country on such a novel expedition, but it must not be inferred that they are savages; on the contrary, the managers of the speculation make no pretence to anything other than purity of race and origin. They were perfectly civilised . . .'

The Aboriginal Touring Team of 1868. *From the MCC Collection*

Surrey won the toss and decided to bat. It was perhaps not Surrey's strongest side, but it did contain at least three of those who had played against England two summers earlier – Jupp, Miller and Noble – and ten of the team were first-class cricketers.

At a quarter past twelve, Jupp and Noble opened the batting for Surrey. Mullagh, the most successful player on the tour, scoring 1698 runs and taking

245 wickets, bowled the first over to a field that consisted of wicket-keeper (doubling slip!), deep slip, point, cover, third man, mid off, mid on, short leg, long leg and longstop – a more attacking field than that set by Spofforth twelve years later.

Mullagh and Lawrence bowled steadily, sending down seven maidens in succession. The fielding was keen, though the throwing lacked accuracy, but too much was expected of Mullagh and Lawrence as bowlers. They bowled 101 overs of the 115 Surrey faced, and, once they tired, Surrey scored more easily. All the Aborigines bowled overarm: Lawrence bowled the occasional underarm lob. Mr W. Baggallay scored 68 for Surrey, in three and three-quarter hours, but half the side were out for 124. The tail wagged, Mr Barton and Mr Hibberd enjoyed a profitable last wicket partnership, and Surrey were all out for 222 at a quarter past five. The Aborigines began their first innings at six o'clock, with an hour left for play, and when stumps were drawn had scored 4 for 34, but Mullagh was still there.

There had been a large crowd at the Oval for the first day's play, over 7000 spectators, and the second day proved as popular. 'Long before Tuesday's business commenced the Oval presented an unusual gathering of spectators,' reported *The Times*. In an hour and ten minutes of the morning session, the Aborigines lost their remaining six wickets for another 49 runs, and were all out for 83. Only Mullagh impressed *The Times* correspondent – 'Their batting is sadly wanting in power'. The Aborigines followed on, faired better in their second innings, being all out for 132, but still lost by an innings and seven runs. Mullagh was top scorer in both innings, making 33 and 73. These were impressive performances, and, though there was a suggestion that Surrey did not bowl their best bowlers until late in the second innings, Mullagh was cheered from the field and awarded a cash prize. The spectators were pleased, the promoters were pleased; more than £600 had been taken at the turnstiles. William Burrup received £150 on behalf of the Surrey Club, the local constabulary received £20 for policing the ground, and a pound was given to each of the umpires, one of whom was Julius Caesar.

The only person who wasn't pleased would appear to have been *The Times* correspondent, who wrote: 'The blacks returned the ball quickly, but not with precision . . . in several instances their batting exhibited on the day in question a great deficiency in those defensive attributes which are requisite for a protracted stand against good bowling. In running between wickets their judgement is much at fault, both on account of slowness and hesitancy. Doubtless, some of these defects will be overcome by the practice with good players during their stay in this country.' For one of the Aborigines, sadly, there was no time to practise his skills. Brippokei, better known in England as King Cole, died of TB in Guy's Hospital on 24th June.

That same summer the Surrey wicket-keeper Edward Pooley made cricket history when he dismissed 12 opponents in the match against Sussex. It's a record that still stands, though it has been equalled twice since, by Don Tallon and H.B. Taber. After Tom Lockyer, Pooley was the second of a long line of outstanding wicket-keepers at the Oval. He was born in 1838, but, when he first applied to join the Surrey staff, he knocked five years off his age, as his father believed he would stand a better chance of being employed if he claimed to be younger. He first played at the Oval, as a bowler, in 1861 for Surrey Colts v Gentlemen of Surrey Club with Hayes and Heartfield. Two years later, he was introduced to wicket-keeping: 'Old Tom Lockyer's hands were bad, and the ground being fiery he could not take his usual place behind the sticks. Mr Miller, the Surrey captain, was in a quandary as to who should relieve him, so I, saucy-like, as usual, went up to him and said "Mr Miller, let me have a try." . . . "Nonsense," said he, and just at that moment H.H. Stephenson came up and remarked "Let the young 'un have a go, sir." Mr Miller thereon relented. I donned the gloves, quickly got two or three wickets, and seemed so much at home that Tom Lockyer was delighted, and said I was born to keep wicket and would have to be his successor in the Surrey team.' (A.W. Pullen – *Talks with Old English Cricketers*) Wicket-keeping was a painful job at that time. Gloves afforded little protection, and there were some wild wickets on which to keep. The Rev. John Mitford, writing in *The Gentleman's Magazine*, gave a vivid description: 'The blood of a cricketer is seldom shed from any part of his body but his fingers; but the fingers of an old cricketer, so scarred, so bent, so shattered, so indented, so contorted, so venerable! are enough to bring tears of envy and emulation from any eye – we are acquainted with *such a pair of hands*, if hands they may be called, that shape have none.' Such a description would have fitted Lockyer, Pooley, or even Strudwick.

For twenty years, Pooley kept wicket at the Oval, until his own hands were ruined and he had no career left. He was a tough character: in 1871 he made 93 against Kent at Canterbury, when batting with a broken finger. He was also not beyond a sharp cricketing practice which he indulged in with the help of a couple of Surrey's close-to-the-wicket fielders. If the bowler bowled down the leg side, Pooley would take the ball, but would immediately turn round pretending he had missed it altogether. Slip and short leg would then set off in pursuit of the mythical missing ball, as though seeking to save four byes. The batsman would look round, see this helter-skelter piece of action, and naturally set off for a run. Pooley would then swing round and stump him. He was alleged to have taken quite a lot of wickets in this way, many of them from the slow off-break bowling of Southerton.

In later years, Pooley fell on hard times. He was frequently seeking shelter in the workhouse, and the minutes of meetings of the Surrey Committee contain several sad references to letters from Pooley or appearances by Pooley, asking for financial support. The Club made regular payments, but Pooley was not able to manage his affairs any more successfully even with this help. His obituary in *Wisden* mentions faults in private character, but concludes that 'even to the last he had a geniality and sense of humour that to a certain extent condoned his weaknesses.' The sad decline of Pooley may be set against happier stories. James Southerton fared far better. Arthur Haygarth's biography records that 'On 20th April 1875, Southerton became "mine host" of the Cricketers Inn on Mitcham Green, but he is (or was) by occupation a hairdresser, and is a popular, temperate, pleasant, and well-informed man on cricket matters, and a favourite with all.'

The summer of 1869 saw several outstanding performances at the Oval, Grace scored 215 for the Gentlemen against the Players, and at least one enthralling finish. Surrey's games against Middlesex have always held a particular fascination – north of the river meeting south of the river, Lords meeting the Oval, patricians meeting plebs, pomposity meeting insolence. When the two sides met in August, Middlesex batted first and were all out in an hour and a half for 76, Bristow (5-29) and Street (4-43) bowling unchanged throughout the innings. Surrey made 353, Jupp scoring 106 not out, and Pooley 88. Middlesex fought back in their second innings, and at twenty to two on the third day they were 4 for 247, only thirty behind and with six wickets in hand, R.D. and I.D. Walker still together after having added over a hundred. Two hours later, Middlesex were all out for 313, and C.W. Potter and W.J. Collyer were opening the batting for Surrey with only 37 wanted to win.

Wisden described the wicket as 'dead but otherwise good'. *The Times* commented that 'most persons present expected to see this magnificent "set" accomplished without much ceremony . . .' The more facetious of Surrey supporters will, however, claim to recognise Surrey's long practised ability to snatch defeat from the jaws of victory, even when, as in this match, the odds were 100 to 1 in their favour.

Howitt and R.D. Walker, for Middlesex, bowled five maidens. This presented no problem for Surrey, there was plenty of time to get the runs. Potter then ran himself out (1 wicket for 0 runs). Jupp came in and scored 14. The crowd perked up. Collyer then had his middle stump uprooted by Howitt (15 for 2). In Howitt's next over, Jupp was caught at short leg by I.D. Walker (16 for 3). R.D. Walker then 'crumpled up' two more Surrey wickets: Stephenson was taken at point by Hearne, and Griffith, seeking to hit his way out of trouble, smote the ball far into the outfield where I.D. Walker took a good catch at long on (16 for 5). Mortlock now joined Humphrey. There followed a leg bye, and a single to Humphrey, and then Howitt knocked Mortlock's off stump out of the ground (18 for 6). Pooley hit his first ball for 4, which 'elicited much applause'. A drive for 3 by Humphrey 'also evoked cheers', but at 26 Humphrey 'laid himself open to the wicket keeper', by which is meant that he was stumped, and 7 wickets were down – 11 runs wanted. 'Mr Ackroyd became Pooley's partner' – cricket must have been the only game in existence that brought two such people together in a common pursuit – but Mr Ackroyd scored only 1 'and retired', by which *The Times* meant was bowled by Howitt (31 for 8 – 6 wanted). 'The

Middlesex captain managed his forces admirably, but he was unable to keep the batting of Pooley in subjection, and the winning hit was affected by a piece of fielding not altogether deficient in novelty and bustle.' How the Oval crowd must have loved that last moment, and what a tragedy that we don't have further details.

Seven years later, in August 1876, Surrey and Middlesex met again and produced an even more exciting result. In fine weather Middlesex batted first and began disastrously, losing their first six wickets (five of them amateurs) for 54 runs. Burghess, one of the only three professionals in the Middlesex side, then put on 59 with Mr Taylor, but the last three wickets fell quickly, and Middlesex were all out at 3.50 for 138, Southerton taking 5 for 38 in 39 (4 ball) overs.

At ten past four, Jupp and Mr Avory opened the Surrey innings, *Wisden* describing Mr Avory as a 'fresh hand'. The much more experienced Jupp was first to go, caught by I.D. Walker off Henderson. Elliott was bowled by the same bowler without scoring, and Surrey were 18 for 2. Avory proved he could 'hit a bit' and had made 31 before he was caught by Webbe off V.E. Walker – three of the seven Walker brothers were in the Middlesex side that day. Surrey slumped to 105 for 6, and Barratt then joined W.W. Read, the Surrey captain. By close of play on the first day, they had put on 54, Mr Read not out 68, Barratt not out 31.

Friday, the second day, was blisteringly hot. In the first hour, Surrey lost their remaining four wickets for 57 runs, Read being bowled by Henderson for 94. Lunch was then taken in the cool of the pavilion, and Middlesex started their second innings at twenty to two. Street quickly got rid of Webbe, but two of the Walkers (I.D. and R.D.) put on 49 before Jones, 'the little lad from Mitcham' – made a capital one-hand catch at slip, and thereby ended Mr I.D. Walker's innings for 25. Mr R.D. Walker and Mr Buller then struck the Surrey bowling for 64 at nearly a run a ball before Mr Buller was caught by Swann off the little lad from Mitcham for 32 (122 for 3, Middlesex 45 runs ahead). Walker and Mr R.J. Webbe, brother of the opener A.J. Webbe, caused a lot of Surrey sweat to be shed, putting on 86 before Webbe was bowled by Southerton. Burghes was similarly dismissed first ball (208 for 5, Middlesex 131 ahead). Lambert was bowled by Street without scoring, but Walker and Mr Turner batted well until Walker was caught in the deep by Jupp off Street for 104 (263 for 7).

The third day, Saturday 12th August, was again hot and a large crowd gathered for the end of the match. Middlesex started the day at 271 for 8, and the last two wickets added another 51 runs, mainly thanks to Mr Turner 41 not out, and V.E. Walker 23. In the second innings, Southerton bowled 65.3 four-ball overs, to take 3 for 88. In terms of a six-ball over, he had match figures of 69.5 overs, an incalculable number of maidens, 126 runs and 8 wickets.

Surrey were left needing 246 to win, and had twenty five minutes batting before lunch. In that time Jupp and Mr Avory indulged themselves and plundered 58 off the Middlesex bowling. Avory was out soon after lunch, caught and bowled by R.D. Walker for 42, and poor Elliott was run out for a 'pair'. Jupp and W.W. Read took the score to 119 before Jupp was bowled for 43. Wickets then fell regularly: 128 for 5 (Pooley lbw), 133 for 6 (Mr Lindsay bowled), 145 for 7 (Read stumped). The little lad from Mitcham joined Barratt, who was batting well, and stayed with him while 46 valuable runs were added. Lambert took a good catch at long-on to dismiss Jones for 16, and Surrey needed 55 to win with only two wickets left.

There was plenty of time left, and no chance of the weather interfering, but Barratt and Southerton played a naturally aggressive game, in the words of *Wisden* they 'got well hold'. The score mounted ... 220 ... 230 ... 240 ... Southerton hit hard and high, and Lambert clung on to the ball at square leg. Six to win, one wicket to fall. Street joined Barratt amidst great excitement. Barratt was now facing R.D. Walker. He pushed the ball away for a single. Street held out for the rest of the over. Henderson bowled to Barratt, who carved him for 3 (9 for 244). Street then managed to score a single, the scores were level, and Barratt (61 not out) was now facing Henderson. The match looked safe for Surrey, but Barratt mistimed his stroke and was easily caught at cover. It was the fourth first-class Tie at the Oval in just over thirty years cricket.

On 2nd and 3rd September 1878, the Surrey Club organised a match between the Australians and Eleven English Professionals. As is so often the case in early September, the weather was fine and warm, and crowds of well over 10,000 gathered on both days. The match was so successful that the original payment of £10 to each English professional was increased to £20, perhaps sowing the seeds of future discord when Abel and company made their demand years later.

It was a low scoring match which the Australians (77 and 89) won by eight runs, dismissing the Professionals for 82 and 76. The finish was exciting enough, but the most remarkable feature of the match was Barratt's bowling for the Professionals in the Australians' first innings. In those days, coverage of cricket matches in the press was spacious. *The Times* could afford a gently unfolding introduction to the story of the first day's play: 'Seeing that the long list of engagements entered into by the Australians is rapidly coming to nought, such a match as that provided at the Oval yesterday could scarcely be wanting in public patronage. It was not. Thousands were attracted to the spot before the umpires set the contenders in array, and the number gradually increased until one of those densely compact circles was formed so characteristic of Kennington when an "event" transpires ...'

Leisurely stuff, and lots of it: in the press-box, sheaf after sheaf of paper was covered with such detail. And yet the only reference to Barratt's achievement that day came in the last paragraph of *The Times* report: 'The bowling of Barratt will be chronicled among the marvels of the season, as in 29 overs for 43 runs he obtained all the wickets.' *Wisden* contained a detailed report of the match – over 1100 words. One line was devoted to Barratt: 'Barratt's bowling captured all 10 wickets – 3 stumped, 7 caught out.'

It was hardly an every day occurrence, having been performed only eleven times in the previous thirty years, though, admittedly, it did happen a little more often on the far more sporting and under-prepared wickets of the 1870s. Maybe the problem was that Barratt was a professional, a left-handed bowler from Durham. Cricket had been invented by amateurs, developed by amateurs. The Oval and the Surrey Club had been conceived and founded by amateurs. In the contemporary press, far more time was devoted to discussing the prowess, gifts, yes, and genius of gentlemen than the earnest endeavours of worthy professionals. Cricket was about batting, at which the gentlemen were extremely good, and professionals were mostly bowlers, who were hired to afford the gentlemen batting practice. Such was the origin of the professional cricketer. For decades, the Gentlemen v Players match at the Oval, and that at Lords up to the last game in 1962, showed the Gents producing a formidable array of batting talent, but scarce able to find an adequate bowling attack.

Or maybe Barratt failed to achieve the fame he deserved simply because, in 1878, the Australians were underrated. The contrast between the coverage of Barratt's '10' and Laker's similar performance against the Australians at the Oval in 1956 is enormous. Maybe Barratt should have waited till after the birth of the Ashes, when Australian cricket was viewed in a totally different light, and when England was embarked, forever, on a quest for revenge.

In all events, it is surely safe to assume that Barratt was suitably grateful for the bonus of £5 he received 'in compliment to the great success of his bowling in obtaining all the ten wickets in Australia's first innings.' He ought to have done much better, financially. An enterprising young couple, claiming to have authority from the Surrey Club, took a collection for Barratt, and then made off with it. 'The pair,' wrote Alcock, 'proved to be members of the light-fingered fraternity, and decamped with their spoils unsuspected.'

Chapter Five

The Golden Age – 1881 to 1900

The Test match of 1880 saw the coming of age of the Oval as one of the major cricket grounds in the world, but, as the report in *The Manchester Guardian* at the time of that Test made abundantly clear, there was a great deal to be done to ensure that the Oval was the right ground for the grand occasion.

In December 1881, the thirty one year lease of the Oval (from 1874) was assigned to Frederick, Earl of Bessborough, to John, Baron Monson, and to Wildman Cattley of 42 Davies Street, Berkeley Square, Middlesex. The rent was £100 per year, and the Oval was described as ' . . . formerly used as a Nursery Ground or Market garden but now and for some time past used as a Cricket Ground by the Surrey County Cricket Club together with the dwelling house then and for some time past used as a Tavern or Public House for the sale of beer and other liquors and refreshments for the accommodation of persons attending the said Cricket Ground.' The lease specifically referred to the tavern, Pavilion, racquet court, out offices, sheds and other buildings.

The Club had become increasingly prosperous. Visits by the Australians in 1878 and 1880 had given cricket a great lift. Large crowds regularly attended first-class matches, and many newspapers carried match reports and details. At the Oval, after the 1880 Test, it was time to arrange accommodation for the Press. To the west of the Pavilion was a stand, and it was proposed to erect a wooden building to adjoin this stand. This new building would be on three floors and would serve three purposes. On the bottom level there was to be a printing room where up-to-date scorecards could be printed during matches. The middle level would serve as a press-box, and the upper level would be for the scorers. It lasted a short time only. Larger crowds meant that the Committee wished to enlarge the West Stand, and the wooden 'annex' was moved to the east end of the Pavilion.

Meanwhile, the excavation of a vast drain, capable of taking the water of the Effra, the stream that bordered part of the Oval, had provided the Club with enough subsoil to build up an embankment round the whole ground, giving standing spectators a much better view. The contractors excavating the drain, not only supplied the soil to the Surrey Club, but made up the embankment and turfed it free of charge. A quarter of a century later, Alverstone and Alcock surveyed the embankment with some pride and not a little wistfulness: 'What a splendid arena it would present, if the whole, or a part of the extensive area, could be covered in wholly or partially . . .! Unfortunately the Surrey authorities are not the freeholders, and cannot do what they like with the ground. In this case many things would be done which, under existing circumstances, have to be left undone, from no fault of theirs . . .'

As well as changes to the ground, there had been changes in the personnel at the Oval. In January 1881, the splendidly named Wildman Cattley was elected Treasurer, replacing his brother (Mark Cattley). A few months earlier, a new groundsman was appointed, following the death of George Street, 'a painstaking and conscientious worker who had taken charge of the ground for some years and with great credit'. Even so, the ground was not reckoned to be in good condition, and the Committee worried over whom to appoint as Street's successor. Eventually they picked John Newton, who had previously worked at the South Essex Club Ground at Upton Park.

Newton had plenty to do. At this time it was the practice to allow several clubs to use the Oval for practice as well as matches. A kind of open house was kept, and, such was the use the ground suffered, both the 'square' and the practice wickets wanted renovation. One of Newton's earliest jobs was to superintend the re-turfing of much of the Oval, and the Committee appear to have been satisfied with his work.

Also in 1881, the decision was taken to roof over the stands to the west of the Pavilion, though the work itself was postponed for a year. A further financial boost was given to the Club by the Australian visits in 1882. It wasn't simply a question of the Test match. The Australians played five matches at the Oval that year, against Surrey, the Gentlemen of England, Players of England, Shaw's Eleven, and, of course, the Ashes Test. Receipts for these matches amounted to £6387.8s.9d, the game against Gentlemen of England bringing in more money than the Test match. This bonanza inspired further ambitious schemes. At that time, a skating rink stood at the Vauxhall end of the ground, covering the area that is presently a car park. It was decided to build a covered stand in front of the skating rink, mainly for use in the winter when football matches were played at the Oval – in fact, for a long time, the stand was known as the Football Stand. In the same year, an asphalt path was laid at the back of the Pavilion, and in 1883, a canvas covering was added to the uncovered stand reserved for members, the tiers of the covered stand were 'tar paved', and the banks on the eastern side of the ground were concreted.

Little was done in the next couple of years to improve the ground facilities, despite another visit by the Australians in 1884. In 1885, however, an agreement was signed for the Tenancy of the tavern 'called The Surrey Club House' for one year renewable, between Bessborough, Monson and Wildman Cattley on the one hand, and Robert Reeder, licensed victualler of Middlesex, on the other. Reeder also held a licence to supply refreshments at Lords. The year's tenancy at the Oval cost him £250, and there was an impressive list of conditions as to the standards of service he was to supply:

1. To provide . . . ready for sale to the Members of the Surrey Cricket Club and all persons attending the adjoining Cricket ground . . . wines, Spirits, Ale and Porter in draught and in bottle lemonade ginger beer soda water seltzer water and provisions and all such other things as ought to be provided in taverns and Refreshment Rooms.
2. List of articles to be sold and prices to be charged to be handed to the Secretary on 1st May each year – to run for one year from that date.

Prices had to be 'fair, reasonable and usual to the satisfaction of the Committee'.

3. List of such prices to be printed in a bold legible manner and published in the Refreshment Rooms, etc.
4. A sufficient number of waiters and other persons and especially when Cricket Matches are about to be and whilst they are being played be employed to attend upon the persons using the premises so as to insure all Visitors and Customers being promptly and properly served.

This clause was to cause problems for the next fifty years.

5. All articles sold to be of best quality.
6 and 7. Furniture, rugs and carpets to be well maintained.
8. Tenant shall manage conduct and carry on business of the premises in a quiet orderly and business like and most approved manner and will not afford any reasonable ground for complaint by any person and shall submit to and carry out all regulations now or hereafter to be imposed by the Magistrates or other authorised granting any licence.

There followed five more conditions covering repairs, no alterations on Reeder's part without permission, no trades to be carried out without the assent in writing of the Surveyor General, nothing to be done that would make Reeder forfeit his licence, and the Tavern to be kept open for the sale of liquors (out of season). In return for all this, the Surrey Club were to insure the Tavern for £3000 and agreed not to let anyone else sell refreshments.

Early in 1887, the Club employed an architect, W. Braxton Smith, to prepare drawings and specifications for additions and alterations to the Pavilion, where the seating needed to be 'augmented', and for a small, new, separate building which was to serve as a dressing room for professionals. New turnstiles were also required at the back of the stand to the west of the Pavilion. In March, the building work was contracted to G. Davenport, a local firm of 100 Warner Road, Camberwell. The Committee was in a hurry to see the work done – what committee isn't – and there was a clause in the contract to the effect that the work had to be completed by the 1st May 1888 (the start of the following season), or Davenport would have to pay £2 per day for every extra day before the work was finished, a hefty sum a hundred years ago. The work on the Pavilion was to cost £729, and the professionals' building £85.

It would appear that the three-way partnership (Committee, Braxton Smith and Davenport) was satisfactory, for, exactly a year later, on 19th March 1888, a second contract was signed, for the addition of another dressing room and bathroom for the players, score-box and press-box, and a boiler-house for the provision of hot water to the dressing rooms. Davenport's potential penalty, if he failed to complete on time, was increased to £10 per day. The following year, a third contract was signed to cover the East Stand. The cost of all this work was £2758, but there was more to be done – a new luncheon room was created at the west end of the Pavilion, turnstiles were provided on the eastern side of the ground, opposite Clayton Street, and the Committee approved improvements to terracing and to the Football Pavilion. In 1890, the centre of the ground was levelled.

2nd July 1891. Gentlemen v Players. W. G. Grace bowling from the Vauxhall end. Grace played in 35 such matches at the Oval (and another 35 at Lords), scoring 2582 runs and taking 110 wickets.
© *Hulton-Deutsch Collection*

The Club was enjoying a period of great success. Surrey won the County Championship in 1890, 1891 and 1892. There were a great many applications for membership and vast crowds attended the most popular fixtures. The traditional August Bank Holiday game against Nottinghamshire in 1892 was reckoned to have attracted over 30,000 spectators on a single day. A vast photo montage hangs on the wall of the present Pavilion, by the door from which you must not exit if the bowling is from the Pavilion end, depicting the members of the Surrey Club in 1894. In the background is the old Pavilion, in the last few years of its life. It is a small, delicate building, and, with the two long and low covered stands to east and west of it, like the wings of some very early monoplane, it looks as though it is about to taxi across the ground preparatory to take-off. Not so the members: those in the foreground of the picture appear men (entirely men, of course, the suggestion of Mr Glanvill in July 1892 that lady members be admitted to the Club 'could not be entertained') of substance, but one cannot be too sure about those in the background. The membership lists at this time suggest that the Club was popular with Army officers, men who had spent the best years of their lives administering the far-flung Empire and had now returned to the mother country, actors, stockbrokers and 'gentlemen'. There are some well known names among them – in 1898 Arthur Boosey, 'music publisher', was elected. P. Stuart Surridge became a member, as did Sidney Pardon, the editor of *Wisden*, and H.S. Altham, who wrote a famous 'History of Cricket'.

Not all, however, was sweetness and light. The behaviour of some gentlemen was less than could be desired. In June 1886, a complaint of 'using foul language' was made against the Captain of the Mitcham Cricket Club. The following month the famous Barratt, one of Surrey's best bowlers, was suspended for a week (' . . . not to enter the ground . . .') and had to apologise to Mr Howe 'to the latter's satisfaction for using insulting language'. By August, the Committee had still heard nothing from Mr Hooper, the Captain of Mitcham, and so it resolved that 'no matches in the future were to be arranged with the Mitcham Club'. That same day came Mr Hooper's apology. There were also problems with members' behaviour. Sir Timothy O'Brien was a dashing cricketer, a fiery Irishman, and a man who enjoyed an altercation. One Bank Holiday, he made a 'scene' at the Oval, and the Committee promptly barred him from the pavilion. Sir Timothy left, and returned not long after, under the sponsorship of another member, who happened to be his butler.

The Oval was a busy place, with lacrosse, football, cycling and skating taking place, as well as cricket. As a result, the playing area itself was taking a battering and needed much constant attention. The groundsman, Newton, lasted only a few years in the post, and was succeeded by another, with the splendidly appropriate name of Over. It's all too easy to envisage confusion and misunderstandings – the umpire calling 'Over!' and the groundsman hurrying out, merely to discover that four balls had been bowled and the action was changing ends –

or convoluted sentences along the lines of: 'We'll have the heavy roller run over the pitch after this over, Over'. Small wonder, perhaps, that Over lasted even less time than Newton. His spell as groundsman was all over in no time – maybe he couldn't stand the jokes. Early in 1887, the Club advertised for a new groundsman, and, from the several well-qualified applicants, they selected Sam Apted, a Surrey man (he had played for the Surrey Colts) who had gained a local reputation at Bickley Park Club, where he had produced 'one of the best run-getting grounds in the kingdom'. He was to stay at the Oval as Head Groundsman for 24 years, sending his requests to the Committee, in neat handwriting, respectfully worded: requests for turf, loam, manure, a horse, new clothes for one of the groundsboys, repairs to the hose, gravel, a new barrow for Martin, brooms, brushes and gully traps.

This may be described as the Age of the Three As, for in 1895 Viscount Oxenbridge resigned as President, and was succeeded by Sir Richard Webster, who was later to become Lord Alverstone. Alverstone, Alcock (the Secretary) and Apted (the Groundsman) looked after the fortunes of the Oval during one of its major periods of growth and re-organisation. Alverstone and Alcock were born within three weeks of each other, in 1842. Alcock was appointed Secretary in 1872. He was a great sportsman, playing cricket for Essex, captaining England at soccer, helping to establish the FA Cup Competition and being a founder member of The Wanderers Football Club who won the Cup several times in its early years, and later becoming Vice President of the Mid-Surrey Golf Club. He was also a JP and a prolific writer. For 26 years he was the editor of *Cricket*, and with Alverstone, he wrote and edited *Surrey Cricket, its History and Associations*, referred to at the Oval today as 'The Old Testament'.

C. W. Alcock who organised the first Test match to be played in England at the Oval. © *Allsport*

Alverstone, too, was an athlete. He was a great middle distance runner, but gave up practising sport at a high level when he entered politics. In 1885, he was appointed Attorney-General in Salisbury's Government, a post that he held, on and off, until 1900. *Who Was Who* gives a mutedly attractive account of him. 'He was not a very clever man, nor a learned lawyer, nor a good speaker – either in the Courts or in Parliament. His equipment as an advocate consisted mainly in a splendid physique, a forcible personality, and immense industry. As a judge, he was dignified, and sitting with a jury was satisfactory, though not distinguished; but the reports will be searched in vain for judgements of his that are expositions of the law. Socially, he displayed a somewhat boisterous geniality which his detractors sometimes regarded as artificial. He was generous with his money, delighted in playing billiards and singing drawing-room songs, and was an assiduous church-goer.' It may well have been hard not to like him.

It was a testing time for the team, as decisions had to be made limiting the free market economy approach to the use of the Oval that had been going on for the last fifty years or more. At a General Meeting in October 1892, Mr J. Shuter (then Captain of the Surrey cricket team) moved that 'at the conclusion of the season, the centre of the ground be carefully roped round and that Football, with the exception of the final tie, be rigidly excluded from the enclosed space'.

Shuter didn't get his way immediately. Football was popular and brought income to the Club during the long winter months. Receipts from football for the winter 1888–89 amounted to well over two and a half thousand pounds. In July 1893, the Football Sub-Committee resolved that football 'be continued at the Oval for the present but having regard to the preservation of the ground . . .' In September 1894, the same sub-committee resolved 'that London Football Association and Crusaders be allowed to play the semi final of the London Senior Cup . . . as before – Crusaders v Westminster on 5th November . . .' It was also decided that football should not be played after 18th March, to give the ground time to recover, but this may well not have proved sufficient time. In July 1895, a Special General Meeting was called to consider a Resolution of the Committee to the effect that 'in their opinion football should not be played at the Oval'. A poll of members was held in September. They decided there was to be no more football at the Oval. 'Since then,' wrote Alverstone and Alcock, 'there has been none, and it is to be hoped in the best interests of cricket, which, after all, is the chief mission of the club, there never will be.'

There was quite enough to be done looking after the cricket ground and the existing buildings if the members were to be kept happy. In the summer of 1891, a problem arose from the proximity of the livery stables to the Members' Luncheon Room. They adjoined each other, and the summer was a hot one. The smell from the stables didn't prevent the members tucking into their mutton chops and rump steaks, but it did lessen their enjoyment. At the same time it was thought advisable to put a door at the entrance to the urinals – better still, to put a door with a spring.

In the autumn of 1891, the Ground Committee had to deal with defective roofs to the Tavern and to the new Luncheon Room. Rain was pouring in. Further improvements were needed to the mens' urinals adjoining the old Luncheon Room. The impression is that the old Pavilion developed piecemeal, with little regard for hygiene. It was years after the urinals had been built that a flushing service was fitted, though in 1895 Mr Jennings agreed to keep the urinals in the Imperial lavatory – on which, presumably, the sun never set – in constant working order for a sum of thirty shillings a year.

In December 1891, the Match Committee placed advertisements in *The Field, The Sportsman* and *Sporting Life* for a cricket instructor ('amateur preferred') for young cricketers of Surrey. The successful applicant would receive all expenses and a salary of £150 per annum.

At the Vauxhall end of the ground, repairs were needed to the dilapidated slipway from the embankment to the Skating Rink. Three weeks later the Committee discussed the question of whether or not to instal a stove in the players' dressing room to 'air damp clothes'. If a stove was fitted there would then be the problem of supplying coal with which to fuel it. It was decided to run water coils from the existing boiler.

More springs were needed on more doors, that to the Members' Luncheon Room, the better to keep out smells from liveries and urinals, and to the door 'admitting to the Pavilion – to prevent slamming'. More refreshment bars were needed, to the east of the Pavilion, opposite the Clayton Street exit, and, consequently, more urinals. After much debate, a telephone was installed in the Pavilion by the National Telephone Company at a cost of ten guineas. The rental was £20 a year.

It was just as well the crowds turned up in their thousands – an average of over 360,000 a year from 1881 to 1897. In 1888, match receipts for cricket alone amounted to over £8000. One hundred years later, in 1988, they amounted to over £760,000, though the vast majority of that came from the Texaco One-Day International and the Cornhill Insurance Test. In 1888, the gate from Surrey v The Australians, a game that was over in two days, realised £2489.10s, nearly a thousand pounds more than the Test match later that year. Even so, at least one member of the Club complained to Alcock about the number of visitors qualifying for free admission and thus depriving paying visitors of their seats. In the late 19th century Surrey, and other clubs, had a policy of giving free admission to certain people in uniform – soldiers, sailors, telegraphists, postmen, railwaymen and firemen. Policemen, too, were afforded this privilege, even if they were in plain clothes. It conjures up a pleasant picture of a plain clothes policeman, an undercover operative maybe, having to reveal the nature of his secret work to one of the stewards at the turnstile. On 9th August 1897, three hundred and sixteen plain clothes policemen reported to the Oval and received free admission. They were rewarded with a wonderful exhibition of batting by Abel and Brockwell, who tore into the Hampshire attack and put on 379 for the first wicket, beating by one run the previous record stand made by Brown and Tunnicliffe, at Sheffield against Sussex, three weeks earlier. The Surrey Committee, however, may not have appreciated the irony of a situation where they were having to pay for the attendance of two inspectors, seven sergeants and sixty constables, on the first day of the August match against Nottinghamshire. It was the price of success, for Surrey won the championship again in 1894, 1895 and 1899.

The Surrey team was full of great players, many of them professionals: Abel, Lockwood, Tom Hayward, Maurice Read, George Lohmann and Tom Richardson. Indeed, the Surrey team had a higher proportion of professional cricketers than almost any other county in the south of England. The Middlesex and Somerset teams were composed almost entirely of amateurs – Kent, Sussex, Hampshire and Essex had more amateurs than professionals in their teams. Then, as now, professionals were paid a retaining salary during the winter months when they could earn nothing from cricket. In the winter of 1895–6, Abel, Richardson and Lockwood were getting thirty shillings a week, and this was reduced in 1897 to twenty shillings. At the same time Yorkshire were paying £2 per week, which 'excited a feeling of anxiety, not to say alarm' (*Wisden*) among other Clubs. In 1909–10, Hitch and Rushby were paid twenty five shillings a week during the winter, but, two years later, the sum had dropped again. Sandham, then a regular member of the first team received only ten shillings a week. As late as 1920, at the height of his career, Jack Hobbs was paid £2 a week out of season. In the late 1890s, top professionals with Surrey were paid thirty shillings a week during the season and £1 a day for matches. They were often given bonuses at the end of the season. In December 1897, Richardson, Wood, Abel, Hayward and Lees each received £20, Baldwin and Brockwell £15, and Marshall and Holland £12.10s. Professionals in the Second Eleven were paid bonuses of between £5 and £7.10s.

In August 1896, Richardson, Abel and Hayward threatened to withdraw their labour. It was not the first time professional cricketers had taken such a step. In 1827, a group had refused to play against Lillywhite's round arm bowling, 'which had so brought Sussex to the front that in this year they were able to beat a picked English team on two occasions.' After one such defeat, some of the England team, including the great Fuller Pilch, met and signed the following document:

> 'We, the undersigned, do agree that we will not play the third match of All England v Sussex unless the Sussex bowlers bowl fair, that is – abstain from throwing.'

In Grace's words 'Reflection brought wisdom', and the third match was played. In 1852, there was further trouble, this time involving William Clarke's All England XI. Several professionals were dissatisfied with Clarke's management, and John Lillywhite, Wisden, and others left Clarke's team and set up the

England v Australia in 1896. There was no play until 4.55 pm on Monday. Giffen had a poor Test, Grace didn't do well, Ranji did worse, but Trumble took 12 for 89. A page from the *Illustrated London News*, with a rare sketch of Craig, the Surrey poet.
© *Hulton-Deutsch Collection*

United Eleven in opposition. They timed their action well, for cricket had become so popular that there was room for both elevens. After Clarke's death, the All England XI and the United XI regularly played each other in aid of the Cricketers Fund Friendly Society. In 1865, Daft, Parr, Tarrant, Carpenter and Anderson all refused to play in the Gentlemen v Players match. The following year the same fixture and the North v South match were 'completely spoiled by the refusal of northern cricketers to take part.' In 1881, the Notts Committee had 'a very disagreeable experience'. Seven of the eleven playing in one match threatened not to play again unless they were selected for the rest of the season. Notts turned to their 'rising talent' to take the places of the 'malcontents', and by the end of the season the matter had been resolved for all but two of the players.

Richardson, Abel and Hayward's complaint, in which they were joined by Lohmann, was that a great deal of money was being made out of extra representative matches arranged against the Australian tourists and out of the Test matches themselves. Early in August, the Surrey Committee met to select the team for the Oval Test – it was still the practice for the 'Home' Committee to do this. Among those chosen were Abel, Richardson, Hayward, Lohmann, and Gunn of Nottinghamshire. The Committee then received a letter from these five professionals asking for £20 each for the match – they had been paid £10 for playing in the Tests at Lords and Manchester, although Alfred Shaw, Morley and Barnes had received a match fee of £20 each when they took part in the first Test at the Oval, back in 1880. The issue had been simmering for some time, and the England professionals had discussed it during the Test at Lords. On that occasion they had played, and then put in a request for a larger sum than £10. The request had been refused.

At Old Trafford, Gunn, Lohmann and Hayward were not selected, and, since the match was away from London, it had been difficult for Abel and Richardson to consult the other players prior to the match. However, these two did, on their own initiative, approach the Lancashire Committee and ask for £5 expenses in addition to the £10 match fee. They received £10, and were told that the question of expenses would be considered. They heard nothing more. It was at this point that the professionals decided that, if chosen for the Oval Test, they would ask 'definitely' for £20, a not unprecedented fee for a representative match. Immediately they heard of their selection, they wrote to the Surrey Committee with their request (4th August), and received an acknowledgement of their letter from Alcock that same day. The timing was important, as the professionals were later accused of making their demand at the final hour. In fact, the delay was largely Surrey's – the Committee did not consider the matter until 7th August, with the Test due to start three days later. Surrey, according to *Wisden*, 'refused point blank to be dictated to.'

There was a great deal of behind the scenes to-ing and fro-ing, seeking to bring the sides together: it would have been a bold selection committee that decided to dispense with the services of the two greatest bowlers in the country and two of the greatest batsmen.

Three of the five professionals were persuaded, two days later, on the opening day of the Test, to write to the Committee:

10th August 1896

Gentlemen,

We extremely regret that you could not see your way clear to grant the request we made but as you know the Australians have made and are making large sums by these fixtures. It seemed to us only reasonable that we should participate in a small way out of the large amount of money received at representative matches. But after further consideration we desire to withdraw our refusal to play and beg to leave the matter in your hands, and we trust in future when these matches are played the matter will not be lost sight of, and at the same time we hope that this will not destroy the good feeling which has existed between us in the past.

We are, Gentlemen,
Yours obediently,

T. Richardson   R. Abel   T. Hayward

Gunn had already decided not to press the demand, and Lohmann was left out in the cold. On the following day (11th August – the second day of the Test), Hayward, Richardson, Abel and Lohmann wrote to the press explaining some of the background to the 'strike', and asserting that they had not waited until the eleventh hour before making their request. The following day, Lohmann wrote his own sad, humble and desperate letter to the Committee. It was printed, with Lohmann's permission, in *The Manchester Guardian* (and other papers) under the headline 'THE "WEAKENING" OF THE SURREY PROFESSIONALS'.

Surrey County Cricket Club, Kennington Oval
12th August 1896

To the Committee of the Surrey Club

Gentlemen,

I beg hereby to express my sincere apologies for my refusal to sign the document placing myself unreservedly in the hands of the Committee. On Monday morning at the time my colleagues signed the withdrawal of the position taken up, I expected William Gunn to be there; and having associated myself with him, merely desired to wait until his arrival before taking any action. I would add that when the original letter was drawn up my idea was that a request was being proferred instead of a demand being made, and that the expression 'demand' which I now see to have been so unfortunate, was inserted against my wish and better judgment. While

tendering my apologies, I wish to seize the opportunity to express my heartfelt gratitude to the Surrey Club for the many great kindnesses I have received at their hands, both in times of health and sickness. My career as a cricketer has been so entirely bound up with the county of Surrey that I should regret if any action of mine caused a rupture with the club with which my happiest days have been spent, and to which I am so much indebted.–
I am, &c.,

G.A. Lohmann

PS At the same time I should like to express my grateful thanks to the members and to the public for their hearty support of my benefit match. – G.A.L.

Hayward, Abel and Richardson had withdrawn their demand on the morning of the 10th of August, the opening day of the Oval Test. They were then selected to play. Lohmann's letter did not reach the Committee until the final morning of the Test. He never played for England again.

It cannot have helped the situation that while Abel and company were making and withdrawing their demand, various newspapers began to report that Club committees were in the habit of making payments to certain amateurs for appearing in representative matches. The villain of the piece, though not the only recipient, was W.G. Grace. *Wisden* defended the practice of making payments to the great man: '"nice customs curtsey to great kings" and the work he has done in popularising cricket outweighs a hundredfold every other consideration'. Nevertheless, the Surrey Committee felt there was a need to clarify and justify their position. On the opening day of the 1896 Test at the Oval, while Abel, Richardson and Hayward were withdrawing their demand, the Club released the following statement:

'The Committee of the Surrey County Cricket Club have observed paragraphs in the press respecting amounts to be paid, or promised to, Dr W.G. Grace for playing in the match England v Australia. The Committee desire to give the statements . . . the most unqualified contradiction. During many years, on the occasions of Dr Grace playing at the Oval, at the request of the Surrey County Committee, in the matches Gentlemen v Players and England v Australia, Dr Grace has received the sum of £10 per match to cover his expenses in coming to and remaining in London during the three days. Beyond this amount, Dr Grace has not received, directly or indirectly, one farthing for playing in a match at the Oval.

Signed on behalf of the Committee,

C.W. Alcock'

The time had come to sign a new lease with the Duchy of Cornwall, but one of the conditions stipulated by the Duchy was that a new pavilion should be built. The Duchy clearly wanted a building of some substance, perhaps to rival Verity's fine new pavilion at Lords, and informed Surrey that they should be prepared to spend £12,000 (at the very least £10,000) on the development. Another new pavilion had recently been built at Old Trafford, and after careful consideration, Surrey accepted plans submitted by the same architects, Muirhead and Baldwin of Manchester.

In the summer of 1897, Surrey were looking for a tender of around £14,000, but costs soared. The estimate which the Committee finally selected, from Messrs Foster and Dicksee of London and Rugby, amounted to £33,558, and the actual cost of the Pavilion and Tavern, including decorations and furnishings, was over £38,000. While the old pavilion was being demolished and the new one built, the Club's headquarters moved to a house by the Crown Baths at Kennington. The work was completed in the astonishingly short time of six months, and was ready for the 1898 season. Alcock was delighted with the new Pavilion; 'The Club now possesses a pavilion beyond a doubt in its internal arrangements second to none in the country, as well as one thoroughly worthy of the Club's importance'.

The Oval's 'nice' new Pavilion at the turn of the century. *From the Oval Collection*

Ernest Ward, writing in *The Times*, 30th March 1898, was complimentary towards the new building. 'The old pavilion and the old tavern with all their cricket traditions have been swept away, and there now stands in their place a handsome red-brick pile of buildings which commands the admiration of all those who pass along the Harleyford-road to Vauxhall and the West-end. Perhaps the disappearance most regretted by old stagers is that of the old players' room, the walls of which could have unfolded many a tale of the great deeds on the Oval in the sixties and seventies . . . The new red-brick building, with Bath stone facings, has a frontage of 300 feet. It much surpasses in its imposing nature its model – the Lancashire pavilion at Old Trafford, Manchester – and also the handsome red-brick and terra-cotta work at Lord's. Nothing has been allowed to interfere with the symmetry of the building; and perhaps the Press, who hitherto enjoyed on the Oval their best view of the game in the kingdom, will be the first to raise an outcry about their position . . . The best places for following the game have been given, and quite rightly, to the gentlemen engaged in the cricket; their dressing and sitting rooms command an exact end-on view of the cricket pitch, while the professionals have almost an equally good position. The Surrey Committee are to be commended for striking out a fresh line in their thought for the players' comfort . . . Apted, the ground man, whose keen interest in his work in looking after the turf, has brought the Oval to better condition than it usually is at this season of the year. There is a fine growth of grass and not a weed is to be seen . . .'

Inside the pavilion, the fittings and furniture, if not of the very finest, were of good quality: linoleum (best plain), American stained oak chairs, solid oak tables, Austrian bent wood chairs, and an American walnut cylinder top writing table for the Secretary's room (£18.10s). There were still one or two problems, however. The Committee couldn't decide where to site the Telegraph Office. The ground floor would be too crowded, 'since as many as twenty operators may be wishing to use the facilities'. And H. & G. Simonds Ltd., The Brewery, Reading, who held the Tavern licence, were concerned as the licensing magistrates insisted upon 'good and adequate urinal accommodation'.

More doors – more springs: but, as the century neared its end, all seemed to be in order.

Wighill Park, Tadcaster   Sept. 20th 1899

My dear Alcock,

Ere long you will be starting to make your next season's programme so I write to say I hope Surrey will give to South Africans and West Indians a chance of playing on your perfect wicket, and inspecting your nice Pavilion . . .

Believe me
Yours very truly

Hawke

A History of The Foster's Oval

PART 2

Chapter Six

The Birth of the Ashes – August 1882

Of the extraordinary events of 28th and 29th August 1882 at Kennington Oval, Neville Cardus once wrote: 'The tale has often been told'. But it is a tale worth telling again, hopefully, and crammed with enough drama yet to provide the backbone of a film or television play. The ingredients are all there – tension, conflict, quest, comedy, tragedy even (one spectator died of heart failure during that final umbrella-handle biting session), prejudice and respect, the trappings and pitfalls of a rigid class system, the cunning and determination of Colonials determined to defeat the mother country, and, ultimately a shocked, stunned and grieving Victorian Society. For many, English and Australian, it remains the greatest match ever played.

Following their defeat of Australia at the Oval in 1880, an English party toured Australia during the winter of 1881–2. They played four Tests, drawing two and losing two. Somehow, these defeats didn't seem to count. They took place 12,000 miles away, and, anyway, it wasn't England's best team, being composed entirely of professionals. Back in dear old Albion, where gentlemen would make up most of the English team, all would be different.

There were one or two signs during the summer of 1882 that this might not be so. The Australians were more than a match for any of the county sides, and could take on the Gentlemen or the Players. In May, when the season was hardly underway, a *Times* leader identified one of the features of the Australians' play which was to prove crucial three months later: 'The Australians . . . present the spectacle of a team which is nothing if not united'. The idea, however, that they could match the cream of England, gentlemen and professionals, had few supporters. The English Eleven, selected by Lord Harris, Mr Burbidge and Messrs V.E. and I.D. Walker, contained only three members of the side that had been beaten in Australia (Barlow, Ulyett and Peate). It was a particularly strong batting side – only Peate, at number eleven, had an average of less than 24. Further, the Australian attack was really comprised of two men only, Boyle and Spofforth, sinced Palmer, who had 'bowled with splendid consistency all the tour' was unable to play.

The Australians were staying at the Tavistock Hotel in Covent Garden. There had been heavy rain in London on the previous Saturday, and more in the early hours of this Monday morning. They awoke on the morning of 28th August to steady drizzle, and by ten o'clock there was a downpour, which drenched the thousands who had already taken their places at the Oval. At eleven o'clock, however, the rain ceased and there was a break in the clouds. The pundits reckoned the Oval wicket would probably deteriorate, and, when he called correctly for the toss, Murdoch decided to bat. A few minutes after twelve, Hornby led out the English team: Barlow, W.G. Grace, Ulyett, Lucas, Lyttelton, Studd, Maurice Read (the Surrey professional who had made a big score against the Australians a few days previously, but whose selection was regarded as 'in the nature of an experiment'), Barnes, Steel and Peate.

It was a strong side, but *The Manchester Guardian* noted that it didn't contain a fast bowler. There were clamorous suggestions from the north that Crossland of Lancashire should have been included, but there were some who considered he 'threw' rather than bowled. There had been a 'most unseemly exhibition of feeling' (*Wisden*) in the Surrey v Lancashire match at the Oval, and Lord Harris viewed Crossland's action with the gravest suspicion. Three years later, in a letter to the Lancashire Committee, his Lordship wrote that he noted that Crossland 'was still . . . bowling as unfairly as in previous seasons.' As a result, the fixture between Kent and Lancashire was cancelled. Therefore there was no way a team picked by Lord Harris would have included Crossland.

A photograph of the Oval ground at the time of the Test in 1882 shows a skyline that has long disappeared. Save the famous five gasholders, no building in the immediate vicinity stands higher than the old pavilion, the five arches of its first floor staring out at the fine turf of the cricket ground. To the west is the long covered stand (one wing of the monoplane). Around the rest of the ground wooden terracing has been erected. There is a large crowd, and, even from a photograph, there is discernible an air of tension, of total concentration. An overcast sky imparts a damp look to the proceedings, as though the scent of wet cloth hung in the heavy August air. It doesn't look as though runs would come easily.

At ten minutes past twelve precisely, Massie and Bannerman descended the few steps of the pavilion to face the bowling of Peate and Ulyett. Lyttelton was the wicket-keeper, and W.G. stood at his customary position of point. In the first over, Bannerman drove Peate for three. Ulyett then bowled a maiden, and in Peate's second over Massie scored a single. With the score at six, Ulyett yorked Massie – 'the early downfall of such a formidable batsman was received with shouts of applause'.

Murdoch joined Bannerman, Peate and Ulyett sent down more than a dozen maiden overs, and Bannerman played a 'clumsy' stroke for 2. With the score at 18, Barlow replaced Ulyett, and he and Peate sent down fourteen successive maidens. The wicket was admittedly slow paced, and the overs were still four-ball, but this was caution taken to an extreme. Murdoch at last scored a single off Barlow, but was bowled by Peate for 13 in the next over (21 for 2).

A hastily erected bank of seats for the Ashes Test, 1882. *From the MCC Collection*

Bonnor lasted a short time only, and was bowled by Barlow for 1 (22 for 3). Bannerman continued to defend, then cut Barlow for three, but was brilliantly caught at point by Grace, low down with his left hand. (26 for 4). Bannerman had been in for an hour and five minutes for 9 runs. Giffen, who joined Horan, has left his own account of the match: 'the way the ball came back on the treacherous wicket put the batsmen through a severe ordeal.' Horan lost his leg stump with the score at 30, and without addition, Giffen was bowled by a 'beautiful ball from Peate, which broke in to him and hit the top of the wicket' (30 for 6).

Garrett and Blackham held out until lunch, forcing Hornby to make a double bowling change, bringing on Steele for Peate and bringing back Ulyett for Barlow. The bell rang for luncheon. Australia had scored 48 in just under two hours play, and the end of the morning session was greeted with a mixture of delight, astonishment, and, for the Australians, disgust. The local crowd, and it was primarily local in those days, would have been well pleased with events. England appeared on the road to victory.

In the first over after lunch, another wicket fell, bringing further joy to the local supporters: 'Young Maurice Read delighted his Oval friends by catching Garrett beautifully at long-off' (H.S. Altham) (48 for 7). Boyle was bowled by a fast rising ball from Barlow. A little rain fell as Jones came out to join Blackham. Blackham cut Peate finely for four, and drove Barlow to the boundary. One run later he skied the ball to point, where Grace took a relatively simple catch.

Spofforth, at number eleven, joined Jones, hit one 4, and then Jones was caught by Barnes at third man off Barlow. The Australians were all out at twenty past three for 63. Peate had figures of 38-24-31-4, and Barlow 31-22-19-5. Converting these figures into six-ball overs, Peate bowled 25 overs for 31 runs, and Barlow 20 overs for 19 runs. In all, Australia batted for 53 'modern' overs. Spofforth was disgusted. Years later he reckoned that Australia should have made 250 on that wicket.

Australian team in England, 1882. *Standing:* G. E. Palmer, H. F. Boyle, W. L. Murdoch (Capt.), P. S. McDonnell, F. R. Spofforth, T. P. Horan, S. P. Jones. *Seated:* C. W. Beale (manager), G. Giffen, A. C. Bannerman, T. W. Garrett, H. H. Massie, G. J. Bonnor. *From the MCC Collection*

At half past three, the Australians came out to field. Their batting had been, according to H.S. Altham, 'in many cases nerveless and unworthy of them, and they must have taken the field a sadly chagrined team'. Barlow and Grace opened for England, to face the bowling of Spofforth and Garrett. Spofforth opened from the Vauxhall end. Barlow settled quickly, pushing both bowlers for singles and a 2. With the score at 13, Spofforth yorked the Champion for 'a paltry 4' (Altham), knocking back the leg stump, and the Australians were 'in a great feather' (Giffen). Ulyett joined Barlow, and had an 'agonising first over' (Altham). Before he had scored, Blackham, standing up to Spofforth, missed a comparatively easy stumping chance.

Ulyett and Barlow added only five runs before Barlow played a ball from Spofforth straight into the hands of Bannerman at forward point. Lucas and Ulyett made the only stand of the innings. Ulyett drove Garrett for four on the off, another 4 came from byes. In thirty five minutes, the England score had risen to 30. Spofforth changed ends, to bowl with the pavilion behind him, and Boyle replaced Garrett. Ulyett was now playing well, driving both bowlers confidently, and the score reached 50. There followed a period of what *The Manchester Guardian* described as slow cricket, both batsmen bogged down by very accurate bowling. Eventually, Ulyett decided the time had come to cut lose. He was always regarded as something of a light-hearted character, and had been nicknamed 'Happy Jack'. It was not a day for dancing down the wicket, however, and when Ulyett jumped out at Spofforth he was easily stumped by Blackham for a hard earned 26 (56 for 3). Three runs were added before Lucas was caught at the wicket off Boyle (59 for 4). Studd fared even worse, being bowled by Spofforth without scoring. 'The ball must have broken back a great deal, for the batsman seemed utterly surprised at finding he was out' (*Guardian*).

Spofforth had now taken four of the five wickets that had fallen. He had been given the name 'The Demon' in 1878, when he had been a genuinely fast bowler, but on his first tour of England he had discovered that the softer wickets enabled him to do a great deal more with the ball. Lord Harris discerned this change in Spofforth: 'Instead of bowling fast with an occasional "judgment" ball, as he called it, he changed to bowling the medium-paced ball as a rule, with an occasional fast one, and so became one of the best bowlers ever seen; in my opinion the best I have ever played.' This was why Blackham was able to stand up for his bowling, and why Ulyett was stumped. Even so, Spofforth was still capable of bowling a very fast, rising ball. Colonel Philip Trevor, writing in *The Strand* magazine forty six years later, recalled that 'Maurice Read heard the hum of Spofforth's fast ball as it whizzed past his ear, and the Grand Old Man picked the bails out of his beard.' Those who knew him, and played against him, agreed, however, that Spofforth's best ball was the one that broke back, the one that dismissed the astonished Studd.

Lyttelton and Maurice Read raised the score to 63, level with that of Australia, before Lyttelton was caught at the wicket off his gloves from the bowling of Spofforth. The lunchtime exuberance in the English camp had long since evaporated, even in the wet atmosphere of the day. Barnes hit a 4, and was then bowled by Boyle (70 for 7). Steel played sensibly, and Read produced one of the best strokes of the day when he drove Spofforth for four. Slowly, steadily, the score rose. Murdoch rested Boyle and brought back Garrett. Steel promptly drove Garrett past cover for four, and Read drove Spofforth to the boundary.

At 96, however, Steel played on to Spofforth. It was time for a captain's innings, but the rain had started once more and the light was described as wretchedly bad. Hornby and Read managed to bring up the hundred, but shortly afterwards, Spofforth bowled Hornby with a brute of a break-back, pitching near the off stump and removing the leg stump. In the same over, Peate was caught by Boyle at short mid off and England were all out for 101 – a lead of 38. Spofforth had bowled unchanged throughout the innings, for the admirable figures of 36.3-18-46-7, in modern statistical parlance 24.3 overs for 46 runs and 7 wickets.

On balance, the Australians were probably reasonably satisfied with the events of the day. Their own batting collapse had been lamentable, but they might well have been facing a far larger deficit. It was still anyone's game, and such advantage as the wicket afforded was with the Australians. The clouds were gathering as they drove back to the Tavistock Hotel from Kennington in a procession of hansom cabs. Altham reported that they ate an 'anxious' meal and went early to bed. Certainly Spofforth deserved a decent night's sleep.

Clouds thickened during the evening, and there was a heavy downpour of rain during the night and another in the morning. 'By ten o'clock there was . . . almost a complete belt of spectators round the field of play, who, protected by umbrellas, macintoshes, &c., maintained their positions throughout all discomfitures' (*The Times*). Those spectators who had purchased copies of *The Manchester Guardian* could read a number of letters from irate northerners, concerning the omission of Crossland from the England team.

> To the Editor of *The Manchester Guardian*,
>
> Sir,
>
> I cannot but regret that Crossland and Pilling have been debarred from upholding against our strong opponents the dignity, honour and ability of, once more, the premier county of England . . . On the first visit of Spofforth with the Australian Eleven to England, his bowling was of general suspicion and a topic of conversation amongst cricketers simply because he displayed such remarkable performances with the ball, and for no other reason. And so it is with Crossland, whose performances this season stamp him as one of the fastest, and, at the same time, fairest bowlers in England.
>
> I am, &c.
>
> C.F.N   Old Trafford

There were other letters of support for Crossland, from "Cover Point", and from "Middle Stump", who cited Crossland's bowling figures against Australia during the tour preceding the Oval Test – 7 for 72 in 49.3 overs – and rejected the notion that Crossland's action was suspect: 'As for getting his wickets by mere brute force, one would almost think from such an epithet that Crossland walks across to the batsmen, knocks them down and plucks the stumps up, instead of bowling from the opposite end.' The Oval crowd, huddling under their umbrellas would probably not have agreed with the tone of the letters. Never overwhelmingly enthusiastic in their support for Lancashire, they might have thought that Crossland's omission was nothing, compared with that of Barratt of Surrey, who had more than proved his worth against the Australians four years earlier.

'Rain before seven, is gone by eleven' – the old adage proved true. Shortly before eleven there was a break in the clouds and the rain stopped. Just over an hour later, at ten past twelve, the Australian second innings began on a wet, slow-paced wicket that probably played better then than at any other time in the match. Conditions for England, bowling and fielding, were abominable. The ball was like soap, and the mud in the bowlers' foot holes was so bad that it had to be dug out and replaced with sawdust.

It was Australia's great chance, and Massie took it. He played one of the great Test match innings, scoring 55 out of 66 in less than an hour. 'He hurled his bat at every ball the slightest loose, and his hits crashed ponderously to the boundary. He was the living image of defiance as he faced the Englishmen, glaring round the field his challenge.' (Sir Neville Cardus). Hornby bowled Barlow (from the pavilion end) and Ulyett without success, though off the second ball of Ulyett's first over, Massie was almost run out. He drove the ball through the covers, but Read, running round the boundary made a good stop. 'In the opinion of many', however, Read threw to the wrong end, and Massie was safely home. With the score at 25, Hornby tried a double bowling change, Peate and Steel came on – with no more success. Australia cleared off the arrears. Studd then bowled a few overs and was replaced by Barnes: six bowlers tried in less than three quarters of an hour. With the score at 47, Massie lifted an immense drive to long on. It was not an easy catch, but relatively straight-forward. The crowd waited for Lucas (local hero) to take it. Lucas (local public enemy) dropped it.

At last Steel induced Massie to play across a straight ball and Massie was bowled for 55, an innings that contained nine 4s, and was to prove far and away the top score in the match (66 for 1, Australia 28 runs ahead). England fought back. Bonnor, promoted to number three, had his middle stump knocked out of the ground by Ulyett's faster ball (70 for 2). Bannerman was then caught by Studd at extra mid-off without any addition to the score. Bannerman had played the anchor role while Massie had hit out, and had scored 13 runs in an hour and ten minutes. Horan joined Murdoch. Hornby switched his bowlers round, and Horan was spun out, caught by Grace at point off Peate (79 for 4). The same combination got rid of Giffen the very next ball (79 for 5). The crowd perked up no end, and cheered enthusiastically.

Blackham and Murdoch played cautiously. Rain, falling steadily, caused lunch to be brought forward by a quarter of an hour. At this point, Australia were 61 runs ahead, with five wickets in hand. The wicket was now extremely difficult to bat on: only for the first twenty minutes of the morning's play, while

August 1882. The Ashes Test, but very much an artist's impression. There appear to be two bowlers, and, understandably, both batsmen are taking strike. © *Hulton-Deutsch Collection*

Massie was getting his eye in, were the batsmen in any sort of comfort. Under these circumstances, the Australians had done well to score 99 runs in just over an hour and a half's play.

The stand between Blackham and Murdoch, which had added twenty valuable runs, was broken without addition in the first over after lunch. Peate bowled his slow left arm spin beautifully, and Blackham edged the last ball of the first over to Lyttelton (99 for 6). Jones held out while Murdoch defended and scored the occasional single. Then came an incident which gave 'great dissatisfaction to Murdoch and other Australians' (*Wisden*). Murdoch drove Peate to leg, and the batsmen crossed for a single. Lyttelton had chased after the ball from behind the stumps, and had thrown at the wicket, hoping to run out Jones. Lyttelton's throw missed the stumps and was fielded by Grace, backing up from point. Jones, having completed the first run, and thinking (wrongly but understandably) that the ball was 'dead', left his ground. Grace broke the wicket, and Jones was given out. The Australians were angry, although at least one of them confessed that, in the situation prevailing, he would have done the same thing. In the rest of the Oval pavilion, the incident was regarded very differently, and one member remarked that 'Jones ought to thank the Champion for teaching him something', at which there was much laughter.

Spofforth failed to score before being bowled by Peate, and, at 117 for 8, Garrett joined Murdoch. The Australian captain had patiently accumulated 29 in a display of defensive skill that won the admiration of Giffen, who described the wicket as being 'as difficult as any bowler could wish'. Now came a piece of ill-luck for Murdoch, though Giffen regarded it as bad cricket, and placed the responsibility for Murdoch's dismissal squarely on Tom Garrett's shoulders. Garrett drove the ball towards the boundary. Hornby, who according to some contemporary accounts didn't have much of a throw, pursued it. The batsmen ran two, Garrett called for a third. Hornby flipped the ball to Studd, who was backing up, and Studd threw to Lyttelton. Murdoch was easily run out (122 for 9). Steel then bowled Boyle, and England were left with 85 wanted for victory.

Nowadays, the Oval crowd seems usually equally divided between optimists and pessimists. It cannot have been all that different a century ago. Contemporary newspaper accounts suggest that the crowd was a knowledgeable one in cricketing terms. The Oval has never been much of a place for dilettantes. They would have assessed the light and the wicket, the strength of England's batting, and the fact that, when all is said and done, eighty five is not an enormous number of runs to make. At 3.40pm, on the afternoon of Tuesday, 29th August 1882, half way through the interval between the innings, the odds would have been in favour of an England win. *The Manchester Guardian* reporter had no doubts: 'Nothing seemed more certain than that the Colonials would suffer a crushing defeat.'

Except in the Australian dressing room. In Spofforth's own account of the match, published in *The Cricketer*, May 1921, he suggests that the Australians had been stung by the incident that had taken place when Jones had been run out. 'It seemed to put fire into (us), and I do not suppose a team ever worked harder to win.' It certainly put fire and determination into Spofforth. He sat there and quietly muttered, 'Boys, this thing can be done.' George Giffen writing in the *Windsor Magazine* of 1898, said: 'England needed 85 runs to win. Would they get them? As we excitedly discussed our chances during the interval, Spofforth said they wouldn't. Spoff's faith in himself, and Murdoch's cheery assurance inspired the rest of us, and we filed out of the dressing room to make the effort of our lives.' Perhaps Altham was exaggerating only slightly when he wrote that the Australian team 'filed down the pavilion steps ready to do or die'. There has always been a ferocious determination about the way any Australian touring party has played cricket, and in the days of Empire and Colonies there were principles at stake for both sides. Here was a group of players, weeks away from home, in a city far less cosmopolitan or antipodean than it is now, representing a continent that was not yet a federation, and that had, but a generation ago been the dumping ground for England's undesirables.

And among them, fuming for victory, was Spofforth. A cartoon of The Demon by Spy now hangs on the wall at the top of the flight of stairs in the Oval pavilion. He is in cricket gear, wearing a blue and white striped blazer and cap. Tall, thin, whip-like, with a smile that contains scorn and mockery in generous quantities, but little humour, if it is a smile at all. Later England batsmen may have seen a similar expression on the face of Dennis Keith Lillee. It is not the smile of one who wishes to make friends. In bowling, he made full use of his height, bringing the ball well down from over the shoulder. His delivery, from its very nature, according to contemporaries, caused the ball to get up quickly from the pitch, but his success was due to the mental influence he brought to bear on his work. It was work, and Spofforth was thorough in his study and practice of it. He learned the greatest secret of bowling – to vary his pitch and speed without giving the batsman the slightest clue as to what was going to happen. But perhaps Neville Cardus has best explained why Spofforth was so deadly on that fateful day. 'It is not possible to account for the prowess of Spofforth by an analysis of his technique. A terrific personal force possessed him . . . A dynamo of hostility worked ceaselessly in Spofforth; he got on the nerves of his opponents; he had the evil eye; he was tall and angular and satanic of aspect.' Spofforth inspired Australia that day because he wasn't acting when he said that they could win. He meant it: he knew it. Forty years later the insistence that England wouldn't get the runs was still with him: 'I never thought they would be got.'

But at 3.45, when Grace and Hornby trotted down the pavilion steps to open the innings for England, there was still all to play for. Spofforth had performed no wonders earlier in the season when he played against Surrey at the Oval – 1 for 65 off 22 overs. Maybe, surely, he could be tamed by the might of England's batting.

The light was grey, there was the bitter-sweet air of autumn that is always so poignant on any cricket field in late August. In almost total silence, Spofforth opened the bowling from the Vauxhall end, long the end favoured by the strike bowler of any team at the Oval. The first over was fast, Blackham had to stand yards back. It was a maiden. Garrett bowled from the pavilion end. Hornby scored a single. Grace scored a single. Spofforth again, and again each batsmen scored a single. Then Hornby opened up and drove Spofforth for 4, and snicked him down the leg side for 2. It was noted by the crowd that Blackham stood up to Spofforth when Hornby was batting, but dropped back for Grace.

The score reached 15 in as many minutes, but in his fifth over, Spofforth uprooted Hornby's off stump. Spofforth's tail was up, and he bowled Barlow with a beauty, first ball (15 for 2). The crowd, who had cheered every run up till then, became silent once more. Four o'clock, and Ulyett, hero of England's first innings, joined Grace. Ten minutes later, the score reached 20. Then Grace on-drove Spofforth twice in one over for a 4 and a 3. The game was sliding England's way. Murdoch rested Garrett, brought Boyle on at the Vauxhall end, and Spofforth changed ends. Ulyett and Grace went carefully on their way, and

F. R. Spofforth. Watercolour by H. S. Tuke. *From the MCC Collection*

each scored a 4 to the deep square leg boundary. At thirty five minutes past four, the crowd applauded the 50 – 35 more wanted and eight wickets in hand.

One run later Spofforth broke the stand. He sent one down just outside the line of the off stump. Ulyett expected the break back, fenced at it, and was well caught by Blackham. Two runs later, Grace attempted to drive Boyle, failed to get to the pitch of the ball and was caught by Bannerman at mid off. Grace had scored 32, and the score was now 53 for 4 – 32 still wanted. Lyttelton joined Lucas. Twelve runs were scored fairly rapidly, including a clean hit to the boundary by Lyttelton off Spofforth. Only 20 needed to win, and six wickets in hand. Spofforth and Boyle strained every nerve and muscle: maiden followed maiden. The tension must have become almost unbearable, but who would have left a cricket match at a time like this. Altogether, Boyle and Spofforth bowled twelve successive maidens; Boyle bowling to Lyttelton, Spofforth to Lucas. Something had to happen to break the deadlock. Spofforth spoke to Murdoch and Bannerman. A plot was hatched. Bannerman deliberately misfielded, and Lyttelton was allowed a single, taking him to the Vauxhall end, where he would have to face Spofforth, with the dark background of the pavilion behind the deadly arm. Four more maiden overs, and then a devastating break back from Spofforth clipped the top of Lyttelton's middle stump (66 for 5 – nineteen wanted to win). Steel joined Lucas, who cut Boyle for 4, relieving some of the tension, but not enough, apparently. 'So very nervous and uncertain became the batting, that Mr Steel, whose style is commonly most finished, played his first two balls from Spofforth as clumsily as a novice'. (*Manchester Guardian*) And this by a man who had already taken two hundreds off the Australian attack that season.

Lucas played a maiden from Boyle, Steel faced Spofforth. He failed to spot the slower ball. 'It pitched about four inches outside his off stump,' Spofforth recalled, years later, 'he started to play forward to it, before he had touched the ball I was off in the direction of silly mid on, and Steel quietly played the ball right into my hands.' (70 for 6). Giffen wrote, later: ' . . . the moment, I fancy, it was really clinched was when Steel was dismissed without scoring.' But all along, the Australians had fielded as though defeat was impossible, setting and maintaining levels of skill and enthusiasm that had rarely, if ever, been seen before. Many spectators and reporters noticed how the field moved in as one when each ball was delivered, that the backing up was faultless, that every Australian on the field was totally and exclusively absorbed in what was happening. It was neither time nor place for faint hearts on either side.

Read, who had made 19 not out in the first innings and who, a couple of weeks earlier, had made 130 when the Players beat the Australians by an innings, was bowled second ball by Spofforth, who had missed the Players match, owing to a strain. *The Manchester Guardian* was scathing in its report next day: 'The placing of Read in the English Eleven was, admittedly, somewhat of an experiment. He has played two or three lucky innings lately, but these do not make a cricketer any more than two or three swallows make a summer.' As poor Read, the Surrey professional, made his way back to the pavilion, and it is a long way at the Oval, the spectators were completely silent. Their thoughts would have been on those tantalising equations which are so often juggled with at cricket matches: did Lucas + Barnes + Studd + Peate = 15 runs?

At first it would seem that they did. Barnes hit Spofforth for 2: the first scoring stroke off that bowler in ten overs. Blackham then made a rare blunder, and the batsmen ran three byes – 10 to win. By way of retaliation, Spofforth let loose a fast yorker, which Lucas came down on, but which then trickled under his bat and dislodged a bail. 'Such was his chagrin,' reported *The Manchester Guardian*, 'that he lifted his bat and struck the dead ball.' He was not, however, summoned to Lords some weeks later to explain his conduct. Perhaps the powers that be had more understanding in those days: perhaps they were aware that Mr A.P. Lucas was a gentlemen. Whatever the case, Lucas had been in a long time for only 5 runs. His defence had been brilliant, but more was needed than defence (75 for 8).

Meanwhile Studd had been pacing up and down in the pavilion, with a blanket round him, presumably shivering with nerves. He now came to the wicket, but Spofforth had finished his over, and Boyle was about to bowl to Barnes from the Vauxhall end. Off the second ball of the over, Barnes nudged the ball with his glove, and was caught by Murdoch at point. In came Peate, the last man, who whacked his first ball for 2, was all but bowled by his second, and flailed like a madman at the third. He was cleaned bowled, Studd watching helplessly from the other end.

When Peate's wicket fell, we are told the crowd sat for a moment voiceless and stunned. Five wickets had fallen in three quarters of an hour for 11 runs. It took a short while for the fact to sink in. Then the crowd roared, and Spofforth was carried shoulder-high to the pavilion. He had taken 7 for 44 in the second innings, again bowling unchanged, and he had match figures of 14 for 90. There have been eight better match figures in a Test match since then, by some of the best and most beautiful bowlers the game has produced – Rhodes, Barnes, Blythe, Briggs, Verity, Laker and Lohmann, with Massie, the lone Australian and perhaps in other ways the odd man out. But nobody has produced the goods on such an occasion as Spofforth did, and nobody has ever so fired a team to pull off the seemingly impossible.

Alcock, the Surrey Secretary, described how he walked from the pavilion to the press box immediately after the match. 'I thought I recognised the form of an old habitué of the Oval on one of the seats in the stand. He was leaning over the seat, and touching him on the back, I asked him if there was anything the matter with him. "Oh, no," was his reply, "only I don't know whether to cry or be sick".'

Punch joined in the many tributes to the Australians over the next few days:

Well done, Cornstalks, whipt us
  Fair and square,
Was it luck that tripped us?
  Was it scare?
Kangaroo land's 'Demon', or our own
  Want of devil, coolness, nerve, backbone?

To many, England's defeat was not a subject for humour or jocularity. The best team the mother country could muster (give or take the argument about Crossland) had been beaten on home territory, just across the river from the Mother of Parliaments, by the wild colonial boys. There was a sense of outrage, of shock, of stunned disbelief. And there was a great outcry that it wasn't fair. The newspapers received many letters from outraged readers and cricket fans.

31st August 1882

Sir,

After the most disgraceful exhibition of England at the Oval v the Australians, is it not possible to select another team to play a final match with our visitors before they depart?

No one grudges the Australians victory less than I do ... Nerve is what these Australians possess, and what our so-called England Eleven does not possess. Possibly the teeth of three of our eleven did not chatter when they walked to the wicket to face the demon bowler; but the remaining eight shivered and funked, and if these remaining eight had played in the same style against fourth form school bowlers they would have fared the same.

Yours truly.
SENEX

Others, including 'One Who Was Present At The Oval', wanted the Players fixture dropped to give England another chance:

'If my suggestion were carried out, a knowledge of the respective teams would be gained, for a majority of seven runs does not reflect much honour on a victorious team, although the Australians played an uphill game (towards the close) with commendable pluck and judgment, which, if their example had been emulated by us, would certainly have changed the match into an easy English triumph. If Mr A.P. Lucas had not missed Massie, who would have been the victorious team?'

Couldn't there be another fixture, another chance for England? One letter suggested cancelling the North of England v Australia match, scheduled for 14th September at Old Trafford, in favour of a second Test. Other letters were emphatic that England had lost through bad luck only, they had not been defeated by the Australians. England had had the worst of the weather, the light, the wicket. And the perennial argument that the selectors had picked the wrong team was advanced. The Lancashire lobby, supporters of Pilling and Crossland were vociferous, prompting a curt reply from "SURREY":

'I saw the letters in your paper complaining of the exclusion of Pilling and Crossland from the English team. If the writers will compare the Lancashire representatives' scores in this great match with those of the representatives of Gloucestershire, Yorkshire and Surrey, I think they will admit that three Lancashire men were quite sufficient a proportion – in fact that to have omitted either Mr Steel or Mr Hornby in favour of some other gentleman or professional might possibly have been an advantage.'

In *The Manchester Guardian* of 1st September, "W.S." wrote a blistering attack on those who reckoned England had lost through bad luck:

'We have lost the great test match, but it is childish to blame the wicket, or the rain, or the light, for all these operated just as much against the one team as against the other, as the small scoring proves . . . we find one of the home team missing an easy catch and another running out of his ground to meet a ball dead on his stumps. That, we are told, was pure "bad luck". The truth is, it was wretched play in both cases. If "luck" had anything to do with the match, the Australians certainly had the worse slice of it in losing Jones in so aggravating a manner, so that the less we say about "luck" the better. The complete "rot" which paralysed the home team's second innings contrasts lamentably with the wonderful pluck of their antagonists, which, combined with the most brilliant attack ever delivered on a cricket field (and they were playing a losing game), literally "pulled the match out of the fire". They played as one man, and all we can do is accept the defeat with the best possible grace, for assuredly the best man won . . .'

"W.S." was in the minority. Most people refused to accept England's defeat. 'In my opinion, the result of last Tuesday was an accident. Had Lucas accepted Massie's chance, the Australians would have been defeated by ten runs, and yet, forsooth, because Lucas missed the catch, the Australians are ahead of us as cricketers . . . last week's match was not decisive enough for us cricket-loving English. No, sir . . . England is still the first and supreme in cricket.'

It was bad luck, it was an accident, it didn't really happen. The awful thing was that news of it would spread, as an article in *Cricket* pointed out:

' . . . the news of the defeat of a picked Eleven of England by the Australian cricketers will have been circulated in every part of the globe. Everywhere where Englishmen assemble the telegraph will have published intelligence of the result which came so unexpectedly on Tuesday evening on the 20,000 spectators present on the Surrey Ground in Kennington. In Australia, where sport is pursued with a keenness unknown even in the mother country, the victory of "the boys" will have evoked a degree of enthusiasm only understood by those who know the interest with which the doings of Murdoch and his men have been followed in the Colonies. And putting aside all questions outside the immediate play, Australia will have just reason to be proud of the success its players have so worthily gained . . .'

However people looked at the events that took place at Kennington Oval on the 28th and 29th August 1882, there was no doubt that they marked, somehow, the end of an era. At the end of the week, the most famous obituary in English history appeared in the *Sporting Times*:

In Affectionate Remembrance
of
ENGLISH CRICKET
which died at The Oval
on
29th August, 1882.
Deeply lamented by a large circle of
Sorrowing Friends and Acquaintances
R.I.P.

N.B. – The body will be cremated and
the Ashes taken to Australia

The hope was, that better fortune would follow Sir Garnet Wolsey's Egyptian Tour that was taking place at the same time, for, on the very day that it reported England's defeat at the Oval, the papers carried ominous headlines:

A GREAT BATTLE IMMINENT IN
THE EGYPTIAN CAMPAIGN
THE HIGHLAND REGIMENTS AT THE FRONT
DESULTORY SKIRMISHES IN ALEXANDRIA

The world had not turned completely upside-down: Sir Garnet won his fixture convincingly.

Charles Hoare, first captain of the Surrey Club, and one of the trio to whom Houghton surrendered his lease of the Oval in 1855. *From the Oval Collection.*

Digby Loder Armroid Jephson: '. . . taken as
a whole the fielding has been bad,
thoroughly bad . . .'
From the Oval Collection.

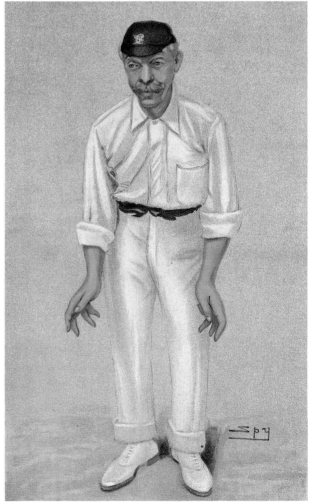

Bobby Abel, Cock Sparrow and Mighty
Atom; thirteen children and seventy five
first-class centuries.
From the Oval Collection.

The Surrey team, officers and members in 1911. *From the Oval Collection.*

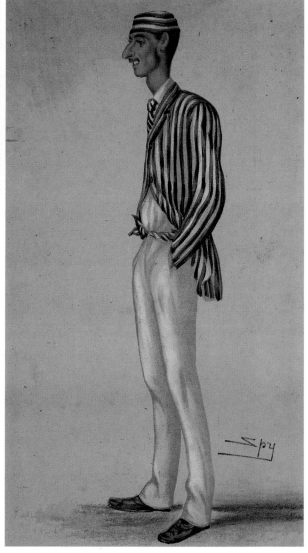

W.E. Roller: '. . . took all the proper precautions . . .'
From the Oval Collection.

The Demon Bowler, F.R. Spofforth: '. . . he had the evil eye; he was tall and angular and satanic of aspect . . .'
From the Oval Collection.

Michael Holding, West Indies v England, 1976. 'It is difficult to believe that there has ever been a comparable sustained spell of accurate and penetrative fast bowling on a slow wicket.' (John Arlott)
© *Patrick Eagar*

(left) The Oval, August 1989. © *Patrick Eagar*

Jubilation on the west terraces, England v India, 1989. © *Patrick Eagar*

England v Rest of the World, 1970, in the days when the Central Press held a photographic monopoly at the Oval and many a fine shot was taken over the wall. © *Patrick Eagar*

Sponsorship may not be to every member's taste, but it has guaranteed the survival of top-class cricket at the Oval.
© *Patrick Eagar*

England v Australia, 1989. A temporary halt to rebuilding. © *Patrick Eagar*

Chapter Seven

'. . . so vast a crowd of workers . . .' – The Matches and Players 1880–1914

A cricket enthusiast born in south London in the 1860s, given good health – not something to be taken for granted in the days before Public Health became politically popular – and a steady job, could have visited the Oval regularly from 1880 to the outbreak of the First World War. Life expectation wouldn't have taken him, or, exceptionally, her, much beyond 1914 unless he came from one of the more salubrious areas south of the Thames – the leafy avenues of Brixton, perhaps, or Streatham, or the heights of Camberwell. Even so, he would have seen the giants of cricket, players whose statistics may be inched lower and lower in the columns of *Wisden*, or even removed entirely from the records, but whose deeds and personalities seem more than life-size, like the monumental statues of the Victorian age in which they were all born. 'Oh, my Hornby and my Barlow, long ago . . .' And my Grace, Lohmann, Abel, Richardson, Jessop, Jackson, Woolley, Hayward and my Hobbs.

They all played at the Oval. Some for England, some for the Players or the Gentlemen, some for the North, some for the South, some for irregular combinations such as 'Kent and Yorkshire', many of them for Surrey. It was a lifetime of great matches and enormous crowds, who came by tram and bus, by train and tube, but mostly on foot to see their heroes. And the heroes themselves might well walk to and from work. Most of the professionals with Surrey were local men – Tom Richardson would bowl his heart out for Surrey all day and then pack his bag and walk home to Mitcham, stopping, it is said, at every pub on the way for his favourite evening tipple, gin and ginger beer. For breakfast, he preferred two bottles of stout.

There were matches where batsmen carved out triple centuries on wickets that should have broken the stoutest hearts among bowlers – Tom Hayward against Lancashire in 1898, Walter Read against eight keen but ineffective young bowlers from Oxford University in 1888, and Bobby Abel against Somerset in 1899. The Champion alone hit nineteen centuries on the Oval, three of them doubles. But there were other games where the bowlers licked their lips and their fingers and sped and spun their opponents to defeat.

G. Burton of Middlesex took all ten Surrey wickets for 59 in 1888. Tom Richardson, with a falling barometer and a south westerly breeze, in generally overcast conditions, on 18th May 1894, clean bowled eight Essex batsmen and finished with 10 for 45. In 1899, W.P. Howell for the Australians took all ten against Surrey.

And there were those matches, perhaps the best in the long run, where nobody achieved any record breaking feat, but the game hung in the balance till the last ball was bowled, and the crowd then ran on to the field to cheer both sides.

In July 1883, the annual Gentlemen v Players match was held at the Oval. It was a low scoring game and on the third day the Gentlemen needed only 150 to win. 'Had the wicket been as hard and fast on Saturday as it was on Friday,' reported the *Morning Post*, 'the runs would undoubtedly have been obtained. The violent storm of Friday night, however, had a considerable effect on the ground and batsmen were thereby placed at an obvious disadvantage.' The Gentlemen faltered to 115 for 8, with only Mr Lucas (local hero) left of the recognised batsmen.

Slowly, carefully, he and Frank pushed the score to 134. Barnes, who had bowled beautifully for the Players, was rested, and Barlow came on to bowl from the Vauxhall end. Lucas scored a single. Fifteen to win, two wickets to fall. Three maiden overs were bowled, 'the bowling being wonderfully straight and good'. Lucas scored another single, and then Flowers beat Mr Frank and the ball just removed the bail (136 for 9). In came Mr Rotherham, the last hope for the Gentlemen. He snicked a ball from Flowers through the slips for 2. There followed a spell of tight cricket on both sides. Four more singles were scored – 142, eight to win. Mr Rotherham 'made a lofty hit to long-on, and looked certain to be out, but to the intense disappointment of the Players, Bates missed a palpable catch, getting the ball in his hands and letting it drop' (*Morning Post*), 'a serious blunder' (*Manchester Guardian*).

Two more maiden overs, 'the excitement being, of course, very great'. Rotherham steered, cut, chopped, snicked (we are not told which) the ball through the slips off Barlow, and the ball went to the boundary – four to win. Rotherham scored a single. Lucas scored a single, though there were those who reckoned it was a chance to Robinson at short mid-on. Rotherham scored another single. The scores were level. The crowd cheered. They could afford to be generous: what did it matter who won, this was neither a county nor an international match. The Players held a consultation and decided, presumably by a democratic decision such as only the Players could arrive at, to replace Barlow with Peate. We shall now never know what was said in the consultation – how Barlow felt, how Peate felt, who steered the committee to the decision it made – for the Gentlemen and the Players, like the Captains and the Kings, are all departed.

But Peate bowled, and with his second delivery spread-eagled Mr Rotherham's stumps. 'It is needless to say that there was plenty of cheering. Everyone seemed delighted to be present at such an extraordinary finish.' There had been no fireworks. It had been desperately slow stuff. The Gentlemen had scored their 149 off one hundred and twenty six four-ball overs, at a modern rate of 1.77 runs per (six-ball) over. But you cannot get closer than a tie, and there hasn't been such a result at the Oval for a very long time.

In the Long Room at the Oval, there is a vast oil painting of W.E. Roller. It was painted in 1883, and was fine enough to be borrowed for exhibition by the Battersea Fine Arts Society in 1892. The artist has depicted the batsman walking down the steps of the old pavilion, pulling on his batting gloves, padded up, bat under his arm. He is wearing a Surrey cap, and a pink and brown tie, and he has the sleeves of his sweater folded back to reveal his strong wrists and the lower part of his forearms. There are several spectators in their seats, wearing a variety of hats – billycock, brown derby, bowler, topper. At the back, leaning against the pavilion wall, is a large man without a hat, and behind him, we can just distinguish the Luncheon Room, with a few members sitting at the tables spread with white cloths.

There is one important detail in the painting. A crumpled and discarded scorecard on the steps of the pavilion suggests that the match in progress is Surrey v Lancashire. Hopefully, the artist has depicted Roller coming out to bat in the second innings, for he scored only 5 in the first, and was injured by a delivery from Crossland, the Lancashire fast bowler whose action many questioned. This incident prompted 'An Old Cricketer' from Erith to write to the *Morning Post*, castigating Crossland, warning against the dangers of 'throwing', and lamenting that 'Mr Roller was so injured by Crossland that he was unable to take any further part in the game until the latter part of the second day'.

So here, in the painting, is Roller going out to bat in the second innings, during the latter part of the second day, when Surrey, needing 234 to win, had lost their first five wickets for only 107. Abel had gone, the Reads had gone, Shuter had gone, Diver had gone. There was much to be done if Surrey were to win, for, with over a day left to play, a draw was out of the question.

As soon as Roller came to the wicket, Barlow, the Lancashire captain, brought back Crossland, an aggressive move. Despite, or maybe because of, his questionable action, Crossland had taken 7 for 34 in Surrey's first innings, and nothing succeeds like success for a fast bowler. But it was Watson, from the other end, who struck, having Henderson caught at the wicket and bowling Bowden (122 for 7, 112 needed to win). Key, a young amateur, joined Roller, and at close of play on the second day they were still together, having made half the number of runs needed.

Surrey hadn't lost a county match at the Oval that year, and a large crowd gathered the following morning. 'The batsmen themselves took all the proper precautions, practising at the nets before play began . . . and running no risks while they were at the wickets . . . They played all the bowling of Lancashire with confidence and coolness, and never faltered for a moment . . .' (*Morning Post*). Barlow tried Crossland, Watson, Nash, Briggs and himself in the fifty minutes that it took Roller and Key to make the 56 runs and give Surrey victory by three wickets. 'Mr Key hit with power and freedom, while Mr Roller showed great judgement in running, and the cheers which greeted their splendid performance were of the most enthusiastic description.'

At ten to one, therefore, Roller would have been walking back up the steps of the pavilion, bat under his arm, success under his belt, but it wouldn't have made such a fine painting. Sadly, it is more than possible that the picture has nothing to do with the Surrey v Lancashire game. Roller has no bandage strapping his wrist where Crossland struck.

In May 1886, the Australians played in London, for the first time on their tour. 'The scene was Kennington Oval, and their opponents the Surrey Eleven, facts in themselves sufficient to account for the immense crowd of spectators present. At the Oval more than at Lords, the former Australian teams have played their most important London matches . . . No wonder, then, that the re-appearance of the Colonial Eleven should be an important day at the Surrey ground. But there was something more than this to mark yesterday as a red letter day in the annals of cricket, for on this occasion the Prince of Wales and Prince Albert Victor witnessed their first cricket match at the Oval. Hitherto it had been rather a reproach to cricket that royalty has not honoured the sport with its presence; the British public delight in the game, society patronises it on two occasions in every year – the Oxford and Cambridge and the Eton and Harrow matches. Royalty, however, has until now stood aloof. Yesterday's visit was particularly well timed, for the Prince of Wales is landlord to the Surrey Club, Kennington Oval being the property of the Duchy of Cornwall, and, thanks to his influence, held at a rent somewhat less than the aggregate of rates and taxes.'

Surrey were a strong side that year, but their achievement in defeating the Australians twice in the season must have come as a surprise to their staunchest supporters. The first match, that witnessed by the Prince of Wales, was a low scoring game which Surrey won by 3 wickets, and which was memorable as being the first time the Australians came across both the batting and the bowling of George Lohmann. He was twenty years old, and in his third season for Surrey. So he still had twelve years of cricket and fifteen years of life left. Sir Pelham Warner reckoned him the greatest all-round cricketer Surrey ever produced, and called him 'glorious'. Many great cricketers have themselves included him in their 'World Elevens'. Shortly before Lohmann's tragically early death, C.B. Fry wrote an appreciation of him as a bowler: 'His normal pace was medium; he took a run of moderate length, poised himself with a slight uplifting of his high square shoulders, and delivered the ball just before his hand reached the top of its circular swing, and, in the act of delivery, he seemed first to urge forward the upper part of his body in sympathy with his arm, and then allow it to follow through after the ball ...'

His action was graceful, his variation of pace masterfully controlled and disguised. He could bowl a very fast off break, a wicked yorker, a ball that appeared to gather pace off the pitch. He was only medium fast, but Fry reckoned him a very hostile bowler – 'he made one feel he was one's deadly enemy, and he used to put many batsmen off their strokes by his masterful and confident manner with the ball.' The Hon R.H. Lyttelton said that 'to see Lohmann bowl on an Oval wicket is an intellectual delight.'

On his first appearance against the Australians, Lohmann top scored for Surrey in their first innings, making 43 not out in a Surrey score of 171. And then he bowled against them, and clean bowled five of them, trapping a sixth lbw, and finished off their first innings with figures of 6 for 36. The Australians were all out for 82, and had to follow on. It seems appropriate that Lohmann scored the winning hit in Surrey's second innings.

The return match took place at the Oval two months later, at the very end of July 1886. Lohmann bowled beautifully in the Australian first innings, and should have had far better figures than 2 for 60. The Australians made 185, and, at close of play on the first day, Surrey had replied with 39 for the loss of their captain, John Shuter. The following day, Abel, Walter Read and Maurice Read pounded the Australians into the ground. Surrey scored at over a run a minute for the six hours of play. Abel and Walter Read put on 135 for the third wicket: Abel and Maurice Read an unbroken 241 for the fourth wicket. The Australians tried thirteen bowling changes. The Surrey score went from 200 to 250 in forty two minutes, from 250 to 300 in 35 minutes, and from 300 to 400 in 95 minutes. 'Late in the afternoon,' wrote the *Morning Post*, 'a collection was made for Abel and Read, and the handsome sum of £68 14s was subscribed and divided equally between them. The wicket played perfectly all day, there was a capital attendance, the number paying at the turnstiles being 5717 ... The Australians took their long outing very well indeed, and the fielding never became careless.'

There was a good deal of rain on the Friday night. Abel didn't add to his score on Saturday morning, but Maurice Read batted on, 'nearly 7000 people paying for admission at the turnstiles, and the members of the Surrey Club mustering in force ... A good many people were evidently counting Read's runs very carefully, for there was a ringing cheer when he passed Shrewsbury's record score of 164 against Australian bowling.' In those days people were already fascinated by cricket's statistical intricacies, but it must have been quite a job keeping up when scoreboards only gave the bare bones of an innings.

Surrey were eventually all out for 501 (Spofforth 1 for 102), Lohmann making a hard-hitting 31 not out. It was a record score against the Australians, but it looked as though the visitors might hold out for a draw. The wicket had started the day behaving awkwardly, but there was further rain, and the wicket even eased a little. Jones and Beaumont got a few early wickets for Surrey, but then

Giffen settled in and McIlwraith began to get his head down. Shuter switched Lohmann to the pavilion end. In six overs he took 3 wickets for 1 run. He had McIlwraith caught by Jones at cover slip, Trumble caught by Roller at mid off, and he clean bowled Jarvis. He ended with figures of 44-19-58-6. 'The result was received with enthusiasm, the people gathering in front of the pavilion and cheering the Surrey Eleven to the echo.' They had beaten the Australians by an innings and 209 runs.

It was an age of massive crowds at the Oval, and occasional poor behaviour. When Surrey played Notts in 1887, 'Alas, this great crowd behaved badly. Probably not expecting such a crowd as assembled, the Surrey Club had not secured a sufficient body of police, and during part of the opening day the boundaries were curtailed by quite twenty yards, a great deal of bottle throwing and other playful eccentricities being indulged in by some of the holiday people.'

It was also an age of massive victories. In 1888, Surrey beat Sussex by an innings and 485 runs, the biggest margin on an English ground until England beat Australia by an innings and 579 runs at the Oval fifty years later. Lohmann, given the grossly prosaic title 'the crack Surrey trundler' by the *Sportsman*, took a dozen wickets for 78, on a hard dry wicket where Surrey had scored 698. It was an age when Surrey could score less than two hundred and still win by an innings. They beat Leicester in a day in 1890. Lohmann took 6 for 20 in the first innings, and Shuter didn't even bother to bowl him in the second.

But it was also an age of some desperately close finishes. In 1894, Lancashire started the last innings of the match needing only 75 to win. The game flipped to and fro. Surrey should have won easily: Lancashire lost their first five wickets for 9 runs. Then Lancashire should have won easily: they needed only 10 with three wickets left and batsmen well set. In the end it was a tie – 'a tremendous finish, and the spectators naturally relieved their feelings by a demonstration in front of the pavilion' (*Morning Post*).

At a time when Surrey had probably its greatest ever bowling attack (Lockwood, Lohmann and Richardson), it seems ironic, cussed almost, that the Oval had the reputation of being a batsman's wicket. Sam Apted, the groundsman during these great years, cut and rolled, and cut and smoothed, and cut his grass again. But the players roughed it up, and the weather made life hard for Sam. The summer of 1888 was not a good one, and it led to some exciting results at the Oval, as elsewhere. 'Surprises have been rampant recently in the cricket world,' wrote the *Sportsman* on 20th July. 'So bad, indeed, are the wickets that cricket, just now, is of a most fluky character. Thus the downfall of the Surrey Eleven on whom most extravagant odds could be laid when the wicket is dry, would not be altogether unexpected. Of course, with the turf in a dry condition, the Oval team might almost play any two counties, but the soft ground has reduced them to the level of other sides . . .'

The match which the *Sportsman* was reporting was that between Surrey and

W. H. Lockwood – one of the great fast bowlers to be seen at the Oval at the turn of the century.
© *Marylebone Cricket Club*

Middlesex, when Burton took all ten wickets. 'There was one especial feature of the match, viz. the bowling of BURTON. In games which come under the category of "first-class" it rarely happens that one man gets the whole ten wickets. Yet Burton accomplished this feat, of which he will be able to boast for many a year. The side he dismissed makes the performance all the greater.' Surrey, needing 52 to win in their second innings, scraped home by 3 wickets at five minutes to six. Burton hardly had time to boast of his feat, before, less than a fortnight later, he took 16 Yorkshire wickets at Sheffield. Two years later, he was gone from the Middlesex side.

It was right and proper that such deeds should have been witnessed by vast crowds. On August Bank Holiday Monday 1896, so many spectators crammed into the Oval that 'after the luncheon interval considerable difficulty was experienced in keeping the playing space reasonably clear. On the whole, however, the people behaved very well, and, though all the boundaries were more or less shortened, things were by no means as bad as on one or two occasions that can be recalled' (*Manchester Guardian*). The crowd got their money's worth. Lohmann was unable to play, but, when Notts elected to bat first, Richardson was 'literally unplayable, fizzing off the pitch and breaking back five or six inches at his full pace' (*Wisden*). He took a fistful of wickets for a handful of runs, though the *Manchester Guardian* reckoned him lucky to have bowled Jones, Shrewsbury and Attewell with three of his famous break-back deliveries, since they were all bowled off their pads. How tightly that august journal supported the north of England in those days.

Others have lavished unstinting praise on Richardson. Jessop said of him: 'No bowler has ever compelled my admiration to such an extent as did Tom Richardson'. Cardus described him as: 'the cricketer whose heart was so big that even his large body hardly contained its heroic energy . . . the greatest cricketer that ever took to fast bowling . . . His action moved one like music because it was so rhythmical. He ran to the wicket a long distance, and at the bowling creases his terminating leap made you catch breath.' And, in this one-sided game against Notts, when 27,000 people paid for admission on the first day, Richardson was entering his prime period at the Oval. In the four seasons from 1894 to 1897 he bowled nearly 30,000 balls and took over a thousand wickets.

He was truly fast, of the speed of Kortright or Kotze, of Larwood, or, much

Tom Richardson: '. . . his terminating leap made you catch breath . . .' (Cardus). *Photograph by George Beldam*

later, of the speed of Tyson. He had amazing stamina, bowling for three hours unchanged, and he was phenomenally accurate. Time and again it was said of him that he almost never bowled a bad ball. He was a man of great heart, as Cardus said, of great sincerity and surprising sensitivity. He rarely bowled short, and, on bad wickets or against understandably apprehensive batsmen, always kept the ball pitched well up. It is said that he even reduced his pace if there was danger of a batsman being injured. Wood, the Surrey wicket-keeper, knew where to stand when keeping to Richardson, but A.A. Lilley of England didn't. He stood up at the stumps, and Richardson lessened his pace, lest he hurt Lilley. Grace told Lilley to stand back, 'He won't bowl full out until you do.'

At Lords in 1896, Richardson and Lohmann bowled out Australia for a measly 53 runs. Sixteen years later they had both died tragically young, far away from the Oval. Lohmann died first, on 1st December 1901, in South Africa, where he had gone to try to stave off the consumption that crippled and killed him. He was thirty six years old. Richardson lasted a little longer. He died at Aix-les-Bains, after a mercifully shorter fight against illness. He was 42.

In August 1896, both men were still in their prime, and both would have played for England in the Test against Australia had it not been for the unfortunate incident that came to be known as the 'Professionals' Strike'. Richardson retracted his demand in time, Lohmann didn't. Richardson played, Lohmann didn't.

The game was played on mud. George Giffen has left no doubt as to what he thought of the pitch: 'What seemed likely to be the game of games, the greatest ever known, was completely spoiled.' Richardson was hardly bowled: he needed hard ground beneath his feet, not a slithery quagmire. It was one of the lowest scoring Test matches ever – 392 runs for all 40 wickets. No one scored fifty – Darling was top scorer with 47 for Australia.

The opening day was preceded by heavy rain, and yet over ten thousand turned up in the hope of seeing some cricket. The *Manchester Guardian* gave a full report of what little action took place, and set the scene in a memorable account that speaks of cricket, or the lack of it, at the Oval over the ages. 'The outlook this morning was decidedly gloomy. Heavy clouds were scurrying over the sky, and an occasional shower driven across the sodden turf by a strong north-west wind made the chances of cricket appear but small. Despite these unpromising conditions the crowds steadily poured into the ground . . . (by half past eleven) all immediate prospects of play vanished. The rain fell in sheets, and the waiting multitude, fringed by a long row of police in their oilskins, was transformed into a mushroom bed of umbrellas . . . It was wonderful how well the vast crowd stood the long and dreary wait. Surrey spectators have not the best reputation for quiet orderly conduct, yet in this case there was nothing in their behaviour to which the most strait-laced member of the MCC could have objected. They realised that the weather was beyond the control of even the Surrey Committee . . .'

On that first day England battled to 65 for 1 before players and spectators had had enough of the foul weather, and the contest was postponed till the following day.

It was a bowler's wicket, almost from the start of play. Heavy rain had saturated the ground, but bright sunshine and a fresh breeze dried the surface of the turf, thereby forming a crust. Once the ball pitched, there were limitless possibilities as to what it might do next. It kicked, crept, broke, twisted, shot 'to the bewilderment of the batsmen'. It was a fearsome day for batting, but a beautiful day to watch cricket, and spectators flocked to the ground. It was estimated that 20,000 were in place when play started at half past eleven, for this was to be the deciding match of the rubber.

'The amount of interest taken in cricket by all classes is thoroughly exemplified at the Oval,' reported the *Manchester Guardian*. 'How so vast a crowd of workers can spare the time from their daily employment is always a mystery. Yet, there they are, labourers and mechanics, clerks and shopkeepers, porters and postmen in their distinctive uniforms, soldiers, sailors, and undoubtedly members of the auxiliary forces, all crowding on the stone ledges to watch every stage of the great struggle, with an interest only borne of genuine enthusiasm for the chief of English games. The warning bell was greeted with warm applause, as is the custom at all important matches at the Oval, and the shouting turned into a roar, as the Australians, led by Trott, descended the pavilion steps . . .'

England were all out for 145, and almost half of that they owed to Grace and Jackson, who had opened the innings when the wicket was still easy, before the crust formed. As has so often happened at the Oval, the damage was done when a bowler, in this case Trumble, switched from the Vauxhall to the pavilion end. He bowled nine overs for ten runs and five wickets; Abel, MacLaren and Hayward among them.

In the interval between innings, the crowd was warned by notices that 'No Promenading on the Field of Play' was to be allowed. It was a wise precaution, taking into consideration the state of the turf, and the fact that the crowd had by then increased to over 25,000. Australia, too, got off to a reasonable start. By lunch on the second day, Darling and Iredale had put on 43 without loss.

And still more people arrived to watch. The ground was so packed by then, contemporary accounts suggest that thousands were probably unable to see the game. Among those who could see, even from the limited accommodation of the old Pavilion, were Lord James, Lord Percy, Lord Ampthill, Sir Richard Webster (of course) and Joseph Chamberlain. Chamberlain was then Colonial Secretary in Salisbury's Government, and was taking time out from dealing with the political mess that had resulted from the Jameson Raid a few months earlier, and from the manoeuvres of the military in the Sudan.

The Australian score reached 75. Then Darling 'fluked' a stroke off Richardson, and attempted to run 5 off it. There was no attempt to rope off only a section of the ground as a playing area in those days, so that matches were held over the whole ground. Even so, to run five was a gamble, and to run five to Ranjitsinhji was asking for trouble. Iredale was run out. Another five wickets fell for the addition of only ten runs. Hearne bowled well to get rid of Darling, Giffen and Gregory, Trott was bowled by Peel, and Hill ran himself out. Only Donnan and Kelly offered much resistance after that, and Australia were all out for 119.

Grace and Jackson came out for England's second innings. The sky was overcast and the light rapidly deteriorated. 'Neither of the batsmen seemed at home with the bowling, and, by their frequent inspections of the wicket, showed how rotten they considered the turf to have become.' Their anxiety anticipated an England collapse. By close of play five wickets were down for 60 runs, giving England an overall lead of only 86, and the possibility of the wicket improving on the next day.

The *Manchester Guardian* sandwiched its account of the third and last day's

Dr. W. G. Grace (1848–1915) and
Sir F. S. Jackson (1870–1947).
From the MCC Collection

play in the Test between a report on the opening of the grouse shooting season, and a description of the Sudan's Expeditionary Force's negotiation of the third cataract on the Nile in their campaign against the Dervishes. The priorities of late Victorian England may be gauged from the arresting opening of the report from the Oval. 'How will the wicket play? That was the sole question . . .' If the wicket had the malice and unpredictability of the previous day, opinion favoured England. There was also the question of the weather. A few spots of rain fell before the start of play, but the skies cleared and play was not interrupted.

The pitch had not improved. 'The batsmen inspected the soft spots at the Pavilion end and shook their heads lugubriously.' Hayward was soon out, playing a leg break from Trumble straight into the hands of Trott at short leg. Peel played his third ball into Giffen's hands at mid off, but the comparatively easy catch was dropped. In the next over, Wynyard was caught behind by Kelly off McKibbin (67 for 7). Trumble was bowling 'a beautiful pitch and break, varying his pace in a most perplexing manner.' McKibbin's leg breaks were also 'practically unplayable'. There cannot have been many times in the history of Test matches at the Oval when two leg break bowlers were operating together. After two maiden overs, Peel played on (67 for 8). Hearne scored a single and was then yorked by McKibbin (68 for 9). 'The cricket had naturally been of the slowest, but with the appearance of Richardson, there came a change. In his old style he hit hard, and soon carried the English lead to a hundred runs.' A great many of the old hands present muttered that England should have hit out much sooner. 'Dreadfully fluky such play would have been, but hitting is the only thing that will save a collapse when a "rot" has once set in. At the worst it could not have resulted in a smaller total. The Australians had dropped back, and both Lilley and Richardson owed their escape to that fact, for each of them had skied the ball which fell short of the fielders.' It wasn't a prolonged last wicket partnership; just sixteen cheerful runs, ten of them to Richardson, before Lilley drove a good length ball from Trumble into the hands of McKibbin at mid off.

England had made 84, and had left Australia with 111 runs to win, an ominous number. Richardson opened the bowling. His first over was a maiden, every ball watched excitedly by the crowd, who, since they numbered less than 8000, could all presumably see. Hearne bowled from the other end, and, in his first over, completely beat Darling with a ball that broke from the off (0 for 1).'Loud and long was the applause as the Australian retired to the Pavilion in not the happiest frame of mind.' After the maiden with which he opened, Richardson bowled no more in the match. Grace, the England captain, brought on Peel. Iredale cut him for three, but good work by Brockwell, who was fielding as substitute, prevented further runs.

Iredale tried to hit his way out of trouble, but was caught by Jackson at mid-on off Hearne. The cricket was slow – seven runs off the first seven (five ball) overs. Giffen was bowled by Hearne, who had sent down five overs and taken 3 for 0. Gregory joined Trott, but the Australian captain was splendidly caught by Brockwell off Peel. 'The substitute fully deserved the applause he obtained. He had some distance to run and when he got to the ball it was almost on the ground. But he managed to get his hands under it . . .' With the score at 7 for 4, Hill came in. Gregory scored a four through the slips, and then Peel bowled Hill (11 for 5). Donnan failed to score, and provided Peel with his one hundredth wicket in Test cricket, a statistic that went unreported and was probably lost on the crowd (11 for 6). 'The procession was almost melancholy . . . there could be little doubt as to whose would be the victory unless something of the most unforeseen nature occurred.' Three runs later Gregory was caught by Richardson off Peel. Kelly and Trumble added a mere five runs before Kelly was out, leg before to Peel (19 for 8).

Jones had a reputation as a hitter, and Grace moved the field back for him. It might have been the correct tactic on Jones's part, but it was not to be his day. He leapt out at Peel, missed and was bowled (25 for 9). It was left to McKibbin to give the Australian total a little respectability. He hit Peel through the covers for four and carted him to the leg boundary. 'However, the pace was too hot to last', and McKibbin snicked Hearne into the slips where Abel made a good one-handed catch, 'the little Surrey man leaping into the air'.

'The moment Lilley saw that Abel had held the ball, he started to run to the Pavilion with the rest of the team at his heels. It was as well they did so, for a wildly enthusiastic mob were hard on their track. Outside the Pavilion there was a dense mass of shouting, cheering spectators, all calling loudly for their particular favourites. Amongst the English team, Peel was unanimously demanded, and after a time the Yorkshireman came out and bowed in some confusion. Then 'Hearne' was the cry and the same scene occurred. After him Grace and finally Trott had to come forth from their retreat and wave their acknowledgements. Then the spectators, feeling that they had done their duty in the matter, retired from the ground and the match was ended . . . Everyone felt that there was not a man in the two teams who had not done his best and done it well. Such a wicket was too heavy a handicap for even the most finished of players . . .'

There were those who said that the Oval wicket was 'ridiculously overprepared' in the 1890s. P.F. Warner was one of them – but what would a man of Lords know. And it didn't stop him helping himself to a century in each innings for The Rest against the Champion County (Notts) in 1907, and a double century for The Rest against Warwickshire in 1911. It was also said that, away from the 'over-marled' Oval pitch, Bobby Abel lacked the skill and agility that he showed on home territory, especially against fast bowling. Yet C.B. Fry remarked that Abel 'gathers runs like blackberries wherever he goes.'

Abel was a small man, who fathered thirteen children and seventy-four first-class centuries. He was the darling of the Oval, the 'Guv'nor', the 'cock-sparrow', the 'little 'un', the 'mighty atom'. To Cardus, Abel was 'the personifica-

In the days before the LCC flats – the Oval looking almost bosky. © *Hulton-Deutsch Collection*

tion of Surrey cricket seen through the air of the Oval; the pert lift of the cap on his head, the slick dexterity of his play, with bat at an impudent angle.' He was the man many in the Oval crowd came to see during the late 1880s and 1890s, when he was Surrey's great professional batsman. It was a position he owed to a change of heart by the Surrey Committee. The county had the greatest of professional bowlers at that time, but had the foresight to see that bowling was not the only function of a professional cricketer. While Gloucestershire, Hampshire and Middlesex played eight or nine amateurs and two or three paid bowlers, Surrey joined Lancashire and other enlightened counties in employing more batsmen. Abel served them well. He had only seventeen seasons in top class cricket, few enough for a batsman, and was in the top three of the national averages for all but four of those years. He stood five feet five inches tall, and, like many small players, used his feet well and excelled at the cut. But he could play all the shots. He was particularly strong on the leg side, and, since he had a surprisingly long reach, he was quick to drive anything pitched up to him, always keeping the ball on the ground.

His most famous innings, and for nearly forty years the highest individual score on the Oval ground, was against Somerset in 1899. Somerset were not a strong bowling side. Nine of them toiled against Surrey during those late May days, even five of the amateurs turning their arms, though the four professionals sent down 137 of the 223 overs that Somerset bowled. Abel mastered them all. 'His great innings was singularly free from blemish . . . all through Abel played very seriously, and he batted quite as correctly after making 300 as at any period in his innings,' wrote *The Times*. 'He never lost his form and always seemed the complete master of the bowling . . . The weather was fine, and the cricket was witnessed by close on 4000 spectators.'

But already, rheumatic infection was working on those bright eyes that smile down from the framed *Spy* cartoon on the wall by the staircase in the Oval pavilion. His sight began to go. He had to wear spectacles ('his only pair' suggested one wag). In 1904, after a thousand innings and thirty three thousand runs, Abel retired from the game and opened a little sports shop very near the Oval. He became blind, but would sit outside his shop, on sunny days, when the crowds were flocking to the ground to see Surrey's new batting hero, and chat with those who still recognised and still remembered him.

There were always other performers waiting in the pavilion at the Oval, for their hours of triumph or their moments of disaster. On the single day in 1890, when Surrey beat Leicestershire by an innings and 80 runs, while Sharpe of Surrey was bowling his way to short-term glory with 9 for 24 in the second innings, six of the Leicestershire team were dismissed for nothing between them. In the following year, another half a dozen of the Warwickshire side failed to score in their first innings against Surrey (Sharpe 4 for 20, Lockwood 6 for 24). And in August 1897, when Abel and Brockwell put on 379 for Surrey's first wicket, the entire Hampshire team bowled, Captains, Misters and plain professionals.

The century died, the old Queen died, George Lohmann died. But they kept playing Test matches at the Oval, and in 1902 the Australians came there on 11th August to play the last game in a five match rubber. It had been a memorable series. In the first Test, at Edgbaston, England had made 376 for 9 declared, and had then walloped into Australia, dismissing them for 36. Only rain had saved the tourists from a crushing defeat. Almost the whole of the second Test, at Lords, had been washed out. Australia, thanks largely to Hill and Trumper, had won the third Test, at Sheffield, by a comfortable 143 runs. The fourth Test, at Old Trafford, had been a cliff hanger. Trumper had scored a century before lunch on the first day. Jackson had scored a century for England, and Australia led by only 37 runs on the first innings. Lockwood then produced bowling that was 'nothing less than a triumph', according to *Wisden*. 'Finer bowling than his on Friday afternoon can rarely have been seen.' Australia were all out for 86, and England, with a batting side that had Rhodes going in at number ten, needed only 124 to win. With three wickets down they needed only 32 to win, but Trumble and Saunders were backed up by wonderful fielding, and Australia won by three runs.

The Ashes were lost, but there was one game left to salvage some prestige, on the ground where England had choked on their pride in 1882. England made a mess of the first innings. Lockwood bowled 'very finely' in Australia's second innings, Trumper slipped and fell flat on his face to be run out for 2, and England went in to bat on the last day chasing a target of 264. MacLaren, Palairet, Tyldesley, Hayward and Braund went for 48, and the odds were then 50 to 1 in favour of Australia. Ben Travers, who saw the whole game, reported that 'quite a number of disgruntled members' gathered up their belongings and departed, 'unable to face the indignity of witnessing England's abasement'. Perhaps the great innings of Botham at Headingley in 1981 may have given us a hint of the emotions and the surging hope that followed.

Gilbert Jessop joined the Hon. F.S. Jackson, with five wickets to fall and 216 wanted for victory. The pitch was soft beneath the surface, but hardening all the time on top. There were still four hours or more left for play, but, so far, care and caution had got England into this sorry mess. Jessop already had a reputation as a hitter, although the Australians had a poor opinion of him in this role. With the advantage of modern cricket statistical data banks, we now know that in his career Jessop scored his 26,698 runs at over 80 an hour, which includes time spent in retrieving balls he hit out of every arena he played on. Like Botham, he used a heavy bat and he played some unorthodox shots, hitting fast bowlers on the rise over cover's head. Like Botham, when he came to the wicket, the crowd expected much of him. Like Botham, he so often met that expectation. His innings broke like thunderstorms across the cricket grounds of England, but, as Cardus described him, 'there is a calm pivoted place at the centre of the wildest cyclone, and so in an innings by Jessop the fury consumed the field and cried havoc and threatened broken shins and heads and the roofs of houses; but the eye of Jessop and the mind were calm and calculating.'

At the Oval he took up his unique and remarkable stance, hunched very low, with his knees bent – 'The Croucher'. When he played a defensive stroke, it was as though he was sniffing at the ball, as an animal sniffs the wind for scent of danger. There was danger in this wicket. R.H. Lyttelton, writing in *The Times* wrote: 'Up to lunch time the wicket was so difficult that nobody could have felt surprised if either batsman had got out . . .' But they stayed, and by the interval had put on 39 runs, of which Jessop had scored 29.

The afternoon belonged to Jessop – the second fastest Test hundred ever, only Gregory of Australia has scored a faster, and that was on a docile South African pitch in the good light of Johannesburg, going in with the score 128 for 2. In 1902, at the Oval, on a brute of a pitch, in the moody light of Kennington, Jessop's achievement is staggering. At the other end, Jackson was often in

'The Croucher' –
G. L. Jessop.

difficulties, but he held on while Jessop hit Saunders for four successive on drives to the boundary. Jackson was out for 49, but Jessop went on, now partnered by Hirst. Trumble bowled over after over – he bowled for the whole of both England innings. Jessop hit him on to the awning above the members enclosure. The ball was retrieved. Jessop hit the next delivery into almost exactly the same spot. The crowd yelled, then quietened as Jessop neared his century. The moment he reached it, there was uproar. 'The conventional Londoner wore a hat in those days,' wrote Travers, 'and the conventional hat he wore was a straw boater. As Jessop made that stroke dozens of straw boaters were sent sailing from the crowd . . .'

Jessop scored 104 out of 139 in 75 minutes, 'reducing to a disorganised rabble an Australian XI which until he came in had been monstrous in its steely efficiency' (Cardus). And then he patted a ball from Armstrong into Noble's hands at short leg, and walked back to the splendid pavilion amid jubilation. 'The rest of the match was simply one crescendo of excitement' (*Wisden*), until Rhodes and Hirst carefully, methodically, pushed their way to the victory that Jessop had already won.

The following day, the headlines in *Sporting Life* proclaimed:

THE PRESTIGE OF ENGLISH CRICKET RESTORED

BRILLIANT BATTING BY JESSOP

but there exists a photograph, by George Beldam, that reveals so much more. The last ball has been bowled, England has won, and the crowd are invading the field as the players dash for the pavilion. In front of the canvas screen at the Vauxhall end, one supporter is caught in the act of throwing his hat in the air, and beyond the screen, figures are bunched in the windows of houses long gone from the area. There is a tree, to remind us that a mere lifetime earlier, this was pasture land. In the middle distance, there is a factory chimney and industrial smoke. And, in the foreground, one of the umpires (Richardson? White?) in a Goon-Show length white coat, is collecting the stumps. Dotted around are the piles of sawdust, evidence of the wetness of the day and the unsuitability of the conditions for fast scoring. The photograph is, of course, in black and white, soot and whitewash, from which it is possible for our modern eyes to register, like light meters, how dark a day it was for such glorious deeds.

13th August 1902. England's great vistory in Jessop's Test: 'The Prestige of English Cricket Restored' *(Sporting Life)*

The heroes came and went. In 1895, Sydney Francis Barnes, the greatest
bowler the world has known, made his first appearance at the Oval. He played
for Warwickshire against Surrey, and Surrey scored 520. Barnes's figures were
33-10-95-2. His second visit was in 1899, this time for Lancashire. Surrey made
556 (Abel 178, Lockwood 131, Jephson 100), but, again, Barnes finished with a
creditable analysis: 44-15-99-3. Altogether, Barnes played at the Oval perhaps a
dozen times. On one occasion, for the Players against the Gentlemen, he had
W.G. caught at the wicket. He appealed for the catch, but the umpire gave
Grace 'not out'. When Grace reached Barnes's end, he said: 'I played it, Barnes.'
'I know you did,' said Barnes, 'and so does everyone else but this chap,' and he
indicated the umpire. Three times, Barnes played in Tests at the Oval – in 1909
and twice in 1912, during the Triangular Tournament. Here, against South
Africa, he was unplayable. He took 13 for 57 on a wicket that was slow after
rain. He played one more game at the Oval, and was gone.

Stricker of South Africa bowled by Barnes in the 1912 Triangular Test. Note the trams.
© *Hulton-Deutsch Collection*

In 1905, John Berry Hobbs made his first appearance at the Oval, in a trial for Surrey on St George's Day. He had twenty minutes net practice, and was then invited to take part in a match. He made 37, and the next day, Alcock called him into the Secretary's office, and offered him the chance to qualify for Surrey on wages of 30/- in the summer and £1 a week in the winter.

oto by R. Scott & Co.,   **SURREY CRICKET CLUB.**   *Manches:*

| Strudwick. | 'Baker. | Marshall. | Holland. | Nice. | Hobbs. | J. N. Crawford. |
| | Hayes. | N. A. Knox. | Lord Dalmeny. | Hayward. | Lees. | |

Surrey XI in 1906. N. A. Knox was a promising fast bowler whose career was sadly cut short by injury. *From the Oval Collection*

Three years later, almost to the day, in cold and wind and snow more suited to winter than spring, The Champion bowed out, and made his last appearance at the Oval, indeed, his last appearance in first-class cricket. Dr W.G. Grace had assembled the Gentlemen of England to play a Surrey team that now included Hobbs, and were more than a match for them. The Gentlemen lost by an innings, but Grace held out for two hours in the first innings, and was one of the few to put up a show of resistance on the last day. 'Dr Grace was only at the wickets for half an hour for his runs (25), and his driving and pulling was an object lesson to many a young player. He put plenty of power into his strokes, and his play was really wonderful considering his age. He was seldom at fault in his timing, and his placing generally was very accurate.' The reporter from *The Times* did not know, nobody knew, that this was the old man's farewell. Grace was nearly sixty – three years earlier, at the age of fifty-seven, he had hit J.N.

Crawford out of the Oval. Now there was to be no more of what Lord Harris called his 'overwhelming excellence'.

But the connoisseur on the Oval benches had plenty more to see in the Golden Age: Bardsley's two hundreds for Australia in the Fifth Test in 1909 (the first time such a feat had been performed in a Test); 'Razor' Smith's incredible 14 for 29 against Northants in 1910, finishing off the match with a hat-trick; Surrey v Middlesex in the same year, when Surrey, needing 79 to win, crashed to 7 for 39 before Leveson-Gower and Smith doubled the score; Hayward's one hundredth century, in the game against Lancashire in 1913; Jessop's whirlwind 81 out of 111 for the Gentlemen, two weeks later; Woolley's all round brilliance in the Triangular Test against Australia in 1912, when he scored 62 and took 5 for 29 and 5 for 20.

19th August 1912. England and Australian teams at net practice together. © *Hulton-Deutsch Collection*

Cardus wrote of the last named: 'Woolley's innings stay with us until they become like poetry which can be told over and over again.' It is hard to equate that with *The Times* leader of May 1913, suggesting that left-handed batting should be outlawed – 'the idea may be rather revolutionary, but it is certainly not unworthy of consideration.'

And, all through the Golden Age, the Oval had its poet – the great Albert Craig, 'the Surrey Laureate', wandering the ground, improvising verse and peddling poetry. His style was appalling, his metre irregular, his rhymes hackneyed beyond repair, but his pockets were weighed down with coppers from his customers, and he could neither do nor say anything wrong as far as the Oval crowd were concerned. He spread compliments as a farmer does manure – 'Yorkshire, my native county; Surrey, my adopted county; Essex my tip for the Championship.' 'All the Gentlemen are Players,' he would declaim, 'and all the Players Gentlemen!' He was famous, friend of the people, darling of the mighty, in his words 'Captain of the spectators'. When he was ill, the Prince of Wales sent a get-well telegram. Once, Bobby Abel walked with Craig from the Oval to Westminster Bridge and attempted to keep count of the number of people who knew and wished to speak to the 'Leno of the Cricket-Field'. There were more than a hundred. The more humbug Craig gave, the more poems he sold. In 1907, he greeted Notts to the Oval for their Bank Holiday game.

> Darling Old Oval, once again we meet,
> One clan to triumph, one to bear defeat;
> Notts, dear old Notts, appear in all their pride,
> We greet them warmly to the 'Surrey Side';
> Some old familiar faces are no more –
> No Shrewsbury – as in happy days of yore;
> No Alfred Shaw, a bright and leading star,
> Immortal Walter Read, alas! has 'crossed the bar'
> Their tasks are o'er, their 'spurs' they nobly won,
> Rest follows toil, their hard day's work is done . . .

Craig lived long enough to praise Hobbs – 'Surrey's coming man . . . Joy reigned in the Pavilion, And gladness 'mongst his clan . . .' – but even Craig's poetry was deteriorating by then. During his life, there was speculation that he owned half Kennington, but when he died in 1909 he was found to be at least as poor as poets are supposed to be. His two great friends, Abel and Richardson, went to his funeral.

Chapter Eight

Members, Menus and Motor-Mowers –
Developments 1900–1914

By the turn of the century, the Oval had come a long way since its foundation as a cricket ground fifty five years earlier, and the whole of Kennington had undergone vast changes. The roads round the Oval were laid out much as they are now, and it was already a built-up area, though none of the blocks of flats that stand today to the east side of the ground and to the north-west of Archbishop Tenison's school had yet been built. Gasholders had long been on the site they still occupy, and the Oval Mansions were part of a much earlier development.

There were also the local factories. Vauxhall's had started life as an iron foundry on the river. Nearer the Oval was the famous Marmite factory, the smell from which, if the wind was in the north, would waft down to a batsman at the pavilion end as though on the panting breath of any fast bowler he faced. Trouble and odour came, it was said, when they opened the valves in the Marmite factory, about noon.

Transport had changed out of all recognition. In 1845, there were two ways of getting to the Oval: in a carriage or on foot. Horse-drawn trams ran from Westminster Bridge to Kennington Park from 1861 onwards, but by the early 20th century, the Oval was on several bus routes, trams clanked past, and there was a station on the City and South London Railway (now the Northern Line) named after the cricket ground. This line, the world's first electric tube line, ran for three and a quarter miles from King William Street in the City to Stockwell. It opened in 1890, and lists of those applying for membership of the Surrey Club, from this date for the next twenty five years, show a considerable proportion of stockbrokers, bankers, and directors who worked in the City, and who must have found the journey to the Oval by underground railway remarkably speedy when compared with any other form of transport. Work stopped early in the City in those days, and luncheon was taken late at the Oval, a joint arrangement that must have seemed alluringly convenient. The management of this railway were not slow in realising the value of the Oval to them as a source of revenue. In May 1900, at the suggestion of a member of the Surrey

Mr Fred Reeves, a
Surrey 'worker'
from 1904 to 1940,
resplendent in his
uniform. *From the
Oval Collection*

Club, a letter was sent to the City and South London, politely complaining about the company's practice of increasing fares on the line whenever there was cricket at the Oval.

Having spent a great sum of money on the 'nice' new pavilion and other developments at the very end of the last century, and having laid twelve thousand new turfs on the playing area, the Club looked forward to a period of growth and assimilation. There was, however, still some fine tuning to be done – maybe there always is. Plans for new stands to the west of the pavilion were sent to the Duchy of Cornwall office, seeking approval. A letter was sent to the Exchange Telegraph Company, accepting their offer to supply a 'Sports Service' for the season. In May 1901, this service was extended to include War news. This was the Second Boer or South African War, which had been spluttering away since the end of the 1899 season. There were no Tests between England and South Africa from April 1899 to January 1906, but by the time the Exchange Telegraph service was installed in the Oval, the news from South Africa was mainly of mopping up operations: there were to be no more Spion Kops and Majuba Hills, and little more guerrilla warfare – well, what could you expect from a country that invented the googly? – and members were, therefore, able to admire the skills of Abel, Hayward and Richardson without fear of bad news from abroad.

The National Telephone Company wished to erect a pole within the precincts of the Oval – the idea was not entertained. There were teething troubles in the new pavilion. Some of the roof tiles had split, and the floor boards were buckling. The Reading and Writing Rooms for Members needed to be 'fitted up'. In 1902, electric lights were added to the large Club Room. Seven years later it was decided to install a new system of electric lights at a cost not exceeding the remarkably precise figure of £12 9s 10d. In the same year there was another innovation at the Oval. In August, Mr R.W. Paul, 60 High Holborn, wrote to the Club asking permission to take cinematograph pictures at the Test and other matches. It was decided that photographers should be allowed to take cinematograph pictures at matches on payment of a fee of ten guineas a day as long as the play and the view of spectators were not interfered with. Five days later, Jessop played one of the greatest Test match innings of all time. Was Mr Paul there with his cinematograph . . .?

In April 1907, the Committee wrote to the London Shoe Black Company, asking them to make arrangements to post a Boot Boy outside the Pavilion, near the paper stall, but the Company replied that they could not see their way to providing this facility. The Committee decided to pay the expenses of Pooley's funeral. A week after the sad news of Tom Richardson's death near Aix-les-Bains was received, the Committee voted a sum of £50 to go to his children. E.H.D. Sewell was appointed Cricket Instructor on the same terms as those previously arranged with Mr W.W. Read – a salary of £37 10s per month. A Sub-Committee was set up to 'inquire into the advisability of having a screen behind the bowler's arm at the pavilion end of the ground, and what effect it would have on the seating accommodation of the Pavilion.' This was in November 1907, and you begin to wonder what it must have been like, in earlier days, taking strike at the Vauxhall end to face Richardson, Lockwood or Lohmann, pounding up with a dark and often moving background.

In July 1905, it was decided to give Shanks Motor Mower a trial. The trial appeared satisfactory, and a year later the Committee decided to purchase such a machine from Shanks and Co. It would mow the ground in six hours, while a horse-drawn mower took ten hours. Six years later, in 1912, the Committee had changed their minds. The mower was in good working order, but unsuited to the Oval. Since Shanks would allow only £20 as a trade-in price, and the Committee wanted at least £80, the recommendation was that it should be sold privately. Seven months later the best offer the Club had received for the mower was £15, and they decided to sell it 'at the best price obtainable'. They were still faced with mowing problems: in December 1913, the mare that pulled the old mower and roller went lame, and had to be destroyed.

It was the age of the Edwards – Windsor and Elgar – of 'Cockaigne' and Coronations, one in 1902, one in 1911. The ground was closed on 27th July 1902 for the Coronation of Edward VII. In June 1911, the Committee voted a sum, not exceeding £10, to be spent on decorations for the Coronation of George V. It was a time of prosperity and order, and a time of growth for the Club. A vast painting adorns one of the walls in the Long Room of the Oval. It is of the Club and members in 1911, many seated in the fine pavilion, the Surrey team standing in front of the little white fence to one side, a group of the Officers of the Club standing boldly to the other side. There is Viscount Alverstone, with topper and sideburns, a stern man, of upright bearing, every inch the aristocrat, and proud of the Club that he loved and documented. And among the members so meticulously recorded by the artist, are Ashley Cooper, 'a man unrivalled as an authority on cricket history', who had spent years in the Reading Room of the British Museum (during the winter months, presumably), combing old newspapers and magazines in search of printed matter about cricket. In his life he wrote 103 cricket books and pamphlets and over 40,000 biographical and obituary notices. He was editor of *Cricket* for five years and for a short while Secretary of the Nottinghamshire County Cricket Club. Today, he is probably best known as the man who, for more than thirty years, compiled the Births and Deaths and Cricket Records in *Wisden*. In the painting of 1911, he sits in the back row of the pavilion, just in front of the Long Room, smiling, and wearing a straw boater.

A few rows in front, and a little to the side, is P. Stuart Surridge, whose firm made cricket bats for Gilbert Jessop, 'The Croucher', the man who put the finest bowlers in the world to the sword, and whose brilliance and audacity changed the course of many a match. Surridge, too, wears a top hat, and smiles happily beneath his waxed moustache. And there, too, is Sir Jeremiah Colman, and other members of the Colman family, scattered about the pavilion like the mustard seed from which they made their fortune. H.S. Altham, in straw hat, has a young, Kippsian look about him. E.H.D. Sewell also wears a straw hat, but looks older and more formidable, despite the vast floral buttonhole. A.M. Latham sits in the front row, a rotund figure with a slightly dispeptic look of displeasure about him – he was vociferous and regular in his complaints about the catering at the Oval. Near the back row, George Mozart, dapper and bright-eyed, has his hands in his pockets, but that is as raffish as they come. The painting is of a well established, well organised, very respectable Club.

The growing membership came from many quarters. The printed lists that came before the Committee included names and of proposers and seconders, and the occupations of the applicants themselves. Among those who joined in 1907 and 1908 were Thomas Geoffrey Blackwell (Partner in Crosse and Blackwell); Fred Earle and Sam Mayo (Musical Hall Artists); Frank Curzon (Theatrical Manager of the Prince of Wales Theatre); F.A. Simonds (Brewer, of Reading); The Sahibzada Nasir Ali Khan, address The Constitutional Club, Northumberland Avenue, WC ('no occupation'); P.F. Knox (Actor), proposed by C. Aubrey Smith; Hon L.H. Tennyson (schoolboy member); Fred Reeves (Musical, Theatrical and Variety Agent); and numerous officers from some of the finest regiments in the Edwardian Army.

They were not the easiest people in the world to please. They may well have enjoyed the cricket, but had many complaints about the catering arrangements. Why could chops or steak not be served until after one o'clock during the matches against Yorkshire and Lancashire in the summer of 1900? The Dinner at the Oval for the Australians in 1899 had been 'very unsatisfactory'. Mr A.M. Latham, scourge of caterers at the Oval for decades, suggested at the Annual Meeting that, in future, such dinners should be held at the Trocadero or the Cecil. He did not, however, get his way. The 1902 Banquet to the 11th Australian Touring Team was held in the Pavilion, on 12th May. The menu comprised:

HORS D'OEUVRES
Anchovies   Caviare

SOUP
Clear Turtle

FISH
Gloucester Salmon, Tartar Sauce
Whitebait

ENTREES
Sweetbreads, Financiere Sauce
Stewed Pigeons and Spinach

REMOVES
Boiled Chicken, York Ham
Roast Lamb and Peas

ENTREMETS
Asparagus
Tomatoes Farcies
Fruit Jellies
Ice Pudding

DESSERT

With this, a certain amount of drink was required: Punch, dry sherry, a *Rudescheimer, Charles Heidsieck 1893, Duminy 1892, Chateau Margaux, Martinez 1880* Port, and liqueurs. An almost identical dinner was given for the 12th Australian team in 1905, except that *Moet 1898* was substituted for *Charles Heidsieck*, and Chicken Fricasee for Stewed Pigeons. Perhaps it was just as well that pigeons were off the menu, as it is all too easy to envisage which part of the Oval those pigeons might have come from – deep square leg, if present grazing ground is anything to go by.

These two meals must, at least, have passed muster, for in the spring of 1909, the President gave a Dinner in the Pavilion to the staff of the Surrey County Cricket Club. The menu was one rung down the gastronomic ladder:

SOUP
Spring Lobster

FISH
Turbot in Lobster Sauce
Fillets of Sole in Dutch Sauce

ENTREE
Mutton Cutlets and Peas

JOINTS
Roast Beef, Yorkshire Pudding, Horseradish
Roast Lamb, Mint Sauce
Spinach, New Potatoes

POULTRY
Boiled Chicken and Ham

SWEETS
Apple Tart and Custard
Wine Jellies

DESSERT

This occasion was enlivened by entertainment. A Programme of Music was supplied by members of the Surrey First Team. For once all the players were styled as 'Mr' on the programme, and each of them sang, or performed, two numbers, accompanied by Mr J. Applegarth. Mr Hayes sang 'Two Eyes of Grey' and 'Would You Care'; Mr Hitch, in Scots mood, sang 'Sandy McNab's Wedding' and 'I Love a Lassie', a big hit at the time; Mr T. Rushby rendered 'Thora' and ''Tis the Day'; Mr E.B. Myers obliged with 'Asleep in the Deep' (possibly long on) and 'The Sailors Dance'; Mr Geo Platt, in comedy vein, convulsed one and all with 'There's a Peculiar Thing' and 'The Old Tin Can'; and Mr G.H. Longman sang 'A Roving' and 'As I Walked Through the Meadows'. The high spot of the evening, however, may well have been Mr W.C. 'Razor' Smith's presentation of 'Didn't I' and 'Four Fingers and a Thumb' – perhaps the same four fingers and a thumb with which he was to take 10 for 51 in the match against Essex a couple of months later.

Ernest Hayes, a fine Surrey all-rounder, who later became coach at the Oval.
From the Oval Collection

In 1909, the Australians returned for a menu that differed in no way from that of 1905, save for the wine list, but in 1912, the year of the Triangular Test Series, the Australians and South Africans were dined at the Savoy, where the menu was very different.

As is the case for any institution, much of the Club's time was spent in matters relating to its staff. At the beginning of 1909, the Committee decided it was time that Hodson, the Night Watchman, retired, and that a younger man be appointed in his place. At the same time, a grant of £25 was voted to Hodson. Three months later, the same Committee met to discuss a letter from Hodson, asking them 'not to dispense with his services'. Another five months passed, and S. Rhodes was appointed night watchman at a weekly wage of 25 shillings. By February 1911, Rhodes was ill, and informed the Committee that he wouldn't be able to carry out his duties for several weeks. In the summer of the same year, Rhodes resigned through ill health and T. Freeman (the T did not stand for 'Tich') was appointed. In January 1911, it was decided that Tom Hayward, who was then approaching his fortieth birthday, should be sent to Matlock Bath for two weeks before the cricket season began. This became a yearly visit for Hayward.

In the 1890s and 1900s, Surrey had been a strong bowling side, with Richardson, Street, Lockwood, 'Razor' Smith, and Lees all capable of running through a side. By 1911, however, although Rushby and Hitch were no mean performers, Richardson had long retired, and the Surrey attack had lost some of its sharpness on a wicket that generally favoured the batsman. There are some unlikely names in the bowling analyses: Hobbs, Ducat, Sandham, Strudwick even. In 1912, the Committee agreed that Mr John Shuter, an ex-Captain of the Club who had led Surrey to six successive County Championships from 1887 to 1892, should write to Woodbrook in Ireland, for full particulars 'as to a certain Clark, who is reported to be a very good googly bowler'. The plan came to nothing.

Although, on the whole, the professionals at the Oval were well looked after, for a while at the very beginning of the century their position became slightly less secure following a letter to the Club from the President, Sir Richard Webster (who later became Viscount Alverstone). Today it is difficult to read the letter without a raising of the eyebrows, if not the hackles:

> ' . . . I have long been anxious that the Surrey County XI should afford greater opportunities to first-class amateurs to play County Cricket. I certainly do not consider that the Championship should be the only object, and while I always wish Surrey to win, I should be sorry if the County Championship remained with Surrey for a long series of years . . . I should like if possible to arrange matters so that at least three places in the XI in all ordinary County Matches should be filled by amateurs . . .'

Such a situation could not exist today, and it seems inconceivable that the

The Pavilion and stands before the War. The awning already spoils the symmetry of the Pavilion, but worse was to come with the erection of the commentators' box on the West end of the Pavilion after the War.
From the Oval Collection

President of any County Cricket Club, even if 'not a very clever man', could even think such things, let alone commit them to paper. Webster appears not to have got his way. Only two amateurs (V.F.S. Crawford and D.L.A. Jephson) turned out for Surrey in their matches at the Oval against Essex and Worcestershire a few weeks later. Possibly Webster would have argued that other counties contained many more amateurs – in 1900, Sussex had five amateurs in their side; Essex six; Middlesex, Kent and Hampshire seven; and Somerset eight. The

Surrey amateurs were both fine players, but Webster's idea would have deprived some similarly talented professional of much needed match money or bonuses.

For professionals at the Oval were still not paid a great sum of money. In the winter of 1900–1901, Abel, Baldwin, Baker, Lockwood, Marshall and Wood were paid thirty shillings a week each, and Strudwick, a comparative newcomer to the ground staff, one pound. During the summer months, junior members of the first team were paid little more. In the spring of 1903, Hobbs and Tom

Rushby were engaged as ground bowlers for the season at wages of thirty shillings a week. The following winter, Rushby was getting ten shillings: Hobbs, having already shown some of his potential, was paid a pound a week to enable him to stay in the County and obtain residential qualifications. A word in Alcock's ear from Tom Hayward also produced a £10 bonus for Hobbs. Surprisingly, Hobbs, a modest and respectful young man, managed to summon up the courage to go back to the Committee four months later, and ask for an increase in winter wages to twenty-five shillings a week – 'as his home was now in the County he could not live off a pound a week'. The Committee decided to pay the increase. Subsequently, it proved money well spent.

That same winter, C.A. Stein, the Acting Honorary Secretary, sent letters to each of the Surrey professionals, enclosing a form to be filled in. The gist of Stein's letter was that the winter wage wasn't meant to be a living wage, but to help them while unemployed and to supplement such earnings as they could secure 'which might possibly be small owing to the employee being only able to take winter work'.The replies from the professionals, and the table below, show what work they did, and how difficult it was to obtain winter employment:

ABEL –	'cricket bat manufacturer'
BALE –	None
DAYS –	None at present
GOATLY –	Has not been able to obtain employment at present
GOODER –	Paperhanger, some weeks 10/-, some weeks 15/-, some weeks nothing
HAYES –	None whatever
HOBBS –	Nothing at present
HOLLAND –	None
JACKSON –	Nothing at present
LEES –	Nothing
LOCKWOOD –	Nothing
MOULDER –	No employment
RUDD –	Nothing
RUSHBY –	Carpenter, probable earnings 30/- a week
SMITH –	None
STEDMAN –	Bricklayer, piece work. Uncertain

Awkward financial questions were asked in May 1901 as a result of an article published in the *Daily Mail*. The article was headed 'PAID AMATEURISM', and pointed the finger at one of the Surrey amateurs, V.F.S. Crawford. Following this article, a letter appeared in the *Daily Mail* a couple of days later, purporting to come from Crawford's father, the Rev William Cobbold Crawford. It criticised the paper, and stated most forcefully that, since Frank Crawford had given up a promising career at Oxford to play for Surrey, and since it was unthinkable that he should play as a professional, it was both understandable and proper that a few right-minded friends had offered to give him backing. The odd thing about this letter was that the Rev Crawford subsequently denied all knowledge of it and claimed that he was not the writer of it.

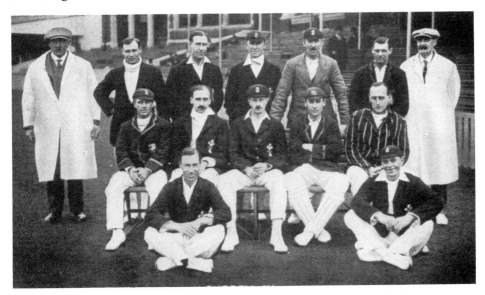

Surrey XI in 1914. The Club emblem now includes the Prince of Wales' feathers.
From the Oval Collection

Crawford's right-minded friends were members of the Surrey Club, among them Lord Alverstone, and a meeting was called to discuss the affair. *The Sportsman* for 3rd May included a report of the meeting.

'In the absence of business of a contentious nature, there was not a very large attendance in the pavilion at Kennington Oval this afternoon, only about 120 members being present, under the Chairmanship of the Rt. Hon. Lord Alverstone, President ... In all the proceedings lasted barely half an hour. After the minutes had been confirmed ... regret was expressed at the death of Sir Frederick Marshall, Vice President, and of John Burrup ... The Chairman, in reply to a question from Mr Gordon, spoke in strong condemnatory terms on the attack which had been made on Mr V.F.S. Crawford in the *Daily Mail*, and trusted that members would be above paying serious attention to what had been said. So far as the Surrey County CC were concerned they would not be directly or indirectly party to any payment as he had said several years ago after dealing with another matter ...'

This was, presumably a reference to the payment of expenses to W.G. Grace.

'. . . it was true that certain gentlemen had assisted to place Mr Crawford in the office of a respectable stockbroker – he was himself a contributor to the extent of a small amount – but if the fact of giving a promising young man a start in life was to be called into question, then goodbye to sport in England (applause).'

In 1914, at the end of the Golden Age, Surrey won the Championship and it was very nearly goodbye to sport in England. A third Edward was in the limelight – Sir Edward Grey, the Foreign Secretary. While he was making his famous speech to the House of Commons on 3rd August, fifteen thousand spectators all but filled the Oval, to see Surrey make 472 for five wickets against Notts (Hobbs 226 not out), and many more than fifteen thousand German troops marched through the Belgian countryside. The following day, the country went to war.

Chapter Nine

Balls to the Ruhleben Cricket Club, Berlin

There still hangs about the outbreak of the First World War, as the smell of linseed oil deep stays long within an old cricket bat, the suggestion that it all happened so fast, so unexpectedly. One moment on a sunny August day, Notts were plodding away at the Oval, facing Surrey's first innings score of 542, and making such heavy weather of it that barrackers were being removed from the ground by police, the next moment Arthur Carr, while at the wicket, was opening a telegram summoning him to join his regiment. Within a matter of days, Jack Hobbs's Benefit Match – Surrey v Kent – had been transferred to Lords, the heroes of the Golden Age, Jessop, Maclaren, Ranji, were all in uniform, urging others to enlist, and the Champion himself was writing to *The Sportsman*: 'I think the time has arrived when the county cricket season should be closed, for it is not fitting at a time like the present that able-bodied men should play day after day and pleasure-seekers look on . . . I should like to see all first-class cricketers of suitable age, etc., set a good example, and come to the help of their country without delay in its hour of need.'

To most full-time cricketers the war was unexpected. The Surrey Committee, at the beginning of 1914, were more concerned with other matters militant, recommending that, in view of the increasing activities of the 'Military' Suffragettes, one extra Night-Watchman be engaged. But there are signs that others, men in more prominent or perhaps more secretive occupations, had some foreknowledge of what was coming. It may even be that the 'game', as it was so often misnamed, against the Kaiser's Germany was a fixture that had long been planned – it was merely a question of finding a suitable date and venue.

On 25th May 1914, an application from the Staff Officer of the Central London Recruiting Depot to place notices inside the Oval, with a view to obtaining recruits for His Majesty's Land Forces, was not entertained by the Surrey Club, but clearly some indication of approaching hostilities was in the air. Indeed, as early as March 1910, the Colonel commanding the 5th London Brigade RFA was writing to the Surrey Club asking for the use of the Oval as a place of assembly for his Brigade should mobilisation for war take place. The Committee gave their permission, and on the evening of 5th August 1914, after rain had ruined the last day of the Surrey v Notts match, the Oval was occupied by the military. It was the first open space in London to be taken over – it's tempting to see some collusion here between government, military and Lords. There were an enormous number of open spaces in London – why the Oval first?

Immediately, it became necessary for the Committee to face at least some of the harsh realities of wartime. Some members of the Surrey staff wasted no time in enlisting, and the Committee had to consider what attitude to take towards such patriots. One of the first from the Oval to join the Territorials was A. Attwater, of the Bowlers' Staff. It was decided that he should receive half his usual summer wages. At the same meeting, a ruling was made that 'no cricket practice should take place at the Oval for the present'. More optimistically, hoping perhaps that 'it would all be over by Christmas', the Committee decided to give Central News Ltd. the option of having the exclusive photographic rights at the Oval for 1915 on the same terms as 1914.

The following week, *Sporting Life* reassured its readers that the worst had not taken place: ' . . . there would be many sentimental reasons for regret were gun carriages and the hoofs of horses digging holes in the delicate turf upon which Hobbs might have been found scoring a charming hundred today in happier circumstances . . . Happily, I can assure those who have a sentimental regard for a classic cricket ground that until Saturday at least the Oval was very much the same as it had been before it came into the hands of the military . . . all that has happened is this: Hurdles have been placed round the playing area some eight yards from the boundary line. Upon that narrow fringe of turf guns have been placed. Horses there are on the ground, but they have not placed a single hoof upon the grass. They are confined to the asphalt space at the Vauxhall end . . .'

The Surrey Committee, meanwhile, had the pleasant task of fixing the bonuses to be paid to the players for winning the County Championship. They decided to give £15 each to Ducat, Hayward, Hobbs, Hayes, Hitch, Rushby and Strudwick; £5 to W.J. Abel, Smith, Goatly and Harrison; and £2 10s each to Platt and Sandham.

The juggernaut of war was, however, gathering momentum. In the first week of September, 175,000 men from Britain volunteered to join Kitchener's New Armies. War fever raged. The Surrey Committee had to deal with a letter from Mr B.B. Turner, who wanted them to dismiss any of their employees eligible to enlist who failed to do so. The Committee tactfully replied that they were 'encouraging their employees to enlist'. By October 1914, an impressive number of Surrey players were in the Forces. Mr C.T.A. Wilkinson, Mr D.J. Knight and Mr J. Howell were in the Artists' Corps; Mr P.G.H. Fender was in the Royal Fusiliers; Myers and Freeman were in the 1st Surrey Rifles; Attwater was in the 7th Sussex Regiment; Bungay was very much at home in the 5th London Brigade RFA, stationed at the Oval; and Hayes, Hitch and Sandham were in the Sportsman's Battalion attached to the Royal Fusiliers. A few weeks later came

Jessop speaking at a recruiting rally early in the
First World War. *From the MCC Collection*

the news that Peach had joined the West Kent Yeomanry, and that Darkwater
(the night watchman at the Oval) was serving with the Royal Marines.

It had become clear, by the late autumn of 1914, that the war would not be
over in a few months. The French, German and British armies had all gone to
earth in Flanders and Eastern France, and already Churchill was hatching
ill-conceived schemes for opening up a second front in the Dardanelles. Should
a great victory and peace suddenly come, however, it was important that plans
be made for the future of cricket. To that end, the Committee met in November
and a provisional list for County Fixtures in 1915 was approved. It was also

decided to play the Champion County v Rest of England match at the Oval, if practicable, on 13th, 14th, 15th and 16th September 1915.

The reality was that the war went on into 1915 and more members of the Surrey staff enlisted. Jennings joined the 13th Reserve Battery RFA. G. Goatly, the Dressing Room Attendant, joined the Royal Fusiliers. An application was received from A.E. Grant, serving with H.M. Forces in France, for some old cricket balls, nets, etc., for use at Rouen. The Secretary was instructed to forward any available materials. Consideration was also given to a request from the Ruhleben Cricket Club in Berlin, for nets, bats, balls etc., for British subjects interned in Germany.

A last photograph of W.G. With him are a nephew of Ranji, A. C. MacLaren, K. S. Ranjitsinhji himself and W. G. Heasman. *From the MCC Collection*

The secretary had a less pleasant task, when he and Mr L.A. Shuter were requested, on behalf of the Committee, to see T. and W. Abel, two members of the ground staff who had not enlisted. The White Feather Brigade had become more and more vociferous, and able-bodied young men not in uniform or engaged in war work were looked on with displeasure. *Wisden* records that, although practice nets were set up at the Oval in 1915, no one wanted to use them, for fear of 'being jeered at by the men on the tram cars'. To be fair to W.

Findlay, who had succeeded Alcock as Secretary, he was himself anxious to enlist, and did so a few months later, his place being taken as Acting Secretary by A.M. Latham, Scourge of the Caterers, and a man who was to fight his battles in the 1920s. The meeting with the Abels took place in March 1915, and it was pointed out to the two Abels that, although they might be employed at the Oval for the summer of 1915, there was a distinct possibility that their services would not be required in the summer of 1916 as they did not propose to enlist. It seems a little like a Catch 22 situation – enlist so that you can't be in our employ anyway, and we'll employ you . . . The Abels had little choice but to take the hint. W.J. Abel gave reasons why he wasn't enlisting, but soon obtained Government work with the Projectile Company of New Road, Wandsworth. T.E. Abel took a job in a munitions factory. They came back to the Oval after the War, and W.J. scored a maiden century for Surrey in 1923.

Most of the Surrey squad survived. Hayes and M.C. Bird were wounded in 1917; Lord Dalmeny was slightly wounded and mentioned in dispatches; Hitch was discharged from the Sportsman's Battalion on the grounds of ill health, but later worked in the Cordite Depot at Stowmarket; Fender was injured in an aeroplane accident; M. Howell was wounded while serving in the Dardanelles. 2nd Lieutenant John Howell, of the King's Royal Rifles Corps, was killed in Flanders on 25th September 1915. Sydney Pardon, writing the young man's obituary in *Wisden* had no doubt of the loss to English cricket: 'Judging from his wonderful record at Repton it is not too much to say that he was potentially an England batsman. But for the war he would have been at Oxford last year and would no doubt have been seen in the Surrey eleven at the Oval.' In a trial match for Surrey at the beginning of the 1914 season he scored 109. He was twenty years old when he was killed.

There was some cricket played at the Oval during the war. The responsibility for arranging such games rested with individuals and organisations rather than with the Surrey Club, and almost all were staged for charity. Archie MacLaren organised such events as a two-day match between Service teams in aid of the Red Cross and Army Service Corps Sick Fund. Hayes organised a match between the Sportsman's Battalion and Surrey Club and Ground. An Amateur Eleven played the Honourable Artillery Company. Aske's School, Hampstead played Strand School, Brixton.

As the War progressed, or perhaps 'degenerated' is a more appropriate word, more cricket was played at the Oval. Its importance to the military steadily decreased, though in July 1917, the Committee had to consider a new request from the Royal Flying Corps. Zeppelin raids over London had become more frequent, and Colonel Bovill and Captain Berrington of the RFC attended a Committee meeting to explain that they wished to use the Oval as a site for filling balloons. The Committee felt that this would not be seriously detrimental to the ground, and gave their permission subject to the consent of the Duchy of Cornwall.

Before the war ended, crowds were returning through the turnstiles to see top quality matches. Many regard the return of 'real' cricket to the Oval as the game played on 5th August 1918 between an English XI and a Dominions XI. It was a day of muddled August weather – frequent showers interspersed with bright sunshine. A strong Dominions team batted first and made 194 for 9, the South African, Herbie Taylor being top scorer with 63. The Dominions bowling attack then began to rip through the England batting, and 6 wickets (including those of Hobbs, Gunn and Woolley) were down for 75 runs. Then Fender 'played an innings worthy of Jessop at his best'. In three-quarters of an hour he scored 70 out of 87 in partnership with the pedestrian J.W.H.T. Douglas.

It was a much needed promise of things to come.

Chapter Ten

And Now, from the Vauxhall End – Developments 1919–1939

The War ended. The military – horses, balloons, hurdles and all – departed from the Oval. There was a great deal of work for the ground staff to prepare the playing area for cricket and the accommodation for spectators, but little damage had been done. In July 1919, the Committee made a final assessment of the claim to be sent to the War Office and put the figure at £3989 4s 3d. Six months later they received £1728 'on account' from the War Office. It was about par for the course.

The first essential was to secure Surrey's tenure of the ground, and a new lease was negotiated with the Duchy of Cornwall in May 1922. The lease was to run for 31 years, and, when the old lease expired, the rent was to be £800 per year and 10% of the profits. That having been established, the next step was to see what needed to be done to restore the Oval to its former glory, and even to improve on that. The Club was not helped in this work by a lorry driver in the employ of Messrs. Scott, Preserve Makers of Silverdale Works, Hayes, Middlesex (it would be Middlesex), who drove into the fence near the Vauxhall gate. The cost of repair came to £6 10s.

One of the first improvements was to cut down some of the trees that surrounded the ground. Those who now look out at the few trees left may consider this an act of the utmost vandalism, but the Committee's problem was that these trees were 'of assistance to people climbing the boundary fence'. It was, therefore, a matter of economic necessity. Not that the Committee objected totally to the idea of people getting in without paying: they approved Douglas Jardine's suggestion that all boys of 12 years or more from any of the local elementary schools within half a mile of the Oval should have free admission. An application for porters and guards of the London and South West Railway to be admitted at half price after four o'clock, was, however, turned down.

The Club was cultivating its sense of History. There were plans to put up a memorial to John Shuter, who had captained Surrey in the years of triumph during the late 1880s and early 1890s. In January 1922, the Finance Committee purchased a complete set of *Wisden*, and decided to sell off its existing 'odd' volumes. The following month, they had a better thought, and authorised the Secretary to buy the necessary volumes to complete the Club's second set. That still left some duplicates, which the Club offered for sale. They had difficulty getting rid of them. Eighteen months later they had to cut the asking prices by 50%. Committees don't always make the right decisions.

The Clayton Street Bar needed rebuilding. The Committee decided to move it and re-erect it behind the East Stand, between the Bowling Green Street entrance and the urinal – an appropriate situation for a Bar – and there it stood until long after the Second World War, indeed the Mound Stand Bar is on the same site today. I can remember, when I first went to the Oval in 1947, gazing up at the long queues of hot, thirsty men in heavy grey and brown clothes, as I dashed to the ferociously pungent urinal during the tea interval. The urinal is still there, but, happily, the smell hasn't lingered on. Other facilities for the general public were improved and extended. Five telephone call-boxes were installed by the Post Office in 1921. The decision was taken to have scorecards printed on all match days, although a loss was made on cards printed for one-day matches.

The lack of success they had had with the Shanks Motor Mower before 1914 had not put an end to the Club's search for a suitable machine. In the spring of 1924, Denis Brothers of Guildford brought a mower to the Oval to show what it could do. The Committee were impressed and purchased the demonstration machine. It gave five years service and the Committee then decided to buy a new 30 inch motor mower, also from Denis Brothers, at a cost of £85, plus a spare cutting cylinder for £5 14s 3d. The old mower was sold for £25, and the new machine gave excellent service. It was still going in 1947, nearly twenty years after purchase. The Committee also bought a Zodex water absorbing roller from Messrs W. Hargreaves and Co. of Old Road, Cheadle, Cheshire, at a cost of £33, 'together with one spare tank at a cost of £1 2s 6d.'

One great area of development in the period between the two World Wars was the introduction and proliferation of broadcasting and filming at the Oval. The Committee gave permission for the Topical Film Company and Central News Ltd. to shoot newsreel material as early as 1921. On the other hand, in September 1924, the Committee turned down an application by Stoll Picture Productions Ltd. to use the Oval ground and pavilion for a 'film picture'. Entertainment, fantasy,'dumb show', call it what you will, had no place at the Oval. If the modern media wished to come to the Oval, then it would have to be to record real deeds of real people. And, in April 1927, the Club gave permission to the BBC to broadcast a 'running commentary' during the first day of the Surrey v Hants game that was scheduled for 7th May. There were, of course, conditions: the Club was to incur no expense, the cost of putting up and removing any soundproof box or other apparatus was to be borne by the Corporation, no spectator was to suffer any inconvenience, the Committee's requirements were to be complied with at all times and in all respects. The BBC had chosen a good day – Surrey scored 439 on a wicket that had not recovered from overnight rain when play began. Hobbs gave 'a masterly display of batting' in scoring 112 (he made 104 in Surrey's second innings), Shepherd made 120, Peach 77, and Fender a lively 53. Further applications came from the BBC that summer, and in 1930, when the Australians toured, came the first broadcasting of a Test match from the Oval, a ten minute account of the events of the day, from 6.30 to 6.40pm each day.

Broadcasting brought in much needed revenue during the Depression. Crowds were still large at the Oval, but a shilling entrance fee at the turnstiles (two shillings if Surrey were playing the Tourists: three shillings if it was a Test match) was a sizeable amount when most working men were getting less than two shillings a day. In the late 1920s and early 1930s, committees were being set up to find ways of making economies. It was decided to make more use of professionals in Club and Ground matches (thereby avoiding having to pay expenses to amateurs), to arrange fewer fixtures for the second XI, the Club and Ground and the Young Players and to terminate the contracts of some of the ground bowlers.

17th August 1926. Early morning refreshments being supplied by the Oval chef – A. M. Latham not in attendance. © Hulton-Deutsch Collection

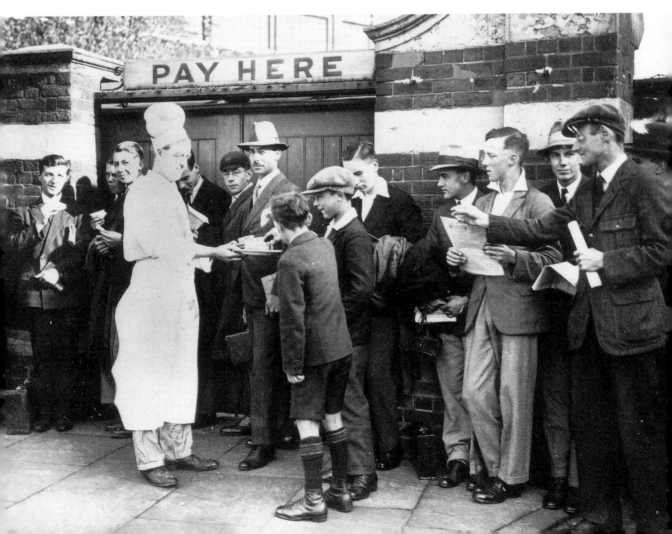

Nevertheless, the Club still employed a large number of players and ground staff. In 1927, Herbert Strudwick, probably the greatest Surrey wicket-keeper, took over as scorer. He was to be paid £4 a week plus railway fares plus twenty shillings for every night slept away from London on Club business plus five shillings for every other day that he scored in any SCCC match. In the mid 1930s, the ground staff were paid on a scale of wages that went from £3 a week for Burls, the Horsekeeper, to 15/- a week each for five 'boys', who were to receive an extra 2/6 a week if they were young cricketers. Among the 'boys' were Arthur McIntyre and Geoff Whittaker, who got a few shillings more 'in view of the heavy work involved in moving the Vauxhall Terraces'. When they joined the Surrey staff in 1938, the Bedser twins were paid £2 a week each, which was supplemented a little by tips earned bowling to members in the Oval nets. As well as paying wages in the summer, and winter retainers, the Club paid for certain expenses incurred by its players. In 1932, the Committee approved a grant of £30 to R.J. Gregory, then a newcomer to the first team, for medical expenses incurred in an operation.

The Club itself was happy to pick up such extra income as £21 from the BBC for broadcasting facilities during the 1934 Test matches, £225 from Gaumont British for Cinematograph Rights to the Oval during the same year, and £100 from Central Press Photos Ltd. for exclusive Press Photographic Rights. By 1938, the BBC was paying £105 for Broadcasting and Television Rights, plus an extra fifty guineas for rights to the Test match against the West Indies in August. County games were reckoned in pounds, shillings and pence – Test matches in guineas. In return for Television Rights to the same Test, the BBC agreed to pay for new gates at a cost of £86 11s, with an extra £10 to the Lambeth Council for a 'crossover' on the pavement. Again, the BBC had picked well. In the Test against the West Indies, 1216 runs were scored at a rate of nearly five an over.

In the run-up to the 1939–1945 War, the Government sponsored a National Fitness Campaign. Part of the campaign was a selection of short films on various sports, and the national Fitness Council were given permission by the Club to take a 'few film shots' of a County Match at the Oval, for 'inclusion in an instructional film'.

There were no advertising boards to be seen around the playing area. In 1932, advertisements appeared for the first time on the backs of scorecards. This led to an increase in revenue from scorecards from £44 to £400 per year. The Committee also managed to increase the takings from the hire of cushions. In 1932, the red and green buttock savers brought in over £100. Something else that lagged behind was hoardings – in 1937, a draft advertisement for Coca Cola was turned down. On the other hand, the Club was itself beginning to advertise cricket at the Oval. In March 1935, it was decided to place one poster on every Southern Railway station in Surrey. This was repeated every year up to the Second World War.

The Committee were still struggling to provide members and the public with

1925 – not a Test match, but one of the regular huge crowds at the Oval. © *Hulton-Deutsch Collection*

satisfactory catering facilities. In 1921, teas for players (amateurs and professionals), scorers and umpires were provided by H. & G. Simonds of Reading,
the contract caterers, at 6d a head. As the national economy began to slump,
prices had to be lowered. In 1922, the Refreshment Committee reduced the
price of players' luncheons from 4/- to 3/6 for amateurs, and from 3/3 to 3/- for
professionals. Cups of tea were reduced from 4d to 3d. The prices on the 1925
Bar Tariff were frozen for 1926, with a few exceptions: Green Chartreuse,
Yellow Chartreuse and Benedictine were raised to 1/9, Creme de Menthe or
Kummel to 1/3.

But 1926 was not a good year for caterers or management at the Oval. On 3rd
May, a complaint was made about the quality of the cheese being sold in the

Members' Dining Room. After due investigation, the problem was found to be not only the quality but also the poor selection of cheese – and 'Cheddar, Gorgonzola and Gruyere were to be available in future'. The following month, complaints were made about the lack of brown bread – 'there should be no difficulty in future with regard to brown bread'. By August, the beer pipes needed re-lining: complaints were many, and presumably bitter, about the state of the beer. And on 23rd August, a salvo of complaints was fired by Brigadier-General F.F. Johnson:

1. Refusal of caterers to supply biscuits *in lieu* of bread with 2/6 luncheon.
2. Refusal of caterers to supply extra butter with 2/6 luncheon.

Mr Latham (S of C) added his voice to the Brigadier-General's, and wanted to know why hard-boiled eggs were not obtainable. The season ended, the complaints continued. On 30th September, there were grumbles about the late arrival of salmon.

Things were no better in 1927. The Secretary reported complaints as to the supply of Turkish and Egyptian cigarettes, and of biscuits. Major Gwynn had several complaints, two of them about lemonade. At the East Stand stall he was charged 5d for a bottle of lemonade. On pointing out that the proper price was 4d, he was informed that the stall was a special one and that special prices were therefore charged. The good Major, no doubt in bad humour, then moved on to the Public Bar, where he again ordered a bottle of lemonade. The glass was half filled from an old bottle, and topped up from a fresh one. 'He questioned the procedure and received unsatisfactory replies.' It really wasn't the Major's day. With blood and steel in his eyes, he strode to the Public Luncheon Rooms where he saw plates of meat brought from the Service Room, piled one above the other in the most unhygienic fashion, and where he was served stale bread and scones. The Committee investigated the Major's complaints. The last three were proved accurate – there was doubt about the first. The overcharging for the bottle of lemonade was 'strenuously asserted by Major Gwynn and equally strenuously denied by Messrs Bertram and Co.'s staff.'

There are no records of complaints for 1928. The only detail would appear to be that non-vintage Bollinger was added to the Wine List in the Members' Dining Room at 17/6 a bottle. It was hardly a time for celebration nationally, however, as the Depression bit deeper and deeper. By April 1929, it was suggested to Messrs Bertram and Co. that they further reduce the price of a cup of tea from 3d to 2d.

Mr Latham now became Chair of the House Committee, and his complaints proliferated. In May, he complained that payment had been demanded of him for an extra piece of cheese in the Members' Dining Room, and that there was a shortage of watercress at teatime, and that 'a very dirty man was employed in the Bar'. By high summer, he had turned his critical attention to the poor quality and lack of variety of ices in the Members' Luncheon Room. On and on he went. In 1933, he found the price of 4d for 'a sardine on toast' or a cold hard-boiled egg more than he could bear. Messrs Bertram agreed to drop the price of both items to 3d.

The members themselves were not above reproach. During the 1920s and 1930s, it would seem that the Oval became a hotbed of gambling. In 1923, the Secretary received reports that card playing was taking place in the Writing Room. Steps were taken to stamp out such wickedness in the Public Rooms of the Pavilion. Worse was to follow: in 1924, Mr A.S. Rintoul and Mr B. Isaacs were found to be taking bets in the Pavilion. The Secretary wrote to them, warning against any repetition of this offence, and notices, to the effect that betting was strictly forbidden, were hung on the walls by the tape machine, whose outpourings of sporting information were fuelling many of the bets. A member of the Exchange Telegraph Company and a reporter on the *Leeds Mercury* misused their Press Passes. In both cases their employers were informed and were asked to deal with the matter.

16th August 1930. '... a hotbed of gambling...' The original caption to this photograph mentions 'followers of Duleep passing away the time with a game of cards outside the Oval...' They were rewarded for their patience: Duleep scored 50 that day. © *Hulton-Deutsch Collection*

All the while, the Oval was a busy place. The Lambeth Wolf Cubs met there. No 1 Group South London Battalion The Boys Brigade held Drumhead Services on certain Sundays on the ground. An application was approved from the Officer Commanding the 26th Air Defence Brigade TA to use the Oval for 'making a searchlight display in connection with a recruiting week 10th to 15th May 1926'. Others were not so lucky. Permission was refused for the Salvation Army to hold their Review at the Oval, and the 3rd (Southwark) Cadet Infantry was denied use of the ground.

A major initiative came from the Duchy of Cornwall. By the early 1930s, there were over two and a half million unemployed in Britain. The Duchy wanted some use to be made of the Oval for unemployed persons, and the Committee unanimously agreed. So the Oval House Club was formed. It was a success. The Prince of Wales (later Edward VIII) visited the Oval and a dinner was given to members of the Unemployed Men's Club. The Prince thanked the Surrey County Cricket Club for the use of their buildings, and said that 'it was a good example which he hoped would be followed by other Cricket Clubs throughout Great Britain'. The Club continued to use the Oval from 1934 to 1937, when it moved to new premises over the Boys' Club in the Harleyford Road.

The biggest changes at the Oval between the Wars took place at the Vauxhall end. In 1921, the Club engaged Edmund Wimperis and Simpson (Architects), of 61 South Moulton Street, W 1, to draw up plans for the development of stands at the Vauxhall end, a stand to the north wing of the main building, the rebuilding of the West Wing of the pavilion (to seat 200 persons and to include Gents lav., press accommodation, scoring-box, tea room and the conversion of the old scoring-box and press-room to four private boxes), the removal of the East Stand, the enlargement of the Members' Dining Room, and the construction of a new Members' Bar.

Estimates were received from a local builder, William Downs Ltd., of Hampton Street, Walworth SE 17. The Vauxhall development was costed at £13,856; the stand to the north of the main building at £6207; the West stand redevelopment £5319; the Members' Dining Room another £2400. In all, the work the Club envisaged was going to cost between £25,000 and £30,000.

Work began in 1923. At first all went well. Indeed, as far as the Club was concerned, the slump appeared to bring a slight bonus, for the wages of the workers on the Vauxhall stands actually fell as work proceeded, from 1/8 a day for mechanics and 1/3 for labourers, to 1/7 ½ and 1/2 ¾ respectively. After a few weeks, however, there was a threatened strike by workmen in the building trades. Trade Union officials refused to allow plumbers to work overtime.

But the great drama began at the end of 1923. There were several parties involved: Wimperis (the architects), Downs (the builders), Selby and Sanders of Caxton House, Westminster (the surveyors), and, of course, the Surrey Club (notably R.C.N. Palairet, the Secretary, and the Earl of Midleton, who was President). The original estimate for work on the Vauxhall stands had been

£19,072. Nine months later this had been increased to £20,184 0s 7d. The architects then wrote to the Surrey Club and said that the real cost was going to be in the region of £21,500, and that the builders (Downs) were not prepared to accept the burden of the extra amount, which was £1324, the difference between the real cost and the second estimate. Surrey, however, were concerned about the difference between the real cost and the first estimate, which amounted to almost £2500.

On 11th June 1924, the Surrey Club wrote to their solicitors, Messrs Bristow, Cooke and Carpmael of Copthal Buildings, EC 2, to see whether there might be an action for negligence against Wimperis. The solicitors wrote back asking Surrey to obtain a full account of the increase from Wimperis. On 8th July, Wimperis wrote to Palairet at the Oval, saying that the increase was due to 'the exceptional conditions of haste under which the work was done'.

Charles Bennett, the Managing Director of Downs, wrote to Palairet on 31st October offering to accept £1500, on top of the original estimate of £19,072, in settlement of the claims, pointing out that 'we shall be practically making a present to the Surrey County Cricket Club of more than £2000'. Bristows and Co. told Palairet to pay £1050. Downs then instructed their solicitors (H.C. Morris and Co, of Walbrook, EC 4) to write to Bristows suggesting arbitration. This seems a reasonable suggestion, for widely differing sets of figures as to what should be paid were now being bounced to and fro by all parties. Bristows saw the matter differently, and wrote back to Morris asking what point there was in going to arbitration.

On 22nd December 1924, Morris informed Bristows that Downs had applied to the President of the Royal Institute of British Architects for the appointment of an arbitrator. Bristows now accepted the idea, and, on 16th February 1925, Major Harry Barnes, of Mitre Court Chambers, EC 4, was appointed Arbitrator. After two postponements, the date fixed for arbitration was 6th April.

On 3rd April, Palairet wrote to his President, the Earl of Midleton. Light was beginning to dawn as to why there was such a discrepancy between estimates and cost. The confusion arose from a mistake made by Wimperis's partner. 'The contract (which I signed),' wrote Palairet, 'was a "qualities" contract and not, as was supposed, a "lump sum" contract; this being the case, I was warned that it might be difficult to resist all the contractors' claims . . .'

William St John Fremantle Brodrick, 9th Viscount Midleton and 1st Earl of Midleton, was in his late sixties. He had been a politician, and was Secretary of State for India in Balfour's Cabinet from 1903 to 1905. In this post, his main achievement appears to have been putting up with Viscount Curzon for a couple of years, but the *Dictionary of National Biography* records that 'to the general public his most notable reform was the introduction (in the 1890s) of a new forage cap for the Brigade of Guards, which came to be known by his name'. He was also 'notable for his sincerity . . . his long experience of men and affairs left him with an unexpected simplicity which was very attractive to his friends.' Like Alverstone, a foggy appeal seems to hang about him. He was not the stereotypical Victorian and Edwardian noble puffing out an anachronistic existence well into the 20th century. But he was resolute, and he was not pleased by the mistake made by Wimperis's partner.

William St John Fremantle, Earl Midleton,
1856–1942. '. . . make him step out . . .'
© *Hulton-Deutsch Collection*

On 4th April, the day he received Palairet's letter, Midleton replied from his residence at Peper Harrow in Surrey:

My dear Palairet,

Your letter, which caught me as I was leaving London, fills me with dismay. I cannot imagine what our architects have intended in advising us throughout that we had taken a 'lump sum' contract. Why have our solicitors not found this out before? It is an astounding lapse.

I am the more concerned about it because I cannot be present at the Arbitration. I have been for weeks engaged all day on Mondays in the

Chair, settling the fate of our County School at Cranleigh in regard to a *great* expenditure on new buildings.

I would have run up to see the lawyers today, but the golf competition for my Captain's prize takes place early today – and I have two meetings in different places afterwards.

I find it very difficult to advise because I do not know exactly what the "quantities" contract would let us in for . . . My general view would be to fight it out. Is this an eleventh hour discovery? If so it should be made clear that we were all along fighting on the understanding of a lump sum and that there is nothing in the correspondence suggesting the reverse.

Tell our Counsel anything like surrender will put us into grave difficulty.

Yours,   Midleton.

Palairet attended the arbitration hearing, and wrote to Midleton informing him that Downs had offered to accept £1250, to pay their own costs and to pay half the Arbitration fees. The Club accepted this solution. A month later, poor Bennett wrote from Downs: 'In accepting £1250 . . . we made a present to the Club of all our profits (£750), hard cash out of our own pockets, and in addition saved the Club from having to pay heavy legal charges . . .' Midleton wrote a polite and placatory letter to Bennett, regretting 'that the difference of opinion as to charges, which has now been adjusted, should have arisen . . .'

Midleton must have had an eye to the further improvements to the Oval that Surrey had planned. By August 1925, the Club were considering spending another £18,700, and, if they were to use the same architects, surveyors and builders, which made sense, it would be as well to promote reasonable relations between all parties. Midleton wanted these improvements as . . . 'enormous crowds now attending certain matches have caused an increasingly difficult problem . . .' He was also fiercely proud of the Oval, and didn't wish to see it take second place to Lords. 'A large expenditure' was 'to be undertaken at Lords before the visit of the Australians next year (1926), although their accommodation is much more ample than that at the Oval. It is necessary to look at the problem from the point of view of the accommodation to be given to the public, although the return may not be as remunerative as was the case when the new stands were recently put up . . .'

The plan this time was for an extension of the East Stand next to the Pavilion, and for the new East Terrace Stand at the Vauxhall end to be enlarged. Once more Wimperis acted as architects, and wrote to the Club in September 1925 estimating the total cost at £15,000. Selby and Sanders, the Surveyors, disagreed with this figure. The cost, they reckoned, would be £7591 for the Vauxhall Stand, and £10,191 for the East Stand – a total of £17,782.

The Club put the work out to tender among builders. Wimperis believed that Messrs Holloway Bros would 'probably compete closely for this work'. In fact, Holloway's was one of the most expensive tenders. The three cheapest were

The subject of a great row and arbitration at the Oval in the 1920s. The Vauxhall Stand. Note the tree: eat your heart out, St Johns Wood. © *The Central Press Photos Ltd.*

Messrs W. Lawrence and Son (£9918), F. Foxley and Co. Ltd. (£10,110), and, hope springing eternal, William Downs Ltd. (£10,290). Not surprisingly, the Club chose Walter Lawrence and Son. There was, however, also work to be done on the West Stand at the Vauxhall end, and Downs sent in a competitive tender for this work. In November 1925, a telegram winged its way from Palairet at the Oval to Midleton at Peper Harrow:

> DOWNS TENDER FOR VAUXHALL STAND
> FOUR THOUSAND POUNDS SHALL I TELL
> ARCHITECTS TO ACCEPT. PALAIRET

and another telegram flew back to the Oval:

> I AGREE. MIDLETON

Rather more care was taken in examining the contracts this time, but even so, all did not go smoothly. In December, a problem arose about the disposal of rubbish and rubble, earth, etc. The Club wanted to know if the earth excavated was of any value. It wasn't. The contractors reported that 400 loads of earth were hampering work at the Pavilion end, and it would cost six shillings and sixpence a load to remove them. At the Vauxhall end there were a thousand loads, but they could stay where they were without causing any hold-ups.

From the Library of the House of Lords, Midleton wrote to Palairet:

> My dear Palairet,
> I think Wimperis should have warned us of this charge and he now puts it to us without an attempt to elude it.
> I can only say if the work is impeded, let the contractors cart away 100 loads at 6/6 a load but make Wimperis put in an immediate advertisement to try and get rid of the remainder.
> It is just what happened before that he puts on an extra which any expert could have foreseen.
> Please make him step out.
>
> Yours vertigo,　　　　　　　　　　　　　Midleton.
>
> I came up today but am at PH hence forward.

After that, all seemed to go well. Ten years later the refurbishment of the Vauxhall end was more or less completed, for the time being, by work on the terraces. In the winter of 1936–7, the terraces to the east of the Vauxhall stand

20th August 1932. Queueing for the Surrey v Yorkshire match in the days before the Hobbs gates were erected. © *Hulton-Deutsch Collection*

were demolished and re-built bringing them in line with the stand itself. The following winter, the same was done to the terraces on the west side of the stand, so that the playing area again became much more a true oval.

Perhaps the most lasting change at the Oval in the period between the two wars, was the rebuilding of the gates at the main entrance. The Committee made the decision to replace the existing gates in January 1934. At first the intention was to erect plain wrought-iron gates with no inscription, but no Club with a feeling for cricket could pass up the opportunity to pay tribute to a player of the calibre of Hobbs. At Lords, the gates were for Grace, a fitting place to honour someone who did so much to advance the quality of cricket. Both men were born many miles away from the sites of the gates that now serve as their memorials, but Grace didn't belong to Lords in the way that Hobbs belonged to the Oval. More than fifty years after his last game, it is still possible, even for those of us who never saw Jack Hobbs, to feel proud that he played at the Oval. The gates *had* to bear his name: THE HOBBS GATES – IN HONOUR OF A GREAT SURREY AND ENGLAND CRICKETER. They were formally opened by the President of the Club, Leveson Gower, on Saturday 5th May 1934 at 11am, the hour when Hobbs so often hurried down the steps of the pavilion and out on to the Oval grass, to do his best for Surrey.

Chapter Eleven

It Isn't Just Cricket

Charles Alcock was a man of many talents. He was also a man of vision. When he succeeded William Burrup in the post of Secretary to the Surrey Club, he was appointed by the Committee as a paid secretary with a salary of £250 a year, with the hope that he would do something for the Club's ailing fortunes. These were not great times for Surrey. The team's performance in no way matched that of the 1860s, and the financial position was far from sound. Alcock reported that 'if the balance-sheet for the year ending March 31, 1872, were reproduced, it would show that both ends had been hardly met.' Burrup had been aware of the difficulties, and had obtained a second source of revenue for the Club in 1870, by the introduction of Association Football.

It made a lot of sense. As a playing area, the Oval was empty for over seven months in the year, and the early fathers of Association Football were looking for suitable venues. Burrup made the initial arrangements, and the first soccer matches were played on the Oval in the winter of 1870. It was an interesting list of fixtures that included matches between England and 'Scotland'. The Scottish team was not truly representative, since it was composed of players of Scottish extraction who happened to be in the neighbourbood. Thus, the team included Quintin Hogg (founder of the Regent Street Polytechnic), W. H. Gladstone (son of W.E. Gladstone) G.G. Kennedy (long distance running champion for Cambridge University) and 'a couple of Old Etonians whose labours in the cause of religious work and charities, as well as for the physical and moral improvement of the working boys of London, have been as successful as they have been unintermittent.' Alcock, who came from Sunderland, captained the North against the South, and was also captain of England.

At first the game came under a great deal of attack from *The Lancet*, since the medical profession regarded it as highly dangerous. Whenever an accident occurred, and in those days of hard boots and heavy leather footballs there were plenty of accidents and injuries, medical opinion was critical, calling for the game to be banned. Public opinion, however, swung entirely the other way, and soccer became swiftly popular. By 1872, when Alcock took over, the Oval had become the headquarters of football in London. Matches were arranged between London and cities such as Sheffield, where football was already popular, and between the Old Etonians and the Old Harrovians. In March 1872, the first FA Cup Final was held at the Oval. The Wanderers (Alcock's Club) beat the Royal Engineers by a goal to nil, despite the 'particularly fine goal-keeping by Captain Merriman of the Royal Engineers,' and 'the conspicuous pluck of one of the Engineer forwards, E.W. Cresswell, who played through the greater part of the game under the serious disadvantage of a broken collar bone.'

One year later, the first representative International in England, between England and Scotland, took place: there had already been one such match in Glasgow five months earlier. The game at the Oval attracted 3000 spectators, who saw England beat Scotland 4–2. Such a turnout was regarded as a great achievement, though Alcock noted, with some humour, how unfavourably it compared with the 'huge gates' attracted by Surrey's cricket matches. Nevertheless, football was doing what it was supposed to do – bringing in much needed cash. At the Annual General Meeting of the Surrey Club on 1st May 1873, Alcock could report a balance in hand of £380.

By the middle of the 1870s, soccer had become a regular institution at the Oval. Oxford and Cambridge met there, Oxford winning the FA Cup in 1874, Harrow school played their only Association Rules game of the year against the all-conquering Wanderers. The Wanderers were a team of ex-Public School players who won the Cup five times in the first seven years of its existence. By the terms of the Association, this entitled the Wanderers to keep the Cup in perpetuity, but the Wanderers themselves suggested that it should be retained by the Association as a perpetual challenge cup, 'never to come permanently into the hands of any club.'

Public school footballers may have been gentlemen in their refusal to purloin the Cup, but they were doughty, and possibly dirty, players. Alcock's report on the Cup Final of 1882, 'memorable for the first appearance of a northern club' (Blackburn Rovers), stresses that the Old Etonians were 'at their roughest as cup fighters'. Though Old Etonians won, by the only goal of the match, they were bewildered by the long passing and rushes of the Rovers. Londoners became accustomed to seeing Blackburn represented at Cup Finals. Blackburn Olympic won the Cup in 1883, and Blackburn Rovers won it three years in succession, 1884, 1885 and 1886.

Further Internationals were held. In 1879, England played Wales for the first time at the Oval, England winning 2–1. London played combined Oxford and Cambridge teams, but were usually outplayed, being thrashed 9–1 in 1883–4. In 1887 and 1888, it was the turn of clubs from the Midlands to win the FA Cup, Aston Villa beat West Bromwich Albion 2–0 in 1887, and they, in turn, beat Preston North End 2–1 the following year. Preston North End beat Wolverhampton Wanderers 3–0 in 1889, a golden year for the Lancashire Club. They were undefeated in the League, scoring 40 out of a maximum 44 points, and conceded not a single goal. Blackburn Rovers returned as champions in 1890 and 1891, beating Sheffield Wednesday 6–1 and Notts County 3–1. The Final of the FA Cup was held for the last time at the Oval in 1892, when West Bromwich Albion beat Aston Villa 3–0.

These were the days when many athletes 'doubled' at cricket and football. At least four of the Notts cricket team played in soccer Internationals at the Oval during the 1880s or 1890s – Dixon, Daft, and two men immortalised on some of the finest cricket bats in the world, Gunn and Moore. From Middlesex came the brothers Edward and Alfred Lyttleton, and P.J. de Paravicini, and from Surrey, W. Lindsay and Alcock himself.

In 1888, the Prince of Wales visited the Oval to see a game of football between a Canadian touring team and the Old Carthusians. Prince Alfred of Saxe-Coburg turned up when a lad to see the Final of the Army Cup, and the Duke of Cambridge was said to be a regular visitor.

In the seventeen years from 1881 to 1897, well over a million people paid to see Association Football at the Oval, fifty thousand members were admitted, and nearly twenty thousand more qualified for free admission – an average yearly gate of approximately sixty five thousand. In 1893, the balance sheet showed the returns from football to be over £3000. The problem was that £2400 of this had to be handed over to the organisers of the matches, to the football clubs themselves. This left Surrey with only £600, out of which they had to pay the cost of labour and repairs to the ground. Apted, the groundsman, was not enjoying the sight of his beloved turf being cut to ribbons by the barbarians from the north and midlands, and it was undoubtedly true that the precious 'square' itself was being harmed. It was decided that no football at all should be played on the Oval during the spring of 1893, to enable Apted and his crew to effect much needed repairs. This meant that the Cup Final had to be held elsewhere, and returns from football were much reduced, as the matches played in the first half of the football season brought in little gate money.

In August 1894, the Football Sub-Committee of the Surrey Club decided to obtain estimates for the erection of an 'unclimbable fence to limit the football ground'. Two months later, they resolved that 'fifty yards of peignon fence be procured at once'. But clubs continued to apply for use of the ground. For the 1894–5 season, the Corinthians Football Club wished to play five fixtures at the Oval, against the Army, Notts County, Aston Villa, Derby County and Queens Park. The terms they offered were 25% of gross receipts – gate enclosure, stands – to be paid to Surrey. The Committee were not overjoyed at these terms, but N.L. Jackson, Secretary of the Corinthians, pointed out that 'these were the terms elsewhere'.

It couldn't last, and in June 1895, 'it was resolved by the Football Sub-Committee to recommend to the Surrey Committee that football should not be played any more on the Oval but that a General Meeting should be called on the subject'. A poll was conducted to assess the views of members. 453 voted in favour of the continuance of football, 1095 against it. Alcock was phlegmatic:

'One may regret, as many undoubtedly do, that the exciting contests in which the giants of football of generation after generaton took part are numbered among the things of the past. But necessity has no law. And in this case one can honestly say, even though a footballer, that it was stern necessity.'

The plain fact was that the Oval has become almost too popular a centre for sport. It was all very well racquets being played there – racquets was played at Lords and it was a tidy game, requiring a court of its own, tucked away behind the pavilion and causing neither interference to cricket nor harm to Apted's magnificent turf. The court was an open one, and was the first thing seen by any visitor on entering the main gates to the ground. The back wall adjoined the east end of the Surrey Tavern. It was a popular venue for some members, including George Boucher, who was the champion racquets player, but its popularity declined. When the time came for urgent repairs to be made, there was insufficient support to keep it going, and it was pulled down. In its place an ornamental flower-bed was planted. Now it is tarmac.

There was also no harm in the occasional Throwing the Cricket Ball Contest. The great W. G. himself liked to perform at the Oval. In 1868, he made three consecutive throws, with the wind behind him, of 116, 117 and 118 yards, and then threw back over 100 yards against the wind. Seven years later, he again showed his prowess, throwing 111 yards 'and back some distance'.

Also welcome, since its members did little or no damage to the premises, was the Surrey Bicycle Club. In November 1872, Mr Alfred Howard of the SBC wrote to the Surrey Committee, proposing the construction of a carriage path round the Oval, for the purposes of cycling. The Committee were in favour of the idea, if Howard could show that he was in a position to carry out such work and if he could give reassurances that any meetings held at the Oval would be confined to Amateur bicycling. By 1874, Howard and the SBC were being allowed four such meetings a year, with practice sessions beforehand. A small fee was paid to the Surrey Cricket Club, and Bicycling became an established sport at the Oval. Between 1881 and 1897, some 290,000 people paid to attend events organised by the SBC.

In 1905, the Club increased the charge to the South London Harriers, of Belmont, South Norwood, to £30 for each meeting staged at the Oval, which prompted an angry reply from the Harrier's Secretary:

> ... Because we have held two meetings which have drawn big gates, you wish to raise the terms of letting the Oval, without taking into consideration the fact that the same amount was paid for several years when our meetings were run at a loss ... How do we know that the next meeting will draw a big gate, or suppose the day be wet? Although I do not complain, yet at the last two meetings 2000 to 3000 persons at least were admitted without payment because they were in uniform ... Could you provisionally book the Oval for Saturday, April 29th?

Like punctures, things were patched up, and the Harriers continued to use the Oval. As late as 1914, Pelham Warner was unable to book the Oval for a three-day match between the Over 35s and the Under 35s as the ground had already been promised to the South London Harriers on one of the days he wanted.

As soon as he was appointed Secretary in 1872, Alcock began to negotiate for the introduction of Rugby Union Football to the Oval. The first match was an International between England and Scotland. In those days teams were twenty a side, and Alcock himself commented on the heaviness of the players – the England team averaged 12 ½ stone, the Scottish team a little over 12 stone. England won by two tries and two dropped goals to a dropped goal. The game also lacked some of the refinements that modern commentators assure us it now possesses, and consisted mainly of prolonged scrummages with the occasional charge of the heavy brigade. The backs were used almost entirely in defensive roles, with two or three full-backs, one three-quarter, and two or three half-backs. That left at least a dozen forwards to monopolise play and do a great deal of damage to the turf on which they played.

In December 1873, the first Oxford v Cambridge game was played at the Oval, resulting in a draw, each side scoring a goal. Within a year or two, more rugger sides were meeting at the Oval. It became the venue for the Inter-Hospital Cup, for North v South, and for Woolwich v Sandhurst. On 19th February 1875, England played Ireland for the first time. 'The Rugby Union game,' wrote Alcock, 'was in its infancy in the sister island. Their representatives knew little of the science of back play, so that their defeat by two goals and a try to nothing was hardly surprising'.

Many of the rugger players were also cricketers of first class ability. A.N. Hornby, of Lancashire and England, played rugger for the North and for England. He scored the only try in the International against Ireland in February 1877, the first match in which fifteen a side were fielded. W.H. Game, a hard-hitting Surrey batsman, also played rugger for Oxford, as did two Gloucestershire cricketers, W.O. Moberley and J.A. Bush. Fred Stokes, who captained the England Rugger team, played cricket for Kent and for the Gentlemen against the Players. These were the days of the 'all-round' sportsman, exemplified by C.B. Fry, who reached the highest levels at two or three different games. H.W. Renny Tailyour played rugger for Scotland, soccer for the Cup winning Royal Engineers, and was, according to Alcock, 'at his best a cricketer with very few superiors'. Harold Freeman was an England three-quarter and also one of the pioneers of tobogganing and winter sports. 'Even now memory lingers over that wonderful drop of his in the Scotch match at the Oval in 1874, when he got the ball about the middle of the field of play, and with a magnificent drop landed it safely over the Scotch bar, giving England a glorious victory by a goal to a try.' In the days of which Alcock wrote, a drop goal counted for 4 points, a try for 3, and Scotch was, apparently, an accepted adjective for more than whisky.

The behaviour of spectators and supporters at both soccer and rugger matches appears to have been good. No special provisions were made for them other than a tent 'for the accommodation of ladies' near the Vauxhall gate. The revenue from rugger was small at first – both soccer and rugger between them produced only £29 in 1873. The charge imposed by the Surrey Club for holding an International at the Oval was £10. Attendances and profit steadily grew, but it was a nightmare for the groundstaff. By the late 1880s, the Surrey Committee had come to the conclusion that rugger would have to go. The last of the Oxford v Cambridge matches took place in 1880, Cambridge winning by two goals to one. Club games continued for a few more years. Middlesex played Lancashire in the Football Jubilee Festival in March 1887, a game attended by the Prince of Wales, who subsequently became patron of the Rugby Union. Rugger's farewell to the Oval took place in March 1891 when Blackheath played London Scottish in a Charity Festival. After that, there were no more scrummages, and Apted could sleep a little more peacefully in his bed.

The game did, however, return to the Oval after the Second World War, and in the 1949–50 season, Harlequins played three rugby trial games.

In 1875, William Michael Adams, of 20 Bridge Row, City of London, gent., approached the Surrey Committee with plans to build a skating rink at the Vauxhall end of the ground. The Committee accepted the idea, and in February 1876, Marshall, Ponsonby and Mortimer signed an agreement with Adams. He was to build two skating rinks, one covered, one open air, within nine months of the agreement and would then be granted a 31 year lease at an annual rent of £250, a considerable sum of money at that time. The agreement also stipulated that the skating rink had to be fenced off so that it was impossible for skaters to gain entry to the cricket ground without having to pass through a turnstile and pay, and there were to be no windows overlooking the cricket ground. On the other hand, members of the Surrey Cricket Club were to have a 120 foot long covered verandah made available to them, from which they could watch the skating, and Adams was to build a urinal at the Vauxhall end 'to which roller skaters were not to have access'. Finally, Adams was to charge not less that 1/- for admission to the rink, and not less that 6d for the hire of skates.

The rink was swiftly built. Within three months, the Duchy of Cornwall Office was writing to the Surrey Club relating to the 'nuisance' caused by music at the skating rink. Almost as swift was Adams's departure. In 1877, the rink was taken over by Messrs Neuburger and Durrant, who, from the word 'go', failed to pay the rent. In June 1877, a Mr Coupe offered to take over the rink, but his proposal was 'not to be entertained'. The rink became more trouble than it was worth, the sport itself lost much of its popularity nationally, and eventually skating, too, came to an end at the Oval.

A much longer life at the Oval was granted to lacrosse. In 1877, the London Lacrosse Club applied to the Surrey Committee for the use of the ground on Easter Monday for a match between North and South of England. Permission was granted, and lacrosse matches were played fairly regularly at the Oval for the next sixty or seventy years. The occasional game has been played in the 1980s. In 1883, a match was staged at the Oval in early June between Canadian and Indian players then touring Britain. One third of the gate went to the Surrey Club, the other two thirds to the promoters of the game. There appears to have been a mixed attitude to the lacrosse on the part of the Surrey Club, and some confusion on the part of certain lacrosse associations as to what they needed. In 1920, the Ladies Lacrosse Association was refused permission to play, but in 1922, the England Lacrosse Association was granted permission and then turned it down as the playing area was deemed insufficient. Later the same year, an application from the South of England Lacrosse Association was turned down. In 1935, however, the same Association was given permission to hold a match between North and South on the Oval at a charge of £10 for the use of the ground plus all expenses. The following year, the All England Ladies Lacrosse Association was refused permission to stage an England v Scotland Interntional in late March. It may well be that the erratic relationship between the Oval and lacrosse was the product of a seasonal near overlap between that sport and cricket, and, at the Oval, cricket, quite rightly, had priority.

Hockey lasted longer at the Oval. It was another innovation of Alcock's time, and in the 1880s and the 1890s attracted an average yearly gate of around 13,000 people. Like soccer and rugger, Internationals were staged at the Oval – in 1935, the Women's Hockey Association paid £50 plus out of pocket expenses to stage the England v Scotland match. The Surrey Committee also promised a longer term commitment to women's hockey, at a cost of £10 per match and 25% of the gross takings, and women's hockey returned in 1947. Matches were regularly played well into the 1950s, and, like Lacrosse, hockey has come to the Oval in the 1980s.

Several other sports made use of the Oval. Baseball was played there in the 1880s. A.S. Spalding, President of the American Baseball Club, arranged several matches which proved very popular. He asked the Surrey Committee for a share of the gate money from the stands as well as the ground, but the application was not entertained. Nor was the idea brought before the Committee by a representative of Messrs Williams Sons and Wallington, Contractors of Shepherds Bush, in 1880, to secure a shoot at the Oval. The representative explained to the Committee that, for the purposes of the shoot, a bank would be built along the west side of the ground, along the Harleyford Road. The Committee was not impressed. The Peckham Athletics Club, and others, had held athletics meetings at the Oval since 1877, and, in the late 1920s and early 1930s, Eric Liddell's trainer had plans to turn the Oval into a major athletics stadium. Until the early 1920s, lawn tennis was played at the Oval.

Acceptance of any of these sports at the Oval depended, of course, on the Duchy of Cornwall. Each lease granted to the Surrey County Cricket Club specified what other sports could be held at the ground without special application being needed. There was rarely any difference of opinion between landlord and tenant on these matters, but in the 1930s, the relationship between Surrey and the Duchy was tested by General Critchley. In July 1931, Critchley approached the Club with the idea of building a Greyhound Racing Track at the Oval. At first, the response of the Duchy was as might be expected. Major McCormick of the Duchy Office wrote to the Surrey Club informing them that 'the proposal to use any part of the Oval for the purposes of greyhound racing is not regarded favourably by the Duchy'. By the autumn, however, the Duchy appeared to have changed its mind and signified that it was prepared to grant a lease to Critchley. The Committee was horrified and a Special General Meeting was called for 30th November at the Great Hall, Winchester House. A Special Sub-Committee was also set up, consisting of Sir Jeremiah Colman, M.R. Jardine (father of Douglas Jardine) and A.M. Latham, with the brief that they were to 'confer with the President as to the tenor of his speech to members at the Special General Meeting'.

The Committee were totally opposed to Critchley's plans, but they could not be certain that the bulk of the membership of the Surrey Club would share their view. It was decided that, should the members reject the Committee's recommendation, the Committee would not resign. A week before the meeting was due to take place, however, the Committee received a letter from Major

15th December 1966. Every little bit helps, financially. Funfair at the Oval. © Hulton-Deutsch Collection

The rock proscenium at the Vauxhall end, complete with classical columns and Neptune figurehead.
© *Central Press Photos Ltd.*

McCormick stating that the Duchy did not wish to proceed any further with negotiations with Critchley and the Greyhound Racing Association. The Committee may have heaved a sigh of relief, but they were also faced with a bill for £64 10s, the cost of calling the Special Meeting. The Surrey Finance Committee wrote to Major McCormick suggesting that this cost be met by the Greyhound Racing Association. McCormick wrote a somewhat stiff letter back, saying that the Duchy was under no obligation to apply to the GRA for the amount spent by Surrey. The Committee, in turn, recommended that Palairet be instructed to express to Major McCormick the Committee's disappointment at his attitude.

Greyhound racing might well have proved a lucrative sideline – it was very popular between the wars – but it is hard to believe that even the most 'sporting' of Surrey members, even the great Percy George himself, would have approved. The nearest that racing came to the Oval would appear to have been in 1906, when the Surrey Committee gave permission for a team of Amateur Athletes to play the Jockeys, at cricket.

Economic necessity, however, has always meant that the Surrey Club have had to look out for alternative ways of raising money. To some, the nadir was reached in the 1970s, when three separate one-day Pop Festivals were held, one in 1971 (Rod Stewart, Lindisfarne, Mott the Hoople, and The Who), and two in 1972 (Linda Lewis and Jeff Beck). They weren't what the Burrup Twins would have 'entertained', nor any of the founding figures of the Surrey Club, but they did bring in £11,000 nett to the Club coffers, more than the gross aggregate receipts from three-day cricket matches in those two years. The ground was packed for all the concerts, and protective coconut matting was laid across the square which had just been re-seeded. New safety regulations meant that the numbers would have had to be limited for subsequent concerts, which would in turn have left little profit after paying the stars.

The 1970s was perhaps the most bizarre period in the Oval's history. It was an extremely difficult time financially, and the Surrey Club were nothing if not inventive in thinking of ways to solve the revenue problem. There was a mammoth Firework Display. In the spring of 1972, the Circus came to the Oval, and the elephants were housed in the groundstaff's workshop. A Donkey Derby was held, and for ten years or so a Sunday Market took place in the car park behind the Vauxhall stand.

There is often plenty of fine weather after the cricket season ends each September, and in the past few years advantage has been taken of this to hold at least two regular fixtures: the Scottish Amicable Baseball Cup – celebrating the centenary of baseball at the Oval in 1989 – and the Australian Rules Football Match for the Foster's Cup, which originated back in 1971 at the Oval. It isn't as iconoclastic as it sounds: in Australia, football is often played on Test match cricket grounds. The Foster's Cup game is scheduled to be held at the Oval well into the next century, and in 1988, it attracted a crowd of 7000.

Aussie Rule Football. © *Around the Foster's Oval magazine, autumn 1988*

There is a rumour, however, that the groundsman likes to go away that weekend, rather than see what is being done to the playing area.

A History of The Foster's Oval

PART 3

Chapter Twelve

'Heat Went With Happiness' – The Matches and Players 1919–1939

To one who never knew the Oval in the 1920s and 1930s, it seems to have been the ground of thousands and thousands of runs, 'Summer-time means Oval-time, and Oval-time means Hobbs' was the old refrain, and it also meant Bradman and Hammond, Pataudi and Duleepsinhji, Leyland and Sutcliffe. The sun was always shining, the bowlers were always sweating. Twenty triple centuries were scored in England in twenty years, three of them at The Oval. Of those three, Hutton's 364 against Australia in 1938 is easily the most famous: few Surrey supporters will still remember Ducat's 300 against Oxford University in 1919, and even fewer Keeton's 313 not out for Notts against Middlesex in 1939, played at the Oval as Lords was wanted for Eton v Harrow – *o tempora, o mores*. The photographs that line the stairs and corridors in the Oval today show sun-scorched turf, glistening batsmen with bats of willow so dark it could almost be ebony, and gasping, panting, heroic bowlers. The scoreboards clanked their way through hundred after hundred: Surrey 428 for the first wicket against Oxford University; England's 534 against South Africa in 1935; Surrey's 540 for 9 declared against Middlesex, 541 for 5 declared (Hobbs 10) against Leicestershire, and 579 for 4 declared against Somerset (Fender 139 in 80 minutes); Australia's 695 against England in 1930, and 701 against England in 1934; finally, on the precarious fringe of what remained of peace, England's 903 for 7 declared against Australia. 'If I was a youngster starting as a batsman,' said Frank Woolley, at the end of this period, 'I think I should like to play always at the Oval.'

The season of 1919 was a strange one for the whole country. After so tumultuous and terrifying a war, after the disappearance of Empires, after the Russian Revolution, even cricket was subject to change, and the authorities experimented with two-day matches with play continuing until half past seven while umpires and players rubbed the muscles of their legs and complained *sotto voce* about their feet. It was also the season that brought home to each and every cricket club the losses it had suffered during the previous four years.

The Oval had been relatively lucky, if such a word doesn't seem in appallingly bad taste when applied to war casualties. Of the eleven who had played in the last first class match at the Oval in August 1914, crushing the ten of Gloucestershire that Dipper left behind when he went off to enlist, all but Hayward were still available in 1919. Hayward had retired, after 21 years and 43,000 runs. He was 48 years old, and cricket had moved into a new age where few quinquagenarians would play: gritty Yorkshiremen like Sutcliffe and Rhodes, and, of course, The Master, proving exceptions. But the familiar faces of the pre-war heroes were back: Hayes, Harrison, Fender, Ducat, Hitch, Sandham, Strudwick and Rushby. And, as the counties visited the Oval in turn, back came Woolley, Hendren, Mead, J. W. Hearne, the Tyldesleys, Hirst, Quaife, Warner, Kennedy, White, Douglas, Root and C. B. Fry.

Perhaps the greatest delight for the Oval crowd after the war was to see Hobbs picking up where he had left off in 1914. He scored over 2500 runs that year, the most exciting of them off Kent in his benefit game, the last of the season at the Oval. For once, the weather was not kind, and Surrey had to get 96 runs in the 45 minutes from 6.45 to 7.30, with banks of grey clouds swirling up from the east and cold rain falling. They got them, notwithstanding the slippery surface on which batsmen had to turn like dancers to make ones into twos, and the rain on Crawford's spectacles as he lashed at the Kent bowling, and the fact that neither he nor Hobbs was in the first flush of youth. They got them in 29 minutes, and the Oval crowd stayed in the cold and damp, cheering and yelling, and dropping £1671 in the collection boxes for Hobbs.

An Australian side toured Britain in 1919. It was not an official Test tour, but it was an extremely strong side. They came to the Oval at the very end of July, to play Surrey. The Australians batted first and made 436. The start of the Surrey innings was disastrous. Hobbs went for 9, Howell for 1, Naumann for 2, Knight and Harrison failed to score. Surrey were then 26 for 5. In an article for *The Cricketer* in 1968, Cardus described what happened next: 'In came J. N. Crawford and launched such an assault on the Australian attack that many watchers babbled of Jessop's incredible foray and 'blitz' on the Australian bowlers of 1902. Crawford actually assaulted the great pace of Gregory, hurled down from a menacing attitude. He hit a six from Gregory, a straight drive on to the awning of the pavilion. In a last wicket stand (Rushby, the accompanying partner, scored 2), no fewer than 80 runs raced and crashed all over the field in 35 minutes: 78 from Crawford's bat.' It must have been good to see such a sight after four empty years.

Surrey were always in with a chance during the 1920s, Fender's eccentric leadership ensured that, but their bowling lacked power and the Oval wicket was cruelly good. They had to fight for their victories – Fender exhausting himself by way of example. Richard Streeton's wonderful biography of Percy George records how Fender slept on a pile of towels in the amateurs' dressing room for three hours after Surrey had beaten Middlesex by 19 runs in 1921. Such was Fender's energy and enthusiasm, however, maybe three hours sleep was all he needed. He led Surrey from the front, the side, in the slips, at mid off, while batting, bowling or fielding. In six years, while he was their captain, the Surrey side were runners-up twice, and never finished lower than fourth in the County Championship. He was a cricketer, footballer, billiards and bridge player, publisher, wine merchant, raconteur and wit. E. W. Swanton has written: 'To the spectators there was something of the wicked Sir Jasper about him that tickled their fancy.' Indeed, it would be impossible to say who was the greater draw at the Oval in the 1920s, Percy George or John Berry.

Also in 1921, nearly 20,000 people a day paid to see Hitch's benefit match against Kent, won by Surrey on the stroke of time. The crowd cheered themselves hoarse for fifteen minutes in front of the pavilion, while passengers in passing trams stood up to see what all the fuss was about.

The Test match of 1921 was reduced to the level of farce on the third day. England led Australia by 14 runs on the first innings, but batted out time as the match crawled to a draw. Hitch injected some life into the torpid proceedings by hitting 50 in 35 minutes, but Armstrong, the Australian captain was so bored that he read a newspaper on the boundary and left his side to organise themselves in the field.

But the sun shone and the crowds flocked to Kennington. In 1922, when Surrey played Hampshire, the sun shone in the eyes of extra cover when he dropped Fender, who had then made 21. The crowd would have roared – nothing pleases Surrey spectators more than seeing one of their own heroes dropped by the opposition – and in this case Fender went on to play the innings of his life. He scored 185 out of 294 in 130 minutes. In a single day, Surrey scored 470 and took a Hampshire wicket when Peach bowled Bowell.

Fender was a bonus for Surrey, a brilliant amateur who needed no salary. Hobbs was a professional, and Surrey were prepared to pay good money to keep him at the Oval. In 1922, he was offered a contract of £440 a year for five years plus talent money, which must have been considerable in the case of The Master. It was good money, and Hobbs gave good value in return. Twenty five thousand people came to the Oval on August Bank Holiday 1923 and saw him make 105 in his best style. In the next four years, Hobbs scored over ten thousand runs. His reliability as well as his artistry bred loyalty among the spectators. They kept coming back, even when the cricket was deadly dull, as it could be on the flawless pitches of 'Bosser' Martin. In the 1926 August Bank Holiday match, the crowd was huge, but subdued. The Notts batsmen did little before lunch, and not even the Simonds Ale in the pavilion or the Watneys available around the ground could dissipate the air of apathy. 'There was no cheering,' reported *The Times*, 'either for fieldsmen or batsmen when the game was resumed; and after three-quarters of an hour, with but 26 runs to show for it, (the crowd) allowed itself a few ironical comments. They were good-humoured and directed mainly at Gunn, who made batting look so easy that he might have been playing a game with himself in which runs counted against him. These protests became a surprised sigh of relief when Gunn played a shade more deliberately than before, and Strudwick asked a question as he took the ball. Gunn had been well over two hours in making 42, and as far as a batsman with his eye and feet can be dull, he was.' Fortunately, Carr, next man in, helped himself to three sixes over a short square leg boundary, which must have woken at least some of the thousands crammed in the terraces.

Two weeks later came far greater excitement. The final Test of the 1926 rubber was to be played to a finish as the previous four had all been drawn after even struggles. England had the better of a strange first day's play. There was a general air of hustle and bustle about the proceedings that seemed out of place in a timeless Test. Hobbs, when set, was bowled by a full toss. Hendren pulled a ball on to his wicket from way outside the off stump. Chapman played as if the match had to be finished that very evening. England were all out in four and a quarter hours for 280. The flurry continued when Australia batted. Macartney hit 25 out of 35 in half an hour, and then hit a long hop onto the stumps. Ponsford ran himself out. At close of play on the first day, Australia had reached 60 for 4.

Early arrivals at the Oval. There is no date on the photograph, but the caps suggest 1930s. © *Planet News Ltd.*

The attendance on the first day had been a little disappointing, by contemporary standards, as some may have stayed away after prophecies of overcrowding and all night vigils. On the second day (Monday), however, the Oval was full. *The Times* reported: 'the gates of the Oval were closed before one o'clock and at the tea interval it seemed that more people had been admitted than the ground would conveniently hold. But the police tactfully and successfully moved back those who had encroached on the playing area, so that a boundary hit was worth four runs to the end of the day.' 'Private Wire', who compiled the London Column for the *Manchester Guardian* at the time, devoted much space to this particular Oval crowd.

'A friend who watched the Lords Test match from the popular side and who was at the Oval early today sends me some reflections on the differences between the two crowds. "I have seen at least one big day's cricket at the Oval every season for the last twenty years, but I have never seen interest so raised right from the start. Generally, even a Test match takes an hour or so to warm up and is seldom really going strong before lunch, but this morning, in spite of uneventful play, the atmosphere was keyed up and tense.

"After Lords it's good to be back at the Oval. Marylebone is too much a social centre and has too little flavour of locality about it. People drop in there to meet friends or to find a seat in the sun, while in Kennington you get real partisan feeling and real knowledge of the game. The popular side at Lords on ordinary days is ignorant and indifferent in comparison to the Oval. For the Test match early this year, there was a strong majority of keen cricketers even at Lords, but there was an irritating minority that had come to 'rubber' because the Press had made the Tests a 'stunt' this year. At the Oval today we were all cricketers.

"I was standing in the fourth row with no slope to let one see over the heads of those in front, having paid my 3/- without being given any hint at the gate that there was only this kind of standing room left. I was annoyed. But I heard no murmur of complaint from those around me, who cheerfully peeped between their neighbours to get a glimpse either of the bowler or the batsman. Both wickets could seldom be seen simultaneously. The ambulance men were busy, and I saw several girls being carried out from the thick of the standing crowd. Yet in spite of all this and of the placid play everyone was pleased and even positively excited.

"I got a hint of how strong a magnet the Oval is these days from the papers that I noticed in one stroll around the ring at lunchtime. There were men reading the Newcastle, Norwich, South Wales and Birmingham papers – to say nothing of the 'MG'."

The enormous second day crowd saw Australia fight for and achieve first innings lead, with a gem of an innings from Gregory, who made 73 out of 103 in an hour and three-quarters. Australia were all out for 302, and England were left with an hour's batting. Hobbs and Sutcliffe took no risks, but made 49 together. That night there was a thunderstorm and a great deal of rain.

The Times opened its account of the third day's play with details of the landlord's trip to his most famous Kennington property. 'The Prince of Wales visited his Oval yesterday and lunched with the contending teams. He saw part of an extraordinarily good batting performance by Hobbs and Sutcliffe, and when he had to leave the ground at three o'clock, England were on the way to victory. Before the close of play, however, the pertinacity of the Australians was rewarded . . . The story of the third day's play begins with the tropical rain that fell in the small hours of Tuesday morning and awakened thousands of England's supporters to blasphemy . . .'

'Private Wire' in the *Manchester Guardian* had another piece on the Oval crowd. 'The Oval was up to its brim again this afternoon, and the crowd, sweltering in the sunshine and ready to be hatless for the sake of the man behind, made coverings of their handkerchiefs, so that the great dark ring round the green seemed to come out in a white rash. On the west side the close packed thousands were getting it quite literally 'in the neck', which is, of course, the danger point, and many were wisely using their handkerchiefs to hang down their backs. Heat went with happiness, and there was no weariness in the applause. The cheering for Hobbs's century held up business for a couple of minutes, and there was an equal enthusiasm for Sutcliffe.

'It would be hard to find a greater mixture of English types than among the "three bobbers" at the Oval. Other sports have their specialised crowds. One knows pretty well who will be at Twickenham or Wembley or in the silver ring at Hurst Park. But Kennington is our true melting-pot. The parsons in tens sat with the clerks in hundreds. The public-school men were shoulder to shoulder with the men whose 'buses they may have been driving under wire netting when the Australians were opening their tour at the time of the general strike.

'There were not many women in the unreserved places, but some mothers of families were bravely seeing it through, and rationing the ginger-beer. The only London type one could not find was the Jew. The Jews cluster where there is money or where there is art, but they do not appear to put cricket in either category.'

In the same paper, Neville Cardus's report concentrated more on the cricket. He headed his piece:

"PROMISED LAND" IN SIGHT – THANKS TO HOBBS AND SUTCLIFFE
CRITICAL PERIOD ON DIFFICULT WICKET
BY CRICKETER

[Despite the three days' play on it the Oval wicket is still in fine condition. Martin, the groundsman, expressed the hope last night that it would last without any serious crumbling until Thursday night.]

'At half past two this afternoon, in the summer sunshine, there was a scene at the Oval which none of us will forget who were privileged to be present. Hobbs played a ball gently to the off side, and, scampering down the wicket like a happy boy, he made a century, his eleventh, and perhaps his last for England against Australia. The great crowd roared out affectionate applause; Collins gave Hobbs a shake of the hand; somebody deep in the encircling multitude called for three cheers, and we sent them in our thousands to Hobbs over his own Oval field. And Hobbs waved his cap at us and then put it on the back of his head – the old beloved attitude . . . our children of tomorrow will envy those who tell them that we once upon a time saw Hobbs and Sutcliffe . . .'

'Cricketer' was wrong about one thing – Hobbs had one more century yet to play against Australia for England, but he caught the spirit of the day. The rain made the wicket dead and easy enough to survive on at first, but after an hour it began to show considerable spite, and the achievement of the England opening batsmen was enormous. Richardson was criticised in *Wisden* for bowling too much 'leg theory' – years before bodyline – which meant that he seldom attacked the stumps, but it should be remembered that the Australian attack comprised Gregory, Grimmet, Mailey and Macartney, as well as Richardson. It is doubtful that any other opening pair could have shown the application and technique displayed by Hobbs and Sutcliffe in the last hour before lunch that day. Hobbs went soon after reaching his century, bowled by Gregory, but Sutcliffe stayed until the last over of the day. When he was bowled by Mailey, he had scored 161, and England were 6 for 375, giving them a lead of 353 runs.

The following day, *The Manchester Guardian* devoted four and a half columns to the Test match, with more space for Australian press comment, and still more for what amounted almost to a Court Circular:

'Prince Arthur of Connaught visited the Oval again yesterday and saw the play in the Test match up to the time rain came on. Mr Stanley Baldwin arrived after lunch and chatted informally with the teams. He reminded the Australians of what he had said about the Worcester cricket ground at the Institute of Journalists' lunch last April, and they all agreed the ground was the prettiest they had seen in England.'

It was very polite of them. By that time they knew they were going to have to make 415 to win the match on a pitch that was certain to be awkward for batsmen, but helpful to both pace and spin bowlers. Tate and Larwood spearheaded the England attack that day, with Geary, Stevens and Rhodes in support. Cardus wrote critically of Larwood: 'Larwood, with careful nursing, might develop into the best fast bowler of recent years, though he is not tall enough to rank ever with the great fast bowlers of Test cricket', but it was Larwood and Riodes who destroyed the Australians that afternoon. The final innings of the match began just after half past three, and Australia were all out some three hours later for 125.

Once again, the crowd raced across the ground to assemble in front of the pavilion. To the tune of 'Bow Bells', they chanted, over and over again:

'We want Chapman, Hobbs and Sutcliffe,
We want Larwood, Rhodes and Geary . . .'

The *Times* was ecstatic: 'We have won! And after all the lean years we were
more than half pleased. We began to cheer when the Australians innings was a
little more than half over, and at the finish we charged, ten thousand of us,
across the ground, and massed ourselves in front of the pavilion, where we
shouted for the eleven men who had won the game, and for the Chairman of the
Committee which selected them. We shouted even more loudly for Mr Collins
and the members of his team. We wanted them to know that we appreciated the
high standard of keenness and honourable conduct which they have set up and
maintained in this and all their other matches.'

Beachcomber in the *Daily Express* was less overwhelmed by the cricket. 'I
wonder which of the earnest statisticians is counting the number of words
written about this Test match. It must be another of the records they love so
well. An amusing effect of the general excitement is that everybody you meet
takes it for granted that there is nothing but cricket in your mind. Papersellers
tell you the score before you ask for the paper, and if you say to a man "What's
the time?" he replies mechanically "432 for nine". If you ask a barber for a
shave, he says "I don't know. He was still in when I last heard."

It was the first time England had won the Ashes since the war in which
patriotism had been strained almost to breaking point, but had clearly survived.
Cardus called on the Muses to help him do justice to the game, others were
content to do their journalistic best with the wonderful material to hand. For
the Australians it was an 'ignominious failure'. For the Oval crowd it was 'a
frenzy of delight'. 'The scene at the Oval immediately after England's remarkable victory was one that will be long remembered by all who witnessed it. The
huge crowd was hushed as Geary prepared for his run of the last delivery of the
match.

'A fraction of a second and then the spread-eagling of Mailey's wicket was the
signal for a frantic outburst of delight and triumph from all over the enclosure.
In the stands erstwhile grave parsons sacrificed their hats, men hugged each
other and danced madly, and women grew hysterical. Colonels leapt the
barriers and scampered madly for the pavilion, and the players were mobbed,
friend and foe alike.

'In a few seconds a huge phalanx of people, fully 10,000 in number, formed in
front of the pavilion to do honour both to their own land and to the vanquished.
First they yelled for the captains and out came Collins and Chapman. The
youthful sunburnt face of the English skipper was the very personification of
joy, and even the grim leader of the Australians, gallant in defeat, had a smile
that would not wear off.

'Mr Sidney Smith, the Australian manager, held very decisive views about the
game. "This will knock the bottom out of the three day Test," he said. "It was a

fine game. I wouldn't have missed seeing it for worlds, and all I can say is I am satisfied."

It was the end of three-day Tests against Australia in England. When the two sides next met in 1930, four days were allotted for each Test. But before that time, there were to be other great matches and great feats at the Oval. In the 1927 Gentlemen v Players game, Kennedy of Hampshire produced the performance of his career when he took all ten wickets in the Gentlemen's first innings. 'On a drying pitch that showed signs of wear in places,' according to *Wisden*, 'Kennedy found a spot in line with the leg stump, and, making the ball get up as well as turn a lot, he compelled eight batsmen to give catches while another was stumped, the ball on only one occasion hitting the stumps.' The following year, Hobbs hit his last Test century in England, appropriately enough at the Oval, scoring 159 against the West Indies. And in 1929, Sutcliffe went one better at the Oval Test, hitting a century in each innings against South Africa.

Notts won the Championship in 1929, and the annual Champion County v The Rest game was played at the Oval in September. The Rest batted first and made 399, Woolley making a lovely 106, and Wyatt 89. Notts were only 35 behind on first innings. When The Rest batted again, Hobbs made 68 and Leyland 75, and Notts were left with 318 to get for victory. Despite a slow and laborious 96 from Gunn, they lost by only eight runs. Nothing hinged on the outcome of the game – the season was already over, the trophy had been won. It wasn't even a game that involved Surrey, save for one or two players. And yet, such was the local love of cricket, and such was the thrill of a close finish, that the large crowd was fired with crackling excitement. Louis Palgrave described the scene at the end of the game: 'Apart from the end of a Test Match, I cannot remember such a scene of enthusiasm as occurred at the Oval at the finish of this game. A huge crowd gathered in front of the pavilion and shouted itself hoarse till the players came out on the balcony. It was George Gunn they most wanted to see, but he sent a polite message to say that he was having a bath.'

The Australians returned in 1930, bringing with them two new stars – Bradman and Jackson. Both men came to England with the highest of reputations, gained on the England tour of Australia in the winter of 1928–1929. Bradman had already hit two centuries in that series, and Jackson had made 164 on his Test debut. In the run up to the Oval Test, England had won at Trent Bridge, Australia had won at Lords, and the Tests at Headingley and Old Trafford had been drawn. Bradman had already scored 741 runs in the series, but Jackson had played in none of the Tests. He had had a disappointing tour until the Australians played a couple of games in the West Country, and was selected only as a replacement for Richardson in the Oval Test.

A great deal of drama surrounded the game. Chapman, although he had proved a popular leader and a successful captain against Australia (and had a batting average of 43 in the first four Tests), was relieved of the captaincy by selectorial myopia, and replaced by R.E.S. Wyatt, a man who had never played against Australia. The public was incensed, the lunatic fringe among it threatening Wyatt with death if he showed his face at the Oval. There was a general feeling, proved correct, that this was to be Jack Hobbs's last Test, and, since the fate of the Ashes hung in the balance, this was to be another timeless Test. Bradman had dozens of Tests ahead of him, Jackson only three more before dying of tuberculosis at the age of twenty-three.

18th August 1930. Wyatt fights back, hooking Grimmett for 4. © *Hulton-Deutsch Collection*

England batted first and made 405. Hobbs scored 47 out of the 68 he and Sutcliffe put on for the first wicket. Sutcliffe went on to score 161, sharing in stands of 65 with Duleepsinhji and 170 with Wyatt, who made a stubborn, possibly life-saving, 64. It was not a bad total, but Australia had made 729 at Lords and 566 at Headingley. It was always doubtful whether it would be enough.

By tea on the second day, Australia had made 159 without loss. Shortly after the interval, Ponsford was bowled by Peebles, and in came Bradman. Rain and bad light postponed the glory that was to come. There was little play on the third day, at the end of which Australia were 215 for 2, Woodfull having been caught at the wicket by Duckworth off Peebles. On the fourth day, Kippax was caught by Wyatt at short leg, also off Peebles, and Australia were 263 for 3. Jackson joined Bradman, and together they put on 243 runs, Jackson's share being a brave 73. It was a difficult partnership, with hostile and accurate bowling from Larwood, Tate, Peebles and Hammond, interruptions for rain and bad light, and for a visit from the Prince of Wales, and, as the partnership progressed into the fifth day, the Oval pitch suddenly becoming menacing. Bradman received a sickening blow under the heart from Larwood after he had made 175, and many believe the Bodyline theory was conceived at the Oval as Bradman and Jackson both tried to dodge the 'fliers' hurled at them. Jackson was battered, hit on the elbow, the jaw, the wrist, hip and thigh. Eventually he was caught by Sutcliffe at extra cover off Wyatt, and Australia were 506 for 4. Bradman went on and on, reaching 232 before being given out, a dubious decision, caught at the wicket off Larwood. McCabe and Fairfax both made fifties, and Australia were all out for 695.

18th August 1930. Boys, aided and abetted by their elders, entering the Oval through a hole in the fence.

And the one who didn't get away.
© *Hulton-Deutsch Collection*

There was just time, before close of play on the fourth day, for Hobbs and Sutcliffe to face a few overs. The crowd cheered them to the wicket, and Woodfull, the Australian Captain, called his men together and called for three cheers for Hobbs. It was the first time such a tribute had been paid out on the playing area in the middle of a Test. Minutes later, Hobbs played on in attempting a forcing shot off Fairfax. In his loving biography of Hobbs, Ronald Mason wrote: 'You could hear the cavernous gasp as the bails fell, the sigh breathed out of all those well-wishing throats as for just that second longer than usual Hobbs stood motionless, looking at the broken wicket...' Hobbs returned to the pavilion, and an appeal was made against the light. The day, the era was over, leaving fifteen thousand to trickle from the ground clutching their disappointment. The fifth day was rained off, and on the sixth day, Hornbrook ran through the England side to take 7 for 92 and to give Australia victory by an innings and 39 runs. It was the first time Australia had won at the Oval since the Ashes Test of 1882, and the thousands who gathered once again in front of the pavilion were as enthusiastic and generous in their cheers for Woodfull as they had been for Chapman four years earlier.

22nd August 1930. Bradman leaving the Oval after Australia regain the Ashes. I particularly like the look of the monocled gent being restrained by the burly constable.
© Hulton-Deutsch Collection

Shortly after the Test, the *Daily Herald* organised the Jack Hobbs Sixpenny Fund, to raise money for the greatest batsman England has ever produced. The Surrey Committee decided not to contribute to the Fund, stating that the Surrey County Cricket Club 'may be relied upon to take whatever steps appear to them to be necessary to secure adequate provision for Hobbs when the proper moment arrives.' Hobbs still had three and a bit seasons left to play for Surrey, and 21 more centuries to score up and down the country, including centuries in both innings against Essex, Somerset and the Gentlemen. He still had four opening partnerships of over two hundred to take part in, and a double century to hit off the West Indians at the Oval when he was fifty years old. Altogether, Hobbs scored ninety centuries at the Oval, delighting generation after generation of spectators. Some may have had the good fortune to have been present at the Oval on two August Bank holidays separated by 19 years. On the eve of the First World War, Hobbs hit 226 off Notts; in 1933 he could manage only 133 against the same county. Alan Pitt Robbins wrote of the two innings in *The Times*: 'In many respects the scene at the Oval seemed scarcely to have changed. There have been minor modifications of the view from the roof of the Pavilion. The gas-holders are in the foreground as of old, but on the skyline Big Ben is in its steel splints and the roofs of the new buildings at Millbank have made for a brighter London. In the Pavilion there are the same portraits and other reminders of the great figures of the past, but there is now a War Memorial to those members of the Surrey Club who made the supreme sacrifice. Around the ground the spectators do not seem to have changed at all . . .'

The games went on and on, with always the hope, often fulfilled, that some great deed would be done. In 1932, Freddie Brown and M.J.C. Allom put on 155 in just over an hour against Middlesex. The following year, Roach hit a century before lunch for the West Indians against Surrey. In the last Gentlemen v Players game to be held at the Oval, in 1934, the players (with a large Surrey contingent) made 651 for 7 declared (J. Arnold 125, Sandham 65, Gregory 51, Squires 119, R. Duckfield 106, Wellard 91), and then Gover, Wellard and Mercer bowled the Gentlemen out for 192 and 154. In 1936, Alf Gover became the first fast bowler to take two hundred wickets in a season since Tom Richardson.

Hobbs was to make one permanent change at the Oval. In 1934, he played his last innings there for Surrey, going in at number four, for some unaccountable reason, and making only 15. But, when he left the ground that night, he would have left through the brand new Gates named after him.

As ever, the heroes came and went. Sandham made his 100th hundred, collected one hundred guineas from the Club (as had Hayward and Hobbs) in recognition of this great feat, played on, but only returned after the War as a member of the Old England side. A new generation of players arrived for Surrey: Squires, Barling, Fishlock, Watts, Parker, Whittaker, Gover, and the Bedsers. In 1931, Hedley Verity made his Test debut at the Oval, taking 2 for 52 and 2 for 33 against New Zealand, while Sutcliffe, Duleepsinhji and Hammond piled up hundreds. In 1933, Charlie Barnett of Gloucestershire made his debut, against the West Indies, going in at number eight and making 52. The honours of the match, however, were stolen by another England player, making his first and only appearance in a Test. 'Father' Marriott, of Cambridge, Lancashire and Kent, approaching his 38th birthday, took 11 for 96 with a mixture of leg breaks and googlies. Sometimes the comings and goings overlapped. In 1937, at the Oval, when Denis Compton and Cyril Washbrook made their Test debuts, Albert Roberts and Henry Vivian of New Zealand bowed out, each making fifties. Others came and went in a single Test: J. C. Clay played in his first and only Test in 1935, against South Africa at the Oval. He did not bat, and took 0 for 30 and 0 for 45.

Norman Oldfield's only Test, against the West Indies in 1939, was more successful – he scored 80 and 19. In the same match, playing for the West Indies in what was to prove his only Test appearance, Victor Stollmeyer scored 96.

The great names of more than a decade of cricket finished their International careers at the Oval: Woolley in 1934, with 4 and 0; Woodfull, in the same Test, with 49 and 13; Ponsford, again in the same Test, but spectacularly with 266 and 22; Cameron of South Africa in 1935; George Duckworth in 1936; R. W. V. Robins in 1937; Jack Fingleton and Leslie Fleetwood-Smith in the 1938 mauling, where Maurice Leyland, in his last Test innings scored 187 in a second wicket partnership of 382 with Hutton, before being run out; Kenneth Weekes with a brilliant 137 for the West Indies in 1939, to be followed by the last Test appearance of Learie Constantine, who flayed the England bowling for 79 and then took 5 for 75. But the gods of cricket are not kind to departing bowlers, not on the Oval wicket. Cruel figures surround those who finished their Test careers on the flawless wickets of Kennington – Cyril Vincent of New Zealand 2 for 188; Morris Nichols 2 for 161 against the West Indies; Reg Perks 5 for 156 in the same Test; and, cruellest of all, Fleetwood-Smith, 1 for 298 in 1938.

For in the 1930s, the Oval was the scene of two of the biggest victories ever in Test or any other cricket. In 1934, Australia had won the first Test, at Trent Bridge, by 238 runs, thanks to the brilliant bowling of Grimmett and O'Reilly. England won the second Test, at Lords, by an innings, Hedley Verity taking 15 for 104. The third and fourth Tests, at Old Trafford and Headingley, were both drawn, with the batsmen very much on top. The two sides came to the Oval to decide the fate of the Ashes.

On the first day, the wicket was hard and fast – it had been a hot, dry summer. Clark of Northants bowled Brown with the best ball of the day early on, and Australia were 21 for 1. Five and a quarter hours later, the second wicket fell when Bradman was caught at the wicket by Ames off Bowes for 244. He and Ponsford had put on 451 for the second wicket, a record that still stands. Bowes, Allen and Clark tried all the theories in the book against Bradman, but none worked. There was no spin in the wicket for Verity, and nothing in wicket or atmosphere for the medium pace of Hammond. The ball scarcely bounced above stump height, and, when the England bowlers dropped short or pitched too far up, Bradman was merciless. The crowd sat back, on their best behaviour, and watched a massacre. The following day, the Surrey Club published an appreciative notice:

> 'The Surrey County Cricket Club wish it to be known that they cannot thank the spectators at the Oval on Saturday sufficiently for their forebearance in refraining from going on to the field of play during the intervals and at the drawing of stumps. Owing to the drought, the turf in the outfield is in a very bad state, and great harm might have been done had the many thousands present trampled over the ground.'

From then on, it was all downhill for England. Australia were finally dismissed for 701 in their first innings. Walters and Sutcliffe put on 104 for the first wicket in reply, but Woolley, Hammond and Wyatt went cheaply, and England slumped to 142 for 5. On the third day, Ames and Leyland made an heroic stand of over a hundred, before Ames had to retire, crippled with lumbago. He took no further part in the match. Later the same day, Bowes was taken into hospital

18th August 1934. The luncheon interval. © *Central Press Photos Ltd.*

20th August 1934.
Ponsford and
Woodfull escort
Ames back to the
Pavilion after the
England wicket-
keeper hurt his
back. Ames took no
further part in the
match. Woolley,
deputising for him,
conceded the record
number of 37 byes
in an innings.
© *Central Press
Photos Ltd.*

for an operation, and it was announced that he too would be unable to play any more. Amazingly, Bowes did return to the Oval to bowl, and bowl well, in the later stages of the Australian second innings. Although England were 381 runs behind on first innings, Woodfull did not enforce the follow-on. *The Times* reported the slaughter that ensued before Bowes struggled back: '. . . what followed when Bradman and McCabe took toll of a bowling side never very strong and now reduced by one can be said in a few words. But first tribute must be paid to McMurray, whose fielding at mid-off, long leg, and extra cover was so superlative that even that master fieldsman, Bradman, was left at times gazing at him in admiration . . .' Tom McMurray 'occasionally played for Surrey', and was fielding as substitute. He was probably better known as a footballer, for he played in turn for Tranmere Rovers, Millwall and Rochdale. You will not find him mentioned in the *Wisden* list of Births and Deaths of Cricketers.

It is sad that young McMurray's efforts were in vain. England, set to get 708 to wing collapsed against Grimmett and were all out for 145, losing by 562 runs. The seeds were sown for the awful defeat inflicted on Bradman and Australia on the same ground four years later.

Revenge is seldom sweet, often grotesque. The Oval Test of 1938 leers at us from the record books, replete with statistics, the worst of which is that England scored their 903 for 7 wickets declared at a rate of 2.69 runs per over. The amazing fact is that the 'timeless' Test was over in four days, the end, at least, being swift and merciful. The wicket was a bowler's nightmare, graveyard, whipping block, sweatshop – anything that breaks body and soul. The weather was cold, damp, unwelcoming much of the time. The crowd was small by Oval Test standards, and Cardus has described it as 'apathetic'. Australia had already made sure of the Ashes, the only thing to play for was revenge.

19th August 1938. Temporary seating accommodation being erected at the last minute among the chimney pots overlooking the ground. © *Hulton-Deutsch Collection*

Old cricketers thronged the ground, gods of the past watching mortals locked in a marathon struggle, from which some would emerge god-like, some remain mortal, and some wouldn't emerge at all. Poor Fleetwood-Smith bowled 87 overs, 11 of them maidens, and took 1 for 298. In the first hour of the third day, when England had already amassed some 650 runs with only half the side out, and when he had been bowling at Hutton for two full days, he bowled beautifully. 'On a fair pitch,' wrote Cardus, ' he would have taken wickets; his fine art was abused by the groundsmen's drowsy syrups . . . The Australians stuck to the hopeless toil philosophically and Bradman changed his bowling, and the umpires counted the overs, and the runs mounted, and the clouds rolled on, and the gas-holder went up and down, and the trams went by the ground, and the hours waxed and waned, and somewhere even the weariest river wound safe to sea.' The timeless Test looked fair to becoming the eternal Test, and Woodfull is said to have asked about the effects of snow on the wicket.

August 1938 – music while you wait.
© *Hulton-Deutsch Collection*

Eventually, Hutton broke Bradman's record, and Hammond's record, and the crowd had something to cheer rather than merely acknowledge, and someone played the cornet and everyone sang 'For He's a Jolly Good Fellow', though not in the same key. And eventually Hutton was out. Cardus observed some Chelsea pensioners watching the cricket and wondered how many of them would live to see the match finished. 700 . . . 750 . . . Hardstaff was still patting half volleys back to the bowler . . . 800 . . . 850 . . . Bradman severely sprained his ankle and had to leave the field, 900 . . . Hammond declared. With Fingleton and Bradman unable to bat, the match was over, but cricket dictates that the game must go on, the bitter cup must be drained. Crazily, there were two endings. In the first, O'Reilly, last man in for Australia, with nearly 600 wanted to avoid an innings defeat, drove Verity high and straight to Hardstaff, waiting in the deep. The stumps were pulled up, the players made for the pavilion. Hardstaff dropped the catch. The second ending was more successful. Fleetwood-Smith was snapped up by Leyland off the bowling of Farnes, and England had won by the biggest margin ever in Test cricket – an innings and 579 runs. 'I wish I had been at the Oval,' wrote the Princess Royal to Sir Pelham Warner. 'However, it was most exciting listening to the wireless and one felt one knew what was going on.' The whole nation listened. Yorkshire almost ground to a halt during Hutton's innings. Had England produced a player to out-Don the Bradman?

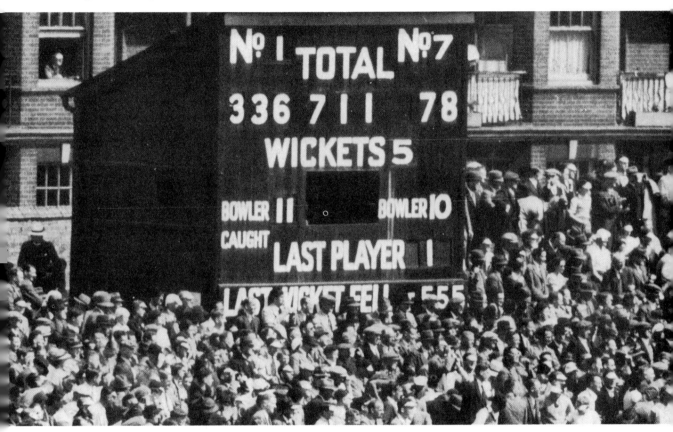

23rd August 1938. The pre-war Oval scoreboard registers that Hutton has passed Bradman and Hammond's previous records.

The receipts for this Test were a record for the Oval – £19,176 3s 0d. Other matches held on the ground between the two wars were less profitable. When Oundle played Stowe, in July 1937, 615 people paid £35 16s 6d. Twenty eight people paid a shilling each to see Clergy of Southwark v Clergy of Chelmsford in June of the same year, and, when the Stoics played the Thespids in August, in front of a crowd of seventeen people, the gate money amounted to 17/6.

There were so many matches at the Oval: RAF v Civil Service, RAF v Army, Royal Navy v RAF, Royal Army Ordnance Corps v RAF, Royal Corps of Signals v Royal Tank Corps, Lords v Commons, Bar v Barristers Clerks, Bar v Stage, Law Society v Chartered Accountants, Old Olavians v Ferrets, Stoics v Incogniti, Epsom College v Cranleigh School. The London Coal Exchange Cricket Club played there, and the London Retail Meat Traders Association – suggesting visions of vast men playing in blood-stained whites. In 1925, the Household Brigade played six days of cricket at the Oval, hopefully not on horseback.

The first match to be staged at the Oval organised by the Women's Cricket Association, took place in June 1935. Prior to their tour of Australia, the England team played the Rest of England in front of a 'goodly crowd'. Shortly after the match began, the rain came down in torrents, and the pitch became a morass. A new pitch was marked out, broadside on to the original one and nearer to the Vauxhall stand. The Rest made 153 for 7 declared (Marjorie Pollard 53 not out), and England were left with 100 minutes to make 151 runs. The rain fell steadily, but 'the last overs of the thrilling finish were wildly cheered by the large crowd that remained to see the last ball bowled, and we went home thoroughly well satisfied . . .' England were only three runs short, with 4 wickets left, at close of play.

10th July 1937. Schoolgirls arriving at the Oval to see the England Women's Cricket team play Australia.
© *Hulton-Deutsch Collection*

The Women's Cricket Association arranged regular fixtures at the Oval. In 1936, they played a combined Surrey, Middlesex and Kent side. Again the match was hit by rain, but Miss A. Brown, Freddie Brown's sister, took several wickets. The following year, an Australian team visited Britain, and three Test Matches were played, the teams came to the Oval to play the deciding game in the series in vile weather. A crowd of 6000 people turned up on the first day, including the Duchess of Gloucester, and saw Australia reach 207 for 9 declared. England then made 308 for 9 declared, Betty Snowball run out for 99 going for the run that would have given her a century. E. W. Swanton reported that there was scarce a dry eye on the ground. In their second innings, Australia made 224, and England needed 124 to win. The weather ruined the match, however, with England 9 for 3 wickets.

The 1930s rolled by – more games were played. The wicket yielded more and more runs. In 1937, Gregory and Sandham of Surrey put on 344 for the second wicket against Glamorgan, Sandham making 239, the last double century of his career. Gregory made the highest score of his career (243) against Somerset in 1938, and a few days later Fishlock made 93 in 75 minutes against the Australians. Holmes relinquished the captaincy in favour of Garland-Wells. Edward VIII abdicated and George VI came to the throne. Halifax replaced Eden as Foreign Secretary.

The nation slid towards September 1939. When the Third Test was played, against the West Indies, there were barrage balloons in the sky, and anti-aircraft guns being wheeled into position. There was more than a sprinkling of uniforms round the ground, and this time they were not those of postmen or firemen or porters of the LSWR. And then, cricket disappeared from the Oval.

Chapter Thirteen

Sandbags on the Square – 1939–1945

Although Hitler had the decency to wait almost until the end of the cricket season before invading Poland, in 1939, even more than in 1914, there were those for whom the war came as no surprise. The fears of war, that had been but temporarily allayed when Chamberlain attempted to play for a draw at Munich and Bertchesgarten, galloped back in the spring of 1939, when trenches were dug in London parks, sandbags filled everywhere, and there was much worried talk of impending air raids.

In May, letters were exchanged between the Surrey Club and the officer in charge of No 3 Section, 303 Anti-Aircraft Company, the battery that would be posted to the Oval in the event of hostilities. The Committee were quite happy to have an Army Telephone party placed on the ground, but pointed out that there was no sleeping accommodation at the Oval, even when Notts were playing. Later the same month, the Committee received a letter from the Land Agent for Eastern Command, stating that the Oval was to be occupied as a searchlight position.

As the last season before the war progressed, cricketers must have found it difficult to keep both eyes on the ball, the tendencies being to look up at the skies for Hitler's openers, Heinkel and Messcherschmidt. The Surrey team went to Edgbaston, where Eddie Watts took all ten wickets against Warwickshire, and then Swansea, before returning to London and to Lords in late August. In these precious few days of peace and sunshine, the West Indies came to the Oval for the Third Test. After that, there was no more first-class cricket at the Oval. The last fixture of the season, between Surrey and Lancashire, was moved to Old Trafford. The season ended in disarray – the game against Lancashire was abandoned after two days.

During the final meeting of the Match Committee held before war broke out, it was recommended that soliciting for autographs in the pavilion be forbidden. Nearly seven years were to pass before this recommendation had the slightest relevance to life. On 21st September, A. F. Davey, the Secretary, reported to the Club that the Auxiliary Fire Service had occupied almost the whole of the pavilion. Helmets had appeared for the first time at the Oval. As the 'blackout' was imposed, and as thousands and thousands of London children were evacuated, the war seemed to come a little closer, and the Committee decided it was time to check insurance against war risks, and to clear the pavilion of trophies, pictures, mementos. The paintings were placed in the cellar, and the Secretary was instructed to inspect them at intervals to make sure they were not being attacked by damp. At the same time, there was still the hope that the war would be over quickly, and the Surrey Committee took the initiative of trying to set up an amended programme of first-class cricket for 1940. The response from other counties was not encouraging.

In January 1940, the Club learnt that it would not be possible to insure against war risks. The war had not yet hit London, that was all to come, but the Committee were faced with numerous financial difficulties. Obviously revenue would be almost non-existent during wartime, although the War Department was paying rent of £472 per quarter. These economic facts of life took a little time to sink in. As late as October 1942, H. D. G. Leveson Gower told the Committee: 'It is generally recognised that the Club at any rate for a time will have to face considerably reduced income . . .' On the other hand, there were still various overheads to be paid. Application for exemption from rates was made, on the basis that the Club were no longer in occupation of the ground, and for an adjustment of income tax demands under Schedule A – income tax had just been increased from 7/6 to 8/6 in the pound. There was also the problem of the Surrey Tavern. The licensees, Bertrams, were understandably not happy about paying rent for the Tavern while it was operating at a loss. They wanted the Club to make a claim against the war department, but eventually gave up their lease, and Watney Combe Reid took over in their place.

The summer of 1940 would have been a good one for cricket at the Oval; many teams and clubs had booked to play there and the weather was fine. Among fixtures arranged that never took place were Wison's Grammar School v St Dunstan's Catford, St Thomas's Hospital v Barts, London Fire Brigade v City of London Police, matches under the aegis of the Women's Cricket Association, and Regular Army v Territorial Army – presumably, in this case, both teams had more important matters to attend to at this time. But the sun shone, the crops ripened, and the phoney war dragged on. In June, the British Expeditionary Force was miraculously saved from Dunkirk, and France fell to Hitler, who then turned his attention to Britain.

The warm-up to the Battle of Britain began in June, when eight people were killed in Cambridge in what was described as an 'incident'. By late July, it was well under way though far worse was to come in August and September. There were two main aims to German strategy – to destroy the Royal Air Force and to destroy civilian morale in London. Both required the most savage use of man-directed air power the world had ever seen. London was saturated with bombs in a blitz that lasted for months. Lords was lucky, so, too, was the Oval. Had either ground been situated a few miles to the east, it might well have been destroyed. As it was, three bombs fell on the Oval on the night of 10th

November 1940. One fell on the Surrey Tavern, one on the Mound Stand to the east of the pavilion, and one fell in front of the pavilion, there being neither long on nor long off posted to catch it.

The blast from the bombs also caused damage to the perimeter wall of the Oval, and the total cost of repairs was reckoned to be approximately £4000. Almost as wounding to the pride of the Club may have been the application from Lambeth Council to use the ground as a coal dump for the duration of the war.

Meanwhile, members of the Surrey team were spread so far and wide in various branches of the Forces. The Bedsers, courtesy of the RAF, went to France, Italy and the Middle East; Freddie Brown and Geoff Whittaker were taken prisoner by Rommel's army in North Africa, Eddie Watts left the Army Physical Training Staff, received a commission and was posted to the East. The bowlers – Gover, Watts, and Allom – tended to join the Army; the batsmen – Barling, Gregory, Parker and Squires – joined the RAF. Laurie Fishlock ended up making aircraft parts, E. W. Brooks was a member for the Police War reserves. Andy Ducat, in his mid-fifties, joined the Home Guard, and died tragically at the batting crease, playing at Lords in 1942. Many cricketers, young and old, were never to return to the Oval. Kenneth Farnes, who'd taken the last wicket in the gruelling, gruesome 1938 Test, was killed piloting his plane. Hedley Verity died of wounds in Italy. Maurice Turnbull, who played at the Oval once in a Test and many times in county games for Glamorgan, was shot by a sniper during the Normandy campaign. Others who had done great deeds at the Oval died more peaceably – Sir Jeremiah Colman, Surrey President from 1916 to 1923, the Earl of Midleton, J. T. Hearne, Archie MacLaren, Bobby Peel, Fred Tate senior.

In March 1942, the War Office hit on a novel use of the Oval, and a prisoner of war 'cage' was erected there to be filled, it was said, with German paratroopers as and when they arrived. It was not a popular move with the Club – it probably wouldn't have been too popular with the prisoners of war, either – since the War Office wished to site the cage on part of the square, doing 'damage to the middle of the ground and much damage to the outfield.' In general, the Oval suffered far more from the efforts of the British than those of the Germans during the Second World War. Also in 1943, the Club received rent compensation of £1942 (covering the period August 1939 to December 1940), £909 for 'dilapidations to the Surrey Tavern', and another £694 for war damage.

The members loyally continued to pay their subscriptions, and the Club saved as much as it could, aware that a great deal of money would be needed to get the Oval back in shape once the war ended. More bombs fell on the Oval in 1943, on the terrace in front of the Long Room, bringing down part of the balcony and roof, and damaging doors and windows. By then, experts reckoned it would take at least twelve months after the war to prepare the Oval for cricket. The 1944 edition of *Wisden* was not optimistic: 'Surrey may find themselves

Andy Ducat – one of the four Surrey players
to make a triple century at the Oval (the
others are Able, W. W. Read and Tom
Hayward).
From the Oval Collection

temporarily homeless when the war ends, and if the Championship is renewed immediately they will face a difficult problem, as it is questionable whether there are enough cricket centres away from Kennington to carry the burden of staging a dozen or more first-class matches without incurring heavy financial loss.'

It was clear that a vast effort would be needed to restore the Oval to playing condition, and a great deal would depend on the Head Groundsman and his staff. In 1940, A. W. 'Bosser' Martin had been granted a testimonial which raised £400, but in 1942 he retired 'after 51 years of faithful service'. He had started work at the Oval in 1891, when Shuter, Abel, Lockwood, Lohmann and the Reads were winning the County Championship for Surrey. To retire in the middle of a cricketless war, as far as the Oval was concerned, must have been a bitter blow. Martin was succeeded by H. 'Bert' Lock, who was then groundsman and professional at Exeter, on the staff of the Devon Cricket Club, and who had worked at the Oval from 1922 to 1932, and had played for the Second XI as a medium fast bowler. Lock was appointed at a salary of £5 a week, pending his release from the RAF.

It was also time to negotiate a new lease with the Duchy of Cornwall, to run from 1943 to 1984. This was done, but not without a certain amount of friction between the Club and the Duchy. The spectre of greyhound racing returned, prompting an irate letter from Lord Russell of Killowen to the President:

> . . . The Duchy seems to be rather greedy as to rent, but I suppose the rent is low. *BUT* I view with grave apprehension the exception and reservation which they propose should be inserted in the lease. It is pregnant with litigation.
>
> Further, the words 'public entertainment or exhibition' may include anything from Buffalo Bill to a Fun Fair. Why can they not trust us to allow proper games in the future as we have done in the past? If they mean 'dogs' we must surely say *NO*. If the thing is confined to 'games' there would not be much harm, but then there would be no need to refer to 'additional buildings, machinery and things' at all.
>
> I thought you might like to have my views for what they are worth . . .

The offer, or plan, from the Duchy was a tempting one financially. Sir Charles Allen wrote to the Club suggesting that a dog racing track be constructed 'out of season' at the Oval. In the early spring each year, the track would be dismantled and removed, and everything would be made good for the start of the cricket. The estimated payment to the Club would be between £15,000 and £20,000 a year. The Committee may well have been tempted, but stuck to their principles. 'The proposition could not be entertained.'

In the autumn of 1944, there was a general feeling that the end of the war in Europe was not far away. Life would still take a very long time to get back to anything approaching normality – there would be little red meat available for budding fast bowlers for years yet – but plans were being made for peacetime. It was a time for looking at the future and the past. In 1945 H. D. G. Leveson-Gower was preparing an article for next year's *Wisden* – 'A Hundred Years of Surrey Cricket'. In it he touched on a happy link with the very early days of the Club. In 1944, A. R. Martingell, great-great-nephew of W. Martingell (the Club's original professional bowler a hundred years earlier), was playing for the Surrey Colts.

In February 1945, the Lands Branch of the War Department offered to return the ground and outbuildings of the Oval to the Surrey Club, but specified that they wished to maintain possession of the main pavilion. A group of SS officers were still miserably in occupation of a Nissen hut at the Vauxhall end, but the first priority was to get the playing area into condition. The military had done their best to make this difficult. Where they had gouged deep holes in the ground, they simply filled them in with sandbags. Forty years later, subsidence from this folly is still plaguing the Oval. Every season small craters appear as the old sandbags rot and settle down further and further in their holes.

Bert Lock took up office without waiting for demobilisation leave, and sent a report to Brian Castor, the new Secretary, outlining his plans for the resuscitation of the ground. The whole area would have to be re-surfaced, Lock strongly advocated re-turfing rather than seeding, as it would be quicker and more reliable. S. T. Mallock, who had supplied the Oval in the past, offered to supply good quality turf at a cost of 34/- per 100, delivered free to the ground. Lock estimated that about 35,000 turfs would be required, and that the cost, therefore, would be about £600. Seed would be considerably cheaper – between £150 and £200. The Committee unanimously recommended turf.

It was clear that the stands, the Tavern, the pavilion, indeed the whole structure, needed a great deal of money spent on it, and, as 1945 was the Centenary year of the Surrey Club, it seemed a good idea to link celebration with need by establishing a Centenary Fund Appeal. A meeting was held at the Savoy Hotel on 30 May 1945, three weeks after Doenitz signed an unconditional instrument of surrender at Eisenhower's headquarters. At the Savoy meeting, the mayors of Guildford, Kingston and Lambeth all suggested other uses for the Oval, and that Surrey should arrange more fixtures in other parts of the county. This had long been an issue. Of all the first-class counties, only Surrey and Middlesex, the two London based clubs, and Notts, were 'one ground' counties. The others all played on a variety of grounds, and even Lancashire, with prestigious headquarters at Old Trafford, managed to play some home games at Liverpool and Blackpool.

Errol Holmes, who had captained Surrey for a couple of seasons, in 1937 and 1938, was appointed Appeal Organizer, in which capacity he drew up a list of functions that he would attend to promote the Appeal. It meant a lot of talking, a lot of listening, a lot of club dinners. In return, he was provided with a car, powerful lungs and good pair of ears. The aim was to collect £100,000, a considerable target. Holmes took teams of Surrey players up and down the county, playing local clubs and scratch teams. Innumerable autographed bats and books were auctioned. Louis Palgrave, who succeeded Holmes as Appeal Organizer, sold 10,000 copies of a Surrey Centenary Souvenir in three months. One of the less successful fund-raising notions was that each member of the Surrey Club should pay £1 for every match that Surrey won during the 1946 season. Surrey played 26 Championship games that year. They drew 9, lost 11, and won only 6, to finish as low in the table as they had ever done.

It is to the credit of the Surrey members that they were more disappointed than relieved.

Chapter Fourteen

The Years of Recovery

Bert Lock was demobbed from the RAF in October 1945. If there was to be cricket at the Oval the following year, he had six or seven months to hack his way through the jungle of outfield, find the square, rid it of weeds, cut the entire ground to a playable level, paint almost everything in sight, make sure the wall was rebuilt, dispose of all the debris left by the military – barbed wire, poles, huts – fill in several craters at the Vauxhall end, and convince Club and players that it would be safe to play. Alec Bedser recorded how Lock and the groundstaff worked long, hard, cold days: 'The practice nets had been gnawed by rats. Bert sat in the east stand, often in freezing winds, repairing the nets to have them ready for the new season in early April.'

Lock walked miles across the Gravesend marshes, looking for weed free turf. Many people doubted that the Oval would be in shape for the 1946 season. Fortunately, a fixture list was arranged for all the counties, so that, when Lock and company had achieved their winter miracle and had produced a square and an outfield, and seats and sightscreens, and a working scoreboard, and all the facilities for the public that are usually taken for granted, there were teams ready to come and play. The Oval was back in business.

Once again correspondence began to flow, and decisions were taken that could be implemented. In February 1946, a new catering contract was awarded to John Gardner and Company. In May, the BBC obtained broadcasting rights at the Oval for the summer for £150 and television rights for a further 125 guineas, subject to certain conditions. These were not met, and, two months later, the Club asked for another 25 guineas. The BBC agreed, but may well have felt that they got little for their money in the end – when England played India in the three-day Third Test at the Oval, most of the first day and all the third day were lost to rain. The following year a milestone was reached in negotiations with the BBC, when broadcasting, as opposed to television, rights were also agreed in 'guineas' – 200 in this case.

One of the celebrations of a hundred years of the Surrey Club was a one-day game, Surrey v Old England. It took place on 23rd May, and 15,000 spectators, including the King, arrived in glorious weather to see Sutcliffe, Sandham, Woolley, Hendren, Jardine, Fender, Tate and Allom playing again at the Oval.

Wisden noted that 'the band of the East Surrey regiment was in attendance, and after the game a dance in the pavilion long room completed the festive occasion.' Less festive was the request, a couple of months later, from neighbouring Archbishop Tenison's Grammar School to use the Long Room for PT, and the Reading Room as a changing room. The Committee agreed, and the Oval once again offered sporting facilities to young people of South London.

Archbishop Tenison's School. It is said that the staff vie for positions on the roof during Test matches.
© *The Central Press Photos Ltd.*

Given the speed at which he had had to get the ground ready, Lock must have watched anxiously that summer, to see how the wicket played. In July, he went before the Committee and discussed his plans for the autumn. He wished to make two experiments on different parts of the middle: to work clay in on two wickets, and to lift the turf on another two wickets, dig down and lay a clay bed, and then replace the turf. Results from the first experiment would be revealed in 1947, but the second experiment would take longer to assess. At the end of the 1947 season, following a year of revenue from cricket, and the crowds had been good that summer, Lock deemed it timely to send a shopping list to the Committee:

> GROUND REQUIREMENTS
> 50 yards Top Spit
> 30 yards Heavy Loam
> 12 bushels Grass Seed for outfield
> 4 bushels Best Mixture Grass Seed
> 10 cwt Anti Clover Dressing
> 5 gallons "Verdone" Weed Killer
> 3 tons Marl for practice wickets
> 5 cwt Worm Killer
> 6 bushels Outfield Mixture
> 2 bushels Best Mixture
> 2500 turfs
> 2 dozen iron pegs for Nets
> More weed killer for "Yarrow"

With the return of crowds to the Oval, came the return of problems with members, guests and visitors. In 1947, an article appeared in *The Cricketer* criticising conditions in the Long Room:

> 'The new Secretary, Mr Brian Castor, has already made many friends by his ability, energy and courtesy, and we hope that during his reign of office he may be able to persuade his Committee to enforce stricter rules in regard to the main room (Long Room) of the pavilion, which at present is rendered unattractive by the custom which allows members to bring their sandwiches, drinks and tea into it. The club would benefit by an improvement in this respect.'

Castor read a letter to the Committee that he had sent in response, pointing out the complete lack of propriety of such a comment made by people, who were not members of the Club, on conditions obtaining in a Club in which they were guests. More indignation was exercised than perhaps the article warranted, but as a result of this altercation, the Committee decided to prohibit the consumption of liquid and other refreshment in the Long Room, a decision that stands today.

Apart from the visits of Denis Compton to the Oval, 1947 was a better year for the Surrey team, and a wonderful year for supporters of cricket. When Middlesex came to the Oval in August, by which time Compton was already poised to break Hayward's record for the most runs in a season and Hobbs's record for the most centuries in a season, a crowd of 30,000 was admitted to the ground on the Saturday and the gates had to be closed at three o'clock. Compton scored a century, and, later in the match, took 12 for 174. Less than a week later, Compton was back at the Oval, scoring 53 and 113 for England against South Africa. Although they lost the series 3–0, the South Africans made a handsome profit from their tour, and generously donated half the gate money from their match against Surrey towards rebuilding the Oval.

The Surrey team performed considerably better in 1947 under Errol Holmes than they had done under N.H. Bennett the previous year. They finished sixth in the Championship, and Captain and Coach made encouraging reports on some of the younger players at the end of the season. J.C. Laker was described as 'a useful all-rounder who must find a regular place sooner or later'. W.S. Surridge was said to be 'a hostile and aggressive fast bowler, and the type of hitter that the crowd likes – might be very useful next year in Gover's absence.' Less fulsome was the praise for Barrington: 'Quite a good bowler for his age and size – spins the ball and has possibilities for this sort of bowling – shapes fairly well with the bat.' The last remark is on a par with the verdict on Fred Astaire's screen test: 'Can't sing, can't act, can dance a bit.'

In 1950, the West Indians toured Britain. They were a popular team with a popular captain, John Douglas Claude Goddard, and they won the Test series 3–1, winning at the Oval by an innings and 56 runs. Test matches had yet to become the life blood of commercial cricket, but they were great occasions – too much so in this particular case. The Committee reported on events in the Players Luncheon Room:

> Here again an extremely unsatisfactory position has arisen. It has been customary in the past at the end of a Test match at the Oval for the two teams, scorers, umpires and visiting team's managers to be provided with champagne. It has always been understood that eighteen bottles was the maximum amount to be supplied, and yet the account is for twenty-seven.

Castor investigated, and discovered that, on demand from the players, the waitresses 'simply drew more from the cellarman.' We do not know which players were especially thirsty, though Hutton, Walcott, Weekes, Rae, Valentine and Goddard all had cause to celebrate. It was the last time that such a 'lax arrangement' was allowed to run, and Castor ended his report with the threat that 'in future years the matter will be dealt with in an entirely different manner.'

The availability of any champagne at all is indication that life was slowly getting back to normal in many ways. There were, however, many post-war restrictions still in force, and the Club had problems in obtaining the necessary licence to rebuild the east terraces, which had suffered from the ravages of time and war. Licences were necessary at a time when raw materials were scarce and there was so much rebuilding to be done. There were also disruptions to the training and coaching of young staff by National Service. The school leaving age was then 15, and, since unemployment was not a problem, it was common for young people to work for two or three years before being called-up. For Surrey, as for any county, this meant that a promising 18 year old would disappear just at the time when he might decide to settle with the Club. In 1953, the Committee therefore agreed that all members of staff should be credited with ten shillings a week while they were on National Service, and should be given the whole amount as a lump sum if and when they re-signed with the Club.

1952 is chiefly remembered at the Oval as the year when Stuart Surridge led Surrey to the first of their seven successive Championships, but it was also the year of several controversies. Early in the season Surrey played Warwickshire, during the course of which match somebody, somehow, managed to doctor the wicket. It remained a mystery as to who had done this, and how or why it was done, but the Committee were satisfied that considerable 'repairs' had been effected, involving substantial time, materials and a tool of some kind, and that the repairs could not have been carried out at night. They interviewed Surridge, Dollery, the Warwickshire captain, and Lock. The match continued, Surrey won, but the mystery remained. It is tempting to believe that a phantom groundsman visited the Oval, armed with spade, brush, knife and watering-can, and crept in between close of play and nightfall, or between dawn and the first arrivals at the ground, to make running repairs to the pitch.

There was no mystery about the plumes of smoke that flooded the ground a couple of months later, when Surrey played the Indian Touring team. The match had already produced plenty of incident. Divecha took a hat-trick in Surrey's first innings, and, when the Indians batted, Umpire Price no-balled Tony Lock for throwing. Price was not the flavour of the month at the Oval in July 1952. In a match three weeks earlier, when the crowd barracked a dour performance by a Yorkshire side intent only in playing for a draw, Price sat down on the grass and refused to let play continue until the barracking stopped. Here he was now, 'calling' Lock from square leg, and causing what *Wisden* described as a 'sensation', it being the first time such a thing had happened to an English bowler for half a century. The ghosts of Willsher and Lillywhite may well have enjoyed the episode, but many mortals were appalled when some of the members booed the umpire. The following day it was difficult for Price to see if Lock was throwing or not, for dense smoke from the Marmite factory at the Vauxhall end drifted across the ground. Resourceful and inventive though he was as a captain, this was not one of Surridge's ploys. He wasn't playing in the match.

Surrey won again in 1953 and 1954, prompting a phone call from Lord Rosebery in Edinburgh to congratulate Surridge and the team. Lord Rosebery had been less happy earlier in the season as a result of an article in the *Evening News* by E. M. Wellings. In an article headed 'Surridge Must Stay As Surrey Captain', Wellings reported that the Surrey Committee might not re-elect Surridge as Captain, and that they were thinking of appointing Peter May. 'More than most counties, Surrey remain eager to have a captain from one of the two major universities. They have never yet had a professional captain, though one of their amateurs had to be subsidised. Surridge was at neither university, nor was he at one of the more fashionable public schools, and his friends have always felt that he held the Surrey captaincy on sufferance.' Wellings went on to say that Surridge's original election had been by a majority of only one, and that his rival, A.C. Burnett, had been favoured by some because he had obtained a Blue at Cambridge. 'Surrey have done some odd things with their captaincy since the war. In 1946, they entrusted it to an unknown, Nigel Bennett. Then they returned to Errol Holmes, who was on the Committee as Organiser of their Centenary Appeal Fund, and next imported Barton, whose former county was Norfolk. In the same period there was a move to bring in another player from outside, Hugh Bartlett, who had then recently been dropped from the Sussex captaincy. Due to all these manoeuvres, a fine Surrey side was kept waiting till 1952 to become sole champions. Had that very good player and senior professional, Stan Squires, been given the job, the honour would surely have come to the Oval much earlier . . .' The rest of the article praised Surridge's innovations, drive, and leadership.

It was a strange piece of writing in one way. Squires may well not have endeared himself to the Committee at the Oval, he used to sing a little song, accompanying himself on the ukelele, the refrain of which was:

> They tell me the Oval's a terrible place,
> The organization's a flaming disgrace . . .

but the sad and insurmountable reason why he had not been made captain of Surrey prior to Surridge was that he had died of leukaemia in 1950.

As an ex-captain of Surrey, Rosebery was hardly likely to take kindly to such remarks, and he had friends strategically placed to whom he could turn. The Committee heard that:

> Lord Rosebery (has) written strongly to Lord Rothermere on the matter saying that the whole of Wellings's article was untrue and completely scandalous. He suggested to Lord Rothermere that some action might reasonably be taken. Lord Rosebery says he has had a reply from Lord Rothermere who has taken the complaint to the Editor of the *Evening News* and in his reply says that he imagines Mr Wellings will be a great deal more careful of what he writes in future.

Wellings's next report on Surrey in the *Evening News*, six days later, was lower key and far more acceptable: 'Glamorgan condemned themselves to bat on a gluey pitch when they chose first innings against Surrey at the Oval today, and they were routed by Tony Lock's left arm spinners . . .'

The 1950s were years of great cricketing success at the Oval, but cricket itself was in decline as a popular spectacle. 1954 was a miserably wet year, and even the touring side, Pakistan, failed to attract the vast crowds that grounds like the

Oval have always needed to keep going. The post-war age of austerity, utility and rationing was over. Many more people had cars, and were looking and going further afield for a day out. Petrol coupons were no longer necessary. Television was biting into leisure time. More and more of the urban population were spending their holidays away from home. One of the Oval erstwhile 'three bobbers' told E.W. Swanton, a few years later, that he put it all down to 'female emancipation'. The weather was similarly dismal in 1955, and even the return of the Australians the following year failed to bring back the crowds. When Surrey won the Championship for the fifth time on the trot, in 1957, gates at the Oval were lower than they had been in the stumbling and fumbling seasons just after the war.

Neither cricket nor the Oval were getting any younger. By 1960, a survey of the ground showed that a great deal of work was needed to keep the fabric in good order. The seating needed renovating, the Tavern needed rebuilding, the terraces and stands needed attention. It was unlikely that revenue for all this would come from the turnstiles. And so sponsorship, one-day cricket and Sunday play came to the Oval as it did to every other county headquarters of cricket, with the same arguments raging over each innovation. When Sunday cricket was introduced, Garland-Wells, ex-captain of Surrey, wrote to the Committee suggesting that a religious service should be held at the Oval before start of play on such occasions. The Committee's view was that a 2 pm start gave everyone ample time to go to church before they arrived at the ground. The Oval may well have seemed a place of little faith, for, although the Boys Brigade had long been given permission to hold Drum Head Services there, a request in the mid 1950s, from the Bishops of Southwark and Winchester, for use of the ground for mass church services had been turned down. Maybe the Oval had long possessed gods of its own. Maybe the church would have found it as hard to summon mass congregations to the Oval as cricket was doing.

The international arenas, Trent Bridge, Old Trafford, Edgbaston, Headingley and the Oval, were relying more and more heavily on Test matches for the main source of their income. In 1987, receipts from the one-day Texaco Trophy game against Pakistan at the Oval were almost double the total receipts from Surrey's Britannic Assurance Championship matches, Refuge Assurance League matches, the Nat West Trophy and Benson and Hedges Cup games put together. In 1988, the Cornhill Insurance Test match against the West Indies brought in well over half a million pounds in paying attendances alone. The only other way to achieve anything approaching a full house was to have success in one of the knock-out tournaments. One day in August 1988, when Surrey played Middlesex in a semi-final of the NatWest Trophy, brought in more money at the gate than the entire thirty-three day County Championship programme.

From 1987, it was possible to look back to 1947, and to two games, forty years apart, where Surrey played Glamorgan at the Oval. In 1947, the ground was full: in 1987, the total paying attendance over three days was 372. From 1960, it was probably not possible to look forward and see all that was to come. Fortunately, miraculously, revenue increased, sometimes dramatically, often slowly and steadily. In 1961, the Financial and General Purposes Committee recommended the purchase and installation of a Fruit Machine for the Members Bar at a cost of £180 – how things had changed from the days when members were disciplined for taking bets in the pavilion way back in the 1920s. Hockey matches that brought in £10 in the old days, brought in £1000 in the 1960s, leading to the suggestion that the Oval might be used for a World Hockey Tournament in 1967. In 1966, the BBC paid £700 to televise some of the play in the Surrey v Yorkshire match in *Grandstand*. The long connection between the ground and the Corinthian Casuals Football Club came to an end in 1963 since the attendances were too small. As an alternative source of income, the Committee looked into the possibility of opening a golf driving range at the Oval. In September 1971 and 1972, three one-day Pop Festivals were held, bringing in £11,000.

Geoffrey Howard, who had been Assistant Secretary at the Oval from 1947 to 1949, returned as Secretary in 1965. It was a crucial time for the Oval. Sponsorship, one-day tournaments, and increased advertising had all helped to bring in revenue, but what was needed was a major development to show that the ground was alive, growing, moving forward. Smaller grounds can exist with a loyal local membership, and there were many who said that Surrey should consider quitting the Oval and moving to a more 'county' based ground. It's all too easy with a ground the size of the Oval for even members of the Club to feel that they are in possession of a vast dinosaur, lumbering its way towards possible extinction. There's a vast difference between an oval shaped piece of ground, with a small pavilion, fringed by one or two pretty villas and a few trees, on which a group of gentlemen besport themselves, and an enormous cricket ground, surrounded by stands and terraces that seat 25,000, on which professional cricketers from all over the world earn their living. The problem was exacerbated at the Oval by a lean spell for Surrey on the field. Just as Surrey had dominated the 1950s, Yorkshire dominated the 1960s, and Surrey didn't win a single trophy. After the years of plenty, the years of famine were not well received.

Since its foundation as a cricket ground, back in 1845, the Oval had enjoyed some major development and improvement roughly every generation: new pavilions in the 19th century, the building of embankments round the ground, the present pavilion at the turn of the century, the Vauxhall stands in the 1920s, a wall to replace the perimeter fence. From the end of the second world war, however, it had been a battle simply to keep things going, it was as though the Oval wasn't breathing as deeply as it had done, its condition was becoming increasingly asthmatic. It needed a whiff of the oxygen of regeneration and innovation.

In this situation, there are really only two things a Club can do: go forward or

go under. Plans were made to go forward. In the 1970s, an ambitious scheme was discussed which envisaged moving the square and developing large sections of the ground. The ultimate aim was to realize some of the dreams of Alcock and others, that the Oval should be completely surrounded by covered stands. At both Vauxhall and pavilion ends there would be further building, with a tower block erected behind the Vauxhall stand. It is still possible that much of this scheme will be realized, for all the building work of the 1980s has been compatible with it, and much has already been done. In 1983, the Taverners Stand, to the east of the pavilion, was reconstructed. The top half was demolished, and a suite of Executive boxes and a restaurant were built and opened in time for the 1984 season. To the east of this stand is another Mound Stand, so that covered accommodation now extends in a broad sweep from the pavilion. With the bowling from the Vauxhall end, mid on or mid wicket have a background of simple but elegant buildings that mask at least some of the old LCC flats. Mid on or mid wicket may well not be grateful – it makes it even harder to focus on a catch. Some of the residents of the flats may not be grateful – they have lost their fine view of the Oval.

Other entertainment boxes were built under the east terraces, and the east side of the ground began to have a solid feel to it – a far cry from the days when sheep were penned there preparatory to grazing the wicket. In 1988, further hospitality accommodation was built in a chalet complex to the east of the Vauxhall stand, including a new press-box with greenhouse effect, which ripened the anger of some of its occupants. Here at least one local resident attempted to halt progress, on the grounds that she was being deprived of her right to light. The protest failed, though it may well be repeated on the west side of the ground, where the flats on the far side of the Harleyford Road have an even better view of play and modern replacement windows through which to enjoy it.

For the obvious next step was a similar development to the west of the pavilion, but that is not yet part of history.

9th June 1986.
Experimental
electronic
scoreboard and
giant video. England
v New Zealand in
the Prudential Cup.
© *Patrick Eagar*

Chapter Fifteen

The Beat of the Drum at the Oval

Between 1880 and 1939, twenty-nine Tests were played at the Oval. Since 1946, over forty Tests have been played there. No cricket fan would ever suggest that this is too much, but the special treat has become the everyday diet and has lost some of its piquancy. It is harder to pick out the plums. It is harder to know where the heroes of today rank beside those of yesterday. Was Lindwall as great a bowler as Lohmann? Was Holding as good as Lindwall? Was anybody as good as Sidney Barnes? Or do we just look at the analyses and the statistics, reckoning that Spofforth's 7 for 44 in 1882 must have been better than Lillee's 7 for 89 in 1981?

Fortunately, cricket isn't merely records and statistics, although there are those in the pavilion at the Oval to this day who talk only a language shot through with decimal points, averages and 'pers'. But when cricket restarted at the Oval in May 1946, a record very soon came along. I was eight years old at the time, and already a desperate Surrey supporter, though I hadn't even seen the Oval. It was with shame and horror, and in tears, that I learnt from my older brother that Surrey had allowed Sarwate and Banerjee, at numbers ten and eleven, to score 124 not out and 121 respectively, in a last wicket partnership of 249, the highest ever in England. I suppose I saw it in very schoolboy terms, supposing that the Surrey team would also be crying with shame, and that somebody, the President of the Surrey Club perhaps, might beat them for their disgraceful performance.

When Surrey played Old England, a fortnight later, the historical significance meant little to me. I was only just beginning to learn the names of the present Surrey team, and knew nothing of the glory and the memories that Sutcliffe and Sandham, Jardine and Fender brought to the Oval. A great crowd gathered to do justice to the occasion, including King George VI, the man who had sent me, and every other schoolchild, a message telling me that the war was over and that we had won. Here, on 23rd May, was proof of that. The match was drawn but the result was of no importance whatsoever. What mattered was that Woolley scored 62 and Hendren 94, that Fender took two wickets and snapped up a catch, that Tate bowled. After the match, Fender wrote a beautiful letter to *The Times*:

11th May 1946. C. T. Sarwate and S. Banerjee, India v Surrey. They put on 249 for the last wicket, a record in England, and 'a lesson in aggression sensibly applied to batting' (E. M. Wellings).

'More than once while we were fielding a thought came to my mind that ... where cricket is concerned, public memory, in spite of the old adage, is not short ... Such a welcome as was given to 'Old England', collectively and individually, must surely be a public assurance that those who can carve for themselves a little niche in the greatest of games can always be sure of a warm place in the hearts of all lovers of cricket.'

23rd May 1946. Old England takes the field against Surrey. From the left: Sandham, Hendren, Freeman, Tate, Allom and Fender

The following year, 1947, I paid my first visit to the Oval. I don't believe I fell in love with it – I don't believe you can fall in love with a cricket ground – but I was entranced. I went then, as I do now, with excitement and reverence warring within me, and always, always with the hope that Surrey will win. Too much I want this, it interferes with my enjoyment of the cricket. Maybe I should move to Leicester, and go instead to Grace Road, where I wouldn't care tuppence who won – unless Surrey were visiting. It hurts, therefore, to record the match that follows.

In August 1947, Surrey played Middlesex. The previous year, at Lords, Compton and Edrich had put on 296 for the third wicket against Surrey. This year, at the Oval, they put on 287 in two and three-quarter hours without being separated. The Surrey scorebook is a sorry sight. Everywhere in the bowling analyses, there are numbers – ones, twos, threes, fours, but strangely no sixes. There are very few dots. Even the Surrey wicket-keeper, McIntyre, bowled. Middlesex declared at close of play on the first day, with their score at 2 for 537. Surrey made a brave response, but by half past five on Monday their first innings ended with a score of 334. Stan Squires made 98, Errol Holmes 61 and McIntyre 51. Compton, showing no signs of tiredness after his 137 not out on Saturday, bowled twenty and a half overs and took 6 for 94. Surrey's second innings was all over long before lunch on Tuesday. This time Compton bowled twenty four overs and five balls and took 6 for 80. Only Fishlock and Barling, with 44 each, offered much resistance, though Surridge made 23 in twenty minutes. Middlesex won by an innings and 11 runs. It was wonderful cricket, and 54,000 people saw it over three days. I stayed at home, hating Compton and Edrich for what they had done to my heroes.

A week later, Compton was back at the Oval, playing for England against South Africa. He made 53 in the first innings, but took an hour and three-quarters over it. England reached a total of 427, but it was slow stuff. Hutton batted two and a half hours for 83, Yardley two hours ten minutes for 59. The South African first innings was also ponderous. They made 302 off 135 overs, largely thanks to Bruce Mitchell, who carried his bat for all but twelve balls in making 120. England's second innings was an altogether brisker affair – 6 for 325 off 77 overs, with Compton making 113 in an hour and three-quarters. Evans made 39 not out in twenty nine minutes, and added 58 in an unbroken stand with Howorth at more than two runs a minute. When stumps were finally drawn at 6.47 pm on Tuesday, South Africa were heading for what would have been a sensational victory. They had been set 451 to win and were 423 for the loss of seven wickets, a mixture of stubborn resistance and a bold attempt to get the runs. Mitchell and Melville had added 184 in 154 minutes for the third wicket, Tuckett and Mitchell an unbroken 109 in 107 minutes for the eighth wicket, a remarkable performance considering they came together with an hour and three-quarters to play and only three wickets left. Mitchell finished with 189 not out, and the match was a draw, though England had already won the series 3–0. The Oval crowd got their money's worth – an average of 136 overs a day were bowled.

The following month Compton returned yet again to the Oval, playing for Middlesex in Champion County v The Rest. It was the first time this fixture had been played since 1935, and only the third time in its history that the Champion County won. On 13th September, Middlesex batted first. Edrich made 180, and Compton made 246. Again, Compton's innings included no sixes, but he scored his runs in only a little over two and a half hours, despite two short breaks for rain and the necessity to retire after a recurrence of his knee trouble. In four innings at the Oval that month, Compton had scored 549 runs, with an average of 183.

When the Rest of England batted (it would have made little difference had it been the Rest of the Universe), Compton bowled 18.4 overs and took 4 for 57. The Rest were dismissed for 246, and followed on 297 behind. In their second innings, Yardley scored 71 and Washbrook 61, but they were all out for 317 early on the fourth and last day. Although the Rest contained seven of the England team, the two that mattered were playing for Middlesex, who won by 9 wickets. It had long been a tradition that the profits from this fixture were donated to various cricket charities. In this year, after paying expenses and Entertainments Tax, there remained a record sum of £1250.

When Australia came to the final Test in 1948, they had already won the

Ashes with big victories at Trent Bridge, Lords and Headingley. It was ten years since the sides had met at the Oval, the last occasion being England's merciless win in 1938. It was time for revenge to swing back to Australia. There had been copious rain before the match, and Lock and his staff had difficulties in getting the ground fit for play. When play did start, both bowlers and batsmen had to use sawdust to obtain firm footholds. There was a lot of cloud, and the weather was humid: on the England scoresheet, the scorer wrote 'weather very dull'. In these conditions, Lindwall, Miller and Johnston bowled superbly for Australia. For once both Edrich and Compton failed, as did everyone on the England team except Hutton. When Hutton was last out, acrobatically caught at the wicket by Tallon off a leg glance, he had made 30 out of a dismal England total of 52. He had been at the wicket for 140 minutes, and was the only English batsman to reach double figures. Lindwall finished with figures of 6 for 20. Vivian Jenkins, writing in the *News of the World*, was inspired:

> 'Magnified Australian cricketers, with huge yellow eyes in the middle of their green caps, cavorted and whirled in a frenzy of destruction.
> Wickets hurtled through the air like flailing boomerangs, gargantuan arms stretched out to take unimagined catches. Round and round the mad vortex went, while in the centre the England batsmen did a pitiful halting little dance of death.'

After this, Barnes and Morris began steadily for Australia, putting on 117 in even time against the bowling of Bedser, Watkins (hardly the most penetrative of opening bowlers in a Test), Young and Hollies. At ten to six on the first day, Hollies had Barnes caught at the wicket by Evans for 61. The stage was set for Bradman.

Though the light was far from perfect, everything else was prepared for the occasion. It was Bradman's Test farewell in England. He needed only four runs to average 100 in Tests. The ground was full. The Oval Test had long been a time and place of reunion for old cricketers, and in the pavilion were many of Bradman's friends and rivals, several of whom had played in the 1938 Test. Bradman had been unable to bat then, having injured his ankle. Now he was fit, and in form, having made 173 not out in his previous Test innings at Headingley. The edge had been more than taken off the bowling, Australia were already in a strong position. He came out of the pavilion, and the crowd rose and cheered and applauded him all the way to the wicket. Once there, Yardley, the England captain, called for three cheers, echoes of Bradman's first Test at the Oval in 1930, when Hobbs had been similarly honoured. 'Evidently deeply touched by the enthusiastic reception,' recorded *Wisden*, 'Bradman survived one ball, but, playing forward to the next, was cleaned bowled by a sharply turning break-back – possibly a googly.' There was no dance of death, no vortex, no whirling. Bradman turned and walked back to the pavilion, and the crowd stood and applauded him all the way. To many, it was the end of an era, and the

14th August 1948. Yardley leading the English team in 'three cheers' for Bradman, making his last Test appearance in England

fact that statistics record that Morris went on to score 196 and that Australia won by an innings and 149 seemed then, as it does now, irrelevant.

In 1950, the West Indians toured Britain for the first time since 1939. They came to the Oval in May to play Surrey, a side fast pulling out of the doldrums of the 1940s. The Surrey attack, consisting of Alec Bedser, Surridge, Parker, Laker, McMahon and Eric Bedser, got two quick wickets, and then Weekes joined Rae to play one of the finest post-war innings seen on the ground. He scored 232 without giving the slightest chance. What intrigued and most excited the West Indian supporters, including his team mates, was that he grew as a batsman with the innings.

14th August 1948. The Don, bowled by Hollies, second ball.

'Until the double century on Saturday 13th May, Weekes had not been known as a hooker or sweeper of the ball on his legs, or just outside the leg stump. Instead he had developed a unique response in which he would step back and slightly away from the wicket on the on side and drive through mid-on or mid-wicket off the back foot . . . relying on his wrists to force the ball. Suddenly, on that Saturday afternoon . . . Bedser bowled one of those in-swingers in which he specialized, but with the direction ever so slightly wayward outside the line of the leg stump. To the astonished delight of his team mates, Weekes stepped inside and hooked the ball. He played the shot with absolute authority, directing the ball downward and past square leg's right hand ... At the other end, Walcott ... applauded with his own bat ...'

Michael Manley – *A History of West Indies Cricket.*

From the Oval, Weekes went to Fenners, where he scored 304 not out, giving him an aggregate of 536 runs for once out in five days.

There were only four Tests arranged for 1950. In the first, at Old Trafford, England won comfortably by 202 runs. In the second, at Lords, West Indies gained their first success in England, winning by 326 runs, thanks to 'those little pals of mine, Ramadhin and Valentine', and to the batting of Walcott, Weekes, Worrell and Rae. At Trent Bridge, Worrell made 261 and Weekes 129, and Ramadhin and Valentine bowled and bowled and bowled 110 overs each, as the West Indies won again, by ten wickets.

At the Oval, the wicket was slow paced at first, and West Indies took longer than usual to pile up 503. Rae and Worrell both made centuries against a much changed England attack, only Bedser remaining of the England bowlers at Trent Bridge. Denys Rowbotham, in the *Manchester Guardian*, described their batting as 'dour, patient and exasperatingly efficient.' The wicket took spin on the first day, and the only England bowler to perform creditably was Doug Wright. 'For Wright the day could hardly have been a more ironic one. On a wicket always easy in its pace, he reduced both Rae and Worrell repeatedly to states of mortal fallibility for which few Englishmen could dare to hope ... neither batsman was certain in picking out his googly from his leg break ... and both were often deceived by his rich, beguiling flight and subtle change of length and pace ...' But Wright was an exceptional spinner, who bowled from a long run and could extract considerable bounce even on a flat wicket. By the end of the day he was tired, having bowled 30 overs, 11 maidens, and taken 1 for 89, that one wicket being off the last ball of the day, when Weekes thumped a long hop straight to Hutton.

The second day was watched by the Prime Minister, Clement Attlee, who had the misfortune to attend on a day when the cricket was, in Rowbotham's words 'interminably bad'. In an innings spread over three days, however, Hutton carried his bat for 202 out of 344 for England and restored at least the *Manchester Guardian's* faith in cricket. There was rain on the second day, and heavy overnight and early morning rain on the third, after which the wicket became treacherous. It passed from 'a sticky one to a worn and dusty one without visible transition', according to Rowbotham. When England lost their ninth wicket with the score at 326, all seemed lost, since to follow on would lead to almost certain defeat. 'Then for twenty five minutes the crowd was put into a state of such palpitating anxiety as had not seemed possible in this match. Wright survived his first few balls, and, without warning, Hutton went for Valentine with a fury almost thunderous. He leapt yards out of his ground and drove him high over mid-off, then waited and swept him soaringly to mid-wicket. He raced out again and took a single to mid-off . . . Wright performed wonders with a straight bat and fixed immobility. He not only survived the occasional balls that Hutton could not help but leave him, but one whole over from Valentine and a second from Ramadhin . . . Hutton glanced Goddard for a four and placed him for a single, (but) he could not score off Ramadhin. This left Wright at Goddard's mercy, and that, in one over, was that . . .' England were left ten short of saving the follow on. Ramadhin and Valentine took nine of the England wickets in the second innings, and the result was a foregone conclusion. England were all out for 103, and the West Indies had won by an innings and 56 runs. Joy, celebration, drums and calypso came to south London, as they had to north London six weeks earlier.

Outside his native Yorkshire, the Oval was one of Hutton's most successful grounds. His record in Tests up to and including the 1950 Test v West Indies was staggering:

> 1937   12 v New Zealand
> 1938   364 v Australia
> 1939   73 and 139 not out v West Indies
> 1946   25 v India
> 1947   83 and 36 v South Africa
> 1948   30 and 64 v Australia
> 1949   206 v New Zealand
> 1950   202 not out and 2 v West Indies.

an aggregate of 1234 runs in 12 innings with an average of 123.40.

It was at least second best, therefore, that in 1951 he scored his hundreth hundred at the Oval, against Surrey. On the opening day Surrey were all out for 156, and by close of play Hutton had scored 61 not out. The following Monday, a crowd of 15,000 turned out to see him reach the precious milestone. The members rose to their feet as, with a 'majestic and characteristic cover drive,' wrote Alex Bannister in the *Daily Mail*, 'the ex-cabinet maker from Pudsey became the thirteenth to hit a hundred hundreds.' It was Hutton's seventh century at the Oval. Yorkshire declared 275 runs ahead, but dropped too many catches in Surrey's second innings. The Surrey tail wagged crucially, Alec Bedser scoring 27 not out and Lock 23, and Yorkshire were left needing 43 in twenty minutes. 'Mad singles were attempted and the batsmen ran to the wicket. Hutton and Lowson hit 11 through the well-spread field in five minutes. Then Bedser struck. Hutton was caught by Constable off a skier, and the next ball Lowson biffed straight to Lock in the deep. Yardley only just saved the hat-trick. Wait's first ball of the fourth over had Yardley caught by Fishlock, which meant that three wickets had tumbled in four deliveries' (Alex Bannister). The frenetic and most uncharacteristic Yorkshire procession to and from the pavilion continued. Keighley and Watson were run out, and Wardle was bowled by Wait with a full toss. That was the end of the circus, and the match finished in a draw.

The 1950s are the years of Stuart Surridge at the Oval, and of unbroken success in the Championship for Surrey. For me it was bliss. Surrey won match after match after match. Reading the papers then, reading old *Wisdens* now, is like reading some fantasy adventure by Tolkien or C.S. Lewis. Surrey seldom faced any difficulties, but, if they did, Surridge (or was it Gandalf?) would conjure up some deep magic and put Yorkshire or Gollamganshire, or some other Force of Darkness, to flight. They won the Championship outright in 1952, the first time since 1914, and their opening county game in May 1953 was a sensation. Warwickshire were beaten in a single day – the first time the Oval had seen so swift an end to a match since 1857. The following year, in August, Worcestershire were beaten by an innings although Surrey declared their first innings closed at 92 for 3. The Surrey team were themselves amazed. They had bowled Worcestershire out for 25 (Lock 5.3–4–2–5) and were settling in on an admittedly tricky pitch. May and Barrington were well set, and most of the Surrey team were looking forward to the rest of the day in the pavilion. Surridge's declaration took all by surprise, but he had phoned the Meteorological Office and had been told that it was going to rain the next day. If Surrey were to win, they had better do so quickly. Two Worcester wickets fell that night, and the rest tumbled helter-skelter in the morning (Laker 17–9–25–4, Bedser 6–3–7–3, Lock 10–7–3–1).

Not all the members were as ecstatic as I was. There were mutterings about falling revenue if Surridge was going to turn three-day matches into one or two-day massacres. There were suggestions that this was not the way to play cricket. Several members were also furious at the way Surridge bellowed at them when they moved behind the bowler's arm, his call to sit down being even more insistent than their call of nature. There were also accusations, from outside the county, that the Oval wicket was being, in some way, specially prepared for Surrey's bowlers. The obvious retort was, if that were so, the wicket would be similarly helpful to seam or spin on the other side. But there was always the knowledge that few bowlers in the country could exploit conditions as Lock, Laker, Bedser, and, later, Loader could. The accusation was much repeated – you still hear of it today. A more probable explanation for Surrey's success is the outstanding commitment to fielding that Surridge inspired. Simply to take the Warwick and Worcester games as examples, of the thirty nine wickets captured by Surrey in those two matches, two were bowled, three were lbw, and one was hit wicket. The rest were all down to the fielders, two run outs and thirty one catches. Under Surridge, fielding became a weapon, an instrument of aggression towards opposing batsmen. It had all been very different at the Oval in 1900, when Digby Loder Armroid Jephson, the Surrey captain, wrote an article on 'Fielding in the Golden Age':

> Taken as a whole the fielding has been bad, thoroughly bad. Men stand in
> the field today like so many 'little mounds of earth', or waxen figures in a

third-rate tailor's shop. The energy, the life, the ever-watchfulness of ten years ago is gone, and in their place are lethargy, laziness and a wonderful yearning for rest. Today a ball is driven through two so-called fieldsmen, and instead of a simultaneous rush to gather it, to hurl it to one end or the other, the two 'little mounds of earth' stand facing each other with a lingering hope in their eyes that they will not be compelled to fetch it.

At the time, the President of the Club, Lord Alverstone, had a different view. 'I defy anybody,' he wrote, 'particularly a first-class field, to keep fit for fielding for four or five months without intermission.' He thought there was too much first eleven cricket. He also thought some catches in the deep were impossible to hold – 'the amount of curl and twist on the ball is such as to defeat the finest field in the world.' He did add, however: ' . . . but a great many catches which ought to be held are lost through sheer carelessness and want of practice . . . You have only to watch the Australian XI in the field to see the justice of these observations . . .'

Surridge proved in the 1950s that it was possible to keep fit for fielding for the whole season. Catches were taken daily which would have astounded and delighted Alf Gover, off whom more catches were dropped than any other bowler at the Oval.

In 1953, the Australians toured Britain for the first time since Bradman's team in 1948. The Ashes had been in Australian hands for twenty years, and England had not won a home Test against Australia since the Oval Test in 1938. The two sides came to the Oval in August after four evenly matched draws on the other Test grounds. With all to play for, a queue began to form outside the ground at lunchtime on the day before the Test. By 2 am on the opening day, over 2000 people had joined the queue, with airbeds, camp-beds and sleeping bags. Some sat all night under the street lamps, reading. Visiting pie and ice cream sellers did a brisk trade. When play began on Saturday 15th August, the ground was full, with over 25,000 people present. By lunch Australia had reached 2 for 98, but during the interval a light rain fell and the pitch woke up. Bedser and Trueman took five more wickets for the addition of only 62 runs, and Australia were 7 for 160. When Bedser caught and bowled Archer, he broke Maurice Tate's record of 38 wickets in an England-Australia series. It was Bedser's last wicket in a Test at the Oval.

Lindwall then played a hard-hitting and stylish innings, and, helped by dropped catches (an unusual sight at the Oval those days), Australia were eventually all out for 275. Cardus was not impressed: 'The play on the whole was commonplace, excepting the gusto of young Trueman, with his sturdy, coltish action, and the liveliness of Evans, who, in coping with Trueman behind the stumps was occasionally obliged to emulate in turn a man on a flying trapeze, an outnumbered goalkeeper, and a fish temporarily flipping about out of water . . . Trueman, attacking from the pavilion end, ran a long, square-

17th August 1953. The Ashes Test, second day's play. England are fighting for first innings lead.
© *Hulton-Deutsch Collection*

shouldered, tight-bottomed course to the wicket with a fast bowler's proper show of hostility . . .'

In rapidly deteriorating light, Miller and Lindwall had time for only one over each. Five years earlier, Lindwall had run through England and he now bowled flat out, a brief object lesson in hostility. 'One ball whizzed like the comet that announces deaths of princes. It streaked upward to a bat held in self defence, and, glancing from it, knocked Hutton's cap from his head and the cap nearly fell on the stumps. Had it done so, Hutton would have been out, and the Oval would have heard again, coming from somewhere not of this world, the devilish laughter heard in Kennington Oval seventy-one years ago, when Peate was bowled trying to drive Boyle and Australia won by seven runs.' Hutton was doubly lucky. The ball that knocked his cap off almost carried to ten hands itching in the slips.

As the Test progressed, it was accorded more and more space on the front pages of the daily papers. The second day's play consisted of dogged resistance by England, reaching 7 for 235 when stumps were drawn, with the game evenly poised. That night, as light rain fell, most of the Australian team went to Her Majesty's Theatre, Haymarket, to see Bobby and Sally Ann Howes in *Paint Your Wagon*. Lindsay Hassett had already seen the show, and, with weightier matters on his mind, did not go with his team. In the morning, the weightier matter of the heavy roller left the pitch easy paced. Both sides struggled for first innings' lead. England's eighth wicket fell at 237, the ninth at 262, with Australia still thirteen runs ahead. Bailey and Bedser fought for every run, and when they finally overtook Australia it was through an unlikely mistake. Bedser lofted the ball over mid-off and Miller assumed it would reach the boundary. It didn't, but the batsmen ran four. Bailey was out just before lunch, having made 64 in three and three-quarter hours. Bedser was not out 22 and the two had put on 44 for the last wicket.

Hassett ordered the heavy roller and the pitch became useful for spinners 'especially of the left arm variety'. Hutton took Trueman off after two overs, and used Lock and Laker on their home ground. An Australian vulnerability against the turning ball was revealed – a sweet foretaste for England of what was to come at Old Trafford three years later. Only Davidson and Archer were able to offer much resistance in a short, aggressive stand. England were left with 132 to win, and the crowd hailed Hutton and Edrich jubilantly to the wicket. Lindwall attacked furiously and almost had Edrich caught in the slips in his first over, but the problem for Australia was that they did not have the bowlers suitable to the pitch. The one Australian present who might have been able to exploit conditions, Bill O'Reilly, was safely occupied with a typewriter in the press-box.

Hutton was run out, having made 17 out of 24. We were staying with my grandfather in Worthing that August, and so we were able to see the drama unfold on his television set. His disgust at Hutton's dismissal was explosive and I suppose I realized for the first time just how important was the fate of the

Ashes. Until then I had cared little for England's cricket success, Surrey was the team that mattered. Now, on a summer holiday where every break in the rain meant a chance to play cricket, on the beach, against the garage doors, in the back garden, we gazed ceaselessly at the black and white television screen as the run stealers literally flickered to and fro.

On the morning of the final day's play, England needed only 94 to win and had nine wickets in hand. Cardus suggested that 'we may surely lay out the red carpet and get the bellringers ready without tempting providence.' That was not how my grandfather felt. Perhaps it was as well that he read *The Times*. But England did win. May was caught by Davidson off Miller with the score at 88, but Edrich and Compton saw us home. And whatever paper you read, there it was on the front page next day. 'WE SAW A MIGHTY VICTORY,' yelled Peter Wilson in the *Daily Mirror*, 'By the beard of W.G. Grace, we've done it!' Cardus recorded how the victory was 'vociferously celebrated'. The crowd, as ever, ran over the field and congealed in a mass in front of the pavilion. 'The heroes were severally hailed, in vocally resonant, if not musical, numbers.' Television brought it all to us, there in Worthing. At the end, Hassett and Morris bowled, with only eight runs wanted for victory. Hassett almost bowled Edrich, and Davidson dived full length to save a boundary when England were only four runs short. My grandfather, glass in hand, snorted with rage, worry and doubt. For him, nothing was certain in cricket. Besides, he had been a Surrey member since the days of Tom Richardson, and it irked him that it was the Middlesex twins who brought England victory when Compton 'pulled' (*Manchester Guardian*) or 'swept' (*Daily Mirror*) Morris for four.

19th August 1953. Crowds invade the ground after England regain the Ashes. © *Hulton-Deutsch Collection*

To my grandfather's great relief, Surrey won the Championship in 1954 and 1955, and in 1956, they not only won the Championship but also beat the Australians, the first county to do so for forty four years. Perhaps not enough significance is attached to Constable's century in paving the way for Surrey's victory, but the outstanding feature of the match was Laker's performance in the Australians' first innings when he took all ten wickets. No English player had accomplished this since 1878, when Barratt had taken all ten wickets for the Players. The scant coverage he had received in the press for this contrasts remarkably with that given to Laker, who shared the front page of the *Daily Mail* with such other items as 'Hanging Back By 4 Votes', and 'Princess Margaret – The Queen Denies Betrothal Report' (who now remembers Prince Christian of Hanover?). Alex Bannister's headline was 'After All Night Vigil with Baby, All Ten Laker Shocks Aussies'. The article described how Laker had asked to come off after he had taken four wickets. 'At tea, he asked Stuart Surridge, Surrey's captain, "Give me a rest – I am tired." Surridge replied, "Not yet, Jim, there are more wickets for you yet, and I'm not going to take you off."' The account of this exchange may well be a paraphrase, but the deed was real and exact. Laker bowled for over four hours, and took 10 for 88. The members

1956, the *annus mirabilis* for Jim Laker, was also a very wet season. Surridge described Laker's bowling as having 'flight, control, variety, intelligence, venom . . . the lot!'
© *Central Press Photos Ltd.*

cheered, and Laker, modestly as ever, acknowledged the applause. 'When I had taken nine wickets,' he said, 'I would willingly have come off, but the thrill of taking ten wickets against the Australians in my benefit year is something I shall never forget.' Did he, did the Australians, have it in mind at Old Trafford later that season?

There are so many departures from the cricket field, so many final farewells to the top class game, that there isn't time to say 'goodbye' to everyone. Many leave almost unnoticed. In August 1960, Alex Bedser played his last game for Surrey, against Glamorgan. The papers had noted his performance in the first innings, when he took 5 for 27 and, with Gibson, dismissed Glamorgan for 101: 'fine seam bowling by A.V. Bedser'. That was all. The next day, Bedser departed, and there were almost more people playing than watching. 'A quiet farewell without trumpets sounding,' wrote Bedser, 'during an ordinary match in front of a few spectators. Just, in fact, how I would have wanted it, for I am sure I would have been too choked inside to have endured a sentimental send-off on a big occasion.' Perhaps he remembered what had happened to Bradman on the same ground in 1948.

The heroes of my childhood all departed from the Oval: Fishlock, whom I worshipped as a batsman and fielder, wishing that I was left-handed so that I could better seek to copy him; Tom Clark; Geoff Whittaker, who once drove the ball through the window of the Secretary's office; Arthur McIntyre, who, of course, I thought should have replaced Evans in the England team; and Jim Laker, whose every movement, gesture, facial expression I perfected. I walked back to my mark like Jim Laker, I glanced up at the school, as he did at the Oval pavilion, turned and gently ran in. And there any similarity ended. I had not a millionth part of his blistering skill, and my tripe bowling was rightly and richly plastered over the entire county of Surrey.

Even the deeds of the heroes went scarcely noticed as the years pattered by. In 1977, when John Edrich reached his hundredth hundred in the match against

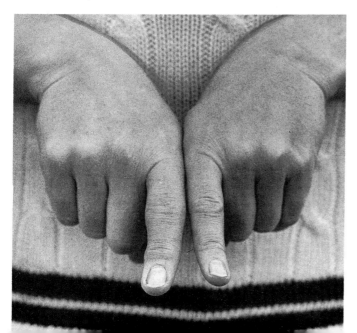

The physical cost of off-break bowling. Laker's right index finger is almost twice as thick as his left. *From the Oval Collection*

Derbyshire at the Oval, a few lines in a few papers sufficed to acknowledge this achievement, and a precious few were there to witness it. The occasion contained elements of the ridiculous. At the end of what was scheduled to be the last over of the match, Edrich was 97 not out. The Derbyshire team turned to leave the field, but sportingly turned back and another over was bowled. The crowd, we learn, cheered Derbyshire 'royally', and Edrich duly completed his century of centuries, the seventeenth player to do so in the history of cricket. But the cheers must have lacked substance, for there were not present the thousands who saw Hayward achieve the same wonderful feat decades earlier. Instead, for Edrich, a light sprinkling of spectators huddled towards the pavilion, and the Vauxhall end was still and empty.

It's a mistake to think that even in the long ago days before mass-produced cars and television, however, the Oval was always crowded. It needed more than Jack Hobbs to bring in theo shining stars were present. Thousands still come to the Oval, less for three-day fixtures than for Cup games, and the biggest crowds of all come for the Test Matches, when the ground is once again full, spectacularly and exuberantly so when the West Indies or the Australians are playing.

A full house saw Trueman take his 300th Test wicket in August 1964. Dexter brought him back on to bowl eight minutes before lunch, when Australia were

26th August 1963. A great West Indian victory. © *The Central Press Photos Ltd.*

190 runs on in the first innings with four wickets left. At that point Trueman had taken 0 for 80, but he now had the share of luck that every record breaker needs. He drew Redpath forward and bowled him, middle stump. His next ball whipped fast outside the off stump, McKenzie fished at it and was caught by Cowdrey at first slip. Lunch intervened. Hawke may well not have eaten a hearty luncheon, but he did prevent the hat-trick. Half an hour later, Hawke fell for the same outswinger that had accounted for McKenzie, and that was Trueman's 300th Test Match wicket. 'Only Trueman,' wrote Denys Rowbotham, 'has taken, and perhaps ever will take, over 300 Test wickets . . .' The record, he thought, was 'beyond challenge'. But new records keep coming, and we lose sight of the first person singular who achieves the staggering. Twenty years later, it was Botham's turn. Matthew Engel in *The Guardian* described how Tavare caught Dujon in the slips and Botham became the fifth bowler to take 300 wickets in Test cricket. Engel ended his report with a note about developments at the Oval: 'The new Executive Boxes, built over the grave of the old Press Box look sumptuous; the new Press Box is unspeakable.'

England v New Zealand 1986. Jeff Crowe is lbw. Ian Botham's 356th Test wicket breaks Lillee's record. He looks quite pleased.
© *Patrick Eagar*

Each year the Test came to the Oval, and most 'years there was something wonderful to see. Graveney's century against the West Indies in 1966, the partnership between Asif Iqbal and Intikhab Alam for Pakistan in 1967, Underwood's 7 for 50 against Australia on a wickedly turning pitch in 1968, when it looked as though a thunderstorm had saved Australia on the last afternoon, but then the sun came out and 5 wickets fell in 35 minutes. 'In many ways,' wrote John Woodcock in *The Cricketer*, 'this last match was a fine one . . . it brought the crowds pouring from the Oval Underground Station, as in days not long ago. Twice the gates had to be closed, and often the players were taken cool drinks on the field, and the Australians made some money . . .'

27th August 1968. After the storm: Cowdrey not yet expecting a miracle. © *Hulton-Deutsch Collection*

The following year, Underwood reaped another fine harvest at the Oval – 12 for 101 against New Zealand. India's first ever victory in a Test in England came in 1971, centuries by the Chappell brothers in 1972, Keith Fletcher's slowest ever first-class century in England in 1974. And still the crowds kept coming, to be rewarded when England played the West Indies in August 1976.

'Those who hear the beat of the drum at Lords and the Oval,' wrote Michael Manley, 'and look across to the "bleachers" – the uncovered, cheap seats – at the gaily coloured shirts and the black, brown and cream faces of the migrants, are observing a new ingredient in English cricket. A witness to the scene does not dissect the throng into its components of Antiguans, Trinidadians, Guyanese, Jamaicans or St Lucians. They do not even distinguish the rhythms that are more reggae than calypso or more mento than both, or sometimes almost purely reversions to African roots. What they see is a largely ethnic army of fans involving people of African, Indian, European, Chinese and other types of origin in a great common experience in which all share, about which all exult, and which in turn can cast all into gloom.'

The West Indies came to the Oval in 1976 having already won the series. It was Harry Brind's first season as groundsman there, and he had inherited a square that had passed the point of burial and needed exhuming. Moreover, it was a hot, dry summer such as few remembered in Britain. In *The Times*, John Woodcock reported that 'even Holding and Roberts found the pitch too slow to think of testing Amiss with the short stuff that unsettles him.' The gates were closed on the first and second days, and the baking crowds saw Richards at his majestic best. Alan Knott broke Godfrey Evans's record for the number of wicket-keeping dismissals in Tests, and only he and Amiss were spared from bowling at Fredericks, Richards, Lloyd, Rowe and King. The West Indies scored 687 for 8 declared at more than a run a minute. 'Weekes, Worrell and Walcott never played any better than Richards,' wrote John Woodcock, 'to say that they played as well at their best, is praise enough. Worrell was more elegant, Walcott more powerful, Weekes was the most like Richards of the three, though I doubt that he hit the ball as hard.'

After the third day, Woodcock described it as 'one of the world's deadest pitches.' Amiss thrived on it, and made 203 out of England's 435. Holding swept in from the pavilion end and took 8 for 92, the first bowler to take eight wickets in an innings in a Test at the Oval since S.F. Barnes in 1912. Even so, it was expected that England would reach a draw with honour. The West Indies did not enforce the follow-on, Fredericks and Greenidge cracked another 182 runs, in only 32 overs, without being parted, and at close of play on the penultimate day, England were 43 without loss. They needed another 392 to win: they had but to bat out the day on a pitch where only 18 wickets had fallen in four days.

In just over an hour's play at the start of the last day, England were crippled at 78 for 5 wickets, four of them to Holding. 'Not often can one be so sure of having been in the presence of a great piece of bowling,' wrote Woodcock. On that morning, Holding walked back past his mark, pacing towards the pavilion, and turned to come in off his long run 'like a gazelle'. His run up was smooth and fast, so light, according to Arlott, 'that umpires often looked round to make sure he was coming up to bowl'; so soft, according to Matthew Engel, that he would have left no footprints in snow. In all he took 14 wickets for 149, while Andy Roberts, at the other end, had to be content with 1 for 139. For England, Willis took 1 for 121 and Selvey 1 for 111. Holding, alone, clean bowled nine victims, and trapped three lbw. It was the first time any bowler had taken 14 wickets in a Test match at the Oval since Spofforth in 1884.

Woodcock concluded his report in *The Times:* 'A word finally for the Oval groundsman. Hindered by a heatwave, he produced a pitch that gave West Indies the opportunity to display some wonderful cricket, and rewarded great batting and great fast bowling. It might have done the same for the highest class of spin had the chance arisen. Mediocrity, whether in the field or with the bat was exposed, much the better side won, medium pace was put firmly in its place, there was scarcely a dull moment. For my money, Mr Harry Brind can take a bow.'

England v India 1979. Venkat is run out for 6, and a great Indian effort fails by 9 runs.
© *Patrick Eagar*

The list goes on and on. Sunil Gavaskar's highest ever innings by an Indian against England in 1979, Botham's 200th Test wicket against Australia in 1981 and his whirlwind 208 against India the following year. Holding's return to his long run, two thirds of the way back to the pavilion, in 1984, and suddenly Broad, Gower and Lamb were swept aside. And it is not always the massive innings or the haul of wickets that stays in the mind of those present. There are beautiful and breathtaking pieces of fielding, a couple of snortingly hostile overs, or a single ball where flight condones spin, and the Devil and the craftsman laugh together. For Ronald Mason, when Botham bludgeoned the New Zealand attack for forty or so runs at the Oval in 1987, it provided 'the only experience of my old age which can balance the exhilaration of my youth.'

Exhilaration is a rare experience, but it has been there for the taking, at the Oval, for nearly a hundred and fifty years now.

Chapter Sixteen

Sweat and Dust and Velvet Grass

In the past 100 years, there have been a score of Prime Ministers of Great Britain, over fifty captains of the England cricket team, and six Head Grounds-men at the Oval. This last is a remarkably low number and will not be increased for years yet, not until the day when Harry Brind, the present incumbent, decides it's time to retire.

To be Head Groundsman at the Oval, would seem, therefore, to be a job that gives satisfaction, though it has never been an easy life. In an article written at the turn of the century, the Reverend T. O. Reay described ground conditions at the Oval fifty years earlier, in the early days of its history. A small pavilion had been built in 1858, but tents were still pitched for the players in the south east corner of the ground. Reay recalled that the wickets ran east-west, though others have disagreed with this view. It seems unlikely that Reay would have been mistaken, as he is very specific about the sun shining straight into the batsman's eyes towards the end of the day. What he describes in more detail is the work of the groundsmen. Sometimes mowers were brought in at four or five in the morning, to scythe the grass while the dew was still on it, but, generally, 'no attempt was made to cut the grass in the long field. Sheep kept it fairly fed down, but thistles and weeds were plentiful . . . The sheep were usually penned up in a corner during the match until play ceased for the day, and then made straight for the tender grass between the wickets . . .' These were the days when there were no boundary boards, no boundary ropes, no boundaries. Everything had to be run for, unless the ball was hit among the ropes of a tent, in which case the batsman was awarded 3 runs.

George Brockwell, one of the two professional bowlers first engaged by the club in 1845, was also one of its first groundsmen. He was a strong man, with an unusual bowling action. As he delivered the ball, he would strike himself, Tarzan like, on the chest with his free hand. As the day wore on, a dark patch would often appear on his shirt front, a mixture of sweat and dust. In 1876, W.H. Gardner was the Groundsman. There is a note in the records of the Surrey Club, that he was to be given two guineas 'for the care he had taken'. Gardner was succeeded by George Street, who had his difficulties with the Committee and who came near to dismissal. Street resigned in 1880 and was in turn

27th August 1968. England v Australia. Dexter and Cowdrey are batting. Connolly is bowling. Dexter will shortly be bowled by Connolly. And a freak storm is not far away . . . © *Central Press Photos Ltd.*

succeeded by John Newton. Newton was probably the first groundsman faced with the task of having to dig up and relay the centre at the Oval. Wickets die eventually, and fail to respond to superficial attention and first aid. Newton was much respected as a groundsman. He came to the Oval from Essex with an excellent reputation, but lasted only a few years in office. His successor, Over, stayed for a couple of seasons, but, in 1887, the Committee were again looking for a new man.

To many, the founding father of the Oval as a Test ground and a square never bettered in the land, was Sam Apted. Apted presided over the Oval during the most important period of its formative years – while the county game was being permanently established with a full programme of fixtures; when Test cricket was introduced; when the basic techniques of modern batting and bowling were pioneered; and when the Oval, with its new pavilion, developed into a ground with accommodation and facilities for very large crowds.

Apted loved the Oval, and he knew it inside out. He was said to have had a different name for each blade of grass. He was a fine, upstanding man – a model late Victorian. In the giant oil painting of the Surrey Club and members, 1911, that hangs in the Long Room, Apted is standing on the well shorn outfield just

in front of the pavilion. In his panama hat and with his white beard, there is a continental, *fin de siècle* air about him. He could be mistaken for an Impressionist painter, or a colleague of Debussy or Chabrier. But, though he dealt in paint, it was for facade and pillar, wall and ceiling, not for paper or canvas. For, as Groundsman, he had to look after the entire Oval complex, not merely the playing area. It was all his to tend, to preserve, to improve.

Those were the days of the gentlemen, of their lordships, and, though the Oval was his, Apted was suitably respectful in his correspondence with the Committee and Secretary Alcock:

26 June 1893

Mr Alcock,
Sir,
I find there is 17,200 square yards in the football ground that will require relevelling and turfing, taking 51,600 of turf and 2,600 of loam. I estimate it will take three to four months to do the work.
Probable cost
    Turf   £325 0 0

Loam	£650 0 0
Labour	£300 0 0
	£1275 0 0

Of course, this is only rough, but I do not anticipate much difference. I should say turf, good, 12s per 100, loam per load 6s delivered on Oval.

Yours respectfully,

S. Apted

The following month, George Hearne, from the cricket ground at Catford Bridge, walked the area with Apted, and they agreed they could make do with 5000 fewer turves, since some of the old football ground could be saved. It was up to Apted and the Committee to find a suitable source of turf. They inspected a field at Mottingham in Kent, but the owner refused to allow turf to be cut once he knew it was for the Surrey Club. Walthamstow, in Essex, proved less chauvinistic, but unreliable with regard to delivery. In December 1893, a representative from Messrs Jas. Carter and Co. attended the Oval and 'reported with regard to turf from the Hermitage Ground, Norbury', a source already inspected and approved by Apted and Alcock. Sam got his turf at last, but the minimum amount of time to lay it before Tom Richardson would come thundering over it once the 1894 season began.

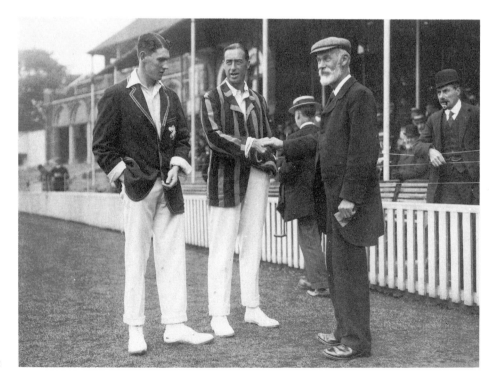

(From the left) M. C. Bird and J. R. Mason, respectively captains of Surrey and Kent, congratulating Sam Apted during his benefit match, August 1910. *From the Oval Collection*

A groundsman's work is never done. Grass grows too fast or not at all. Rain is unevenly distributed in our fickle climate. Football, lacrosse and hockey are no respecters of the good grass made available to them. Staff and equipment become old or poorly. In 1894, Apted had to buy a new large roller (for £8 5s 0d) and two more horses to pull it. Apted sent the Ground Committee a list of his needs and of the work to be done:

> Loam at 7 shillings 61 load remainder of 200
> New barrow for Martin 28/-
> Clothes for the boy
> Horse of I.M. Taylor £5
> Blinds for the pavilion (estimate £5.17.0)
> New rope for the playing staff
> Flags – repair if possible
> Hydrants to be overhauled
> Old hose and reel to be repaired
> 8 New lengths of hose and connections
> Old fence repairs
> New fence – Davenports – £29.10
> Broom and brushes
> Castles Seating Bolts and Co.
> Gravel – about 4 yards
> 15 old seats repaired £3
> Electric board
> Gulley traps – Davenports contract
> Basin and taps in Bowlers Room
>   Everything to be branded with SCCC

The Committee made sure Apted had all this. He would have been a brave and foolish soul who told Apted how to do his job. And they listened to his grumbles and his grievances, deciding, in the autumn of 1894, that football should not be played after the following 18th March, and that the football ground should be fenced off from the cricket ground.

With each new season came a new list of requests. Apted wrote again to Alcock on 29th March 1895:

> To C.W. Alcock, Esq.
>
> Sir,
> The following is a list of what is necessary
> 1 Horse for large Roller
> 1 Horse for Mowing Machines
> 20 bushels Carters Grass Seed
> 1/2 ton Carters Manure
> 6 New Wing Nets

5 New Back Nets
6 Old Wing Nets want repairing
5 Old Back Nets want Replacing
Horse Feed
Turfing banks
Sun Blinds
Patent Score Board
Boys
Boys Uniforms
Austen Martin's wages 25/-

In November 1896, Apted reported on the state of the playing area to the Ground Committee:

> 'If given fine weather today and tomorrow I shall get all the returfing finished. I have had 14,600: my estimate was 15,000. I came out very close indeed to this. There may be a few places to do in the spring that do not show at present. Only be a matter of two or three hundred. On the whole the Turf is doing well, very free indeed from weeds. The frequent rain made it very bad cutting . . . The state of the ground at this time of year (all over) is very satisfactory, the grass has made good bottom growth which is very important.'

He is proud of his accurate assessment of the number of turfs needed – 'I came out very close indeed to this'. The letter is that of a man who knows what he is doing, and the Surrey Club recognised that they had an outstanding Groundsman. In the autumn of 1896, he was voted an extra grant of 15 guineas. In 1899, his wages were increased to £200 p.a.

The century came to an end, Victoria died, Lord Salisbury lost an election, Bobby Abel and Tom Richardson retired, Apted continued in charge at the Oval. He patrolled his territory, noting what needed to be done, where his beloved Oval was being abused. On 30th April 1901, he wrote to the Committee complaining of the condition of the passage behind the pavilion after smoking concerts in the Tavern. It was this attention to detail that made him respected, trusted and appreciated, and prompted the Surrey Committee to take an unprecedented step in 1910. 'Tomorrow and the following days the profits from the Kent and Surrey match will be given to the benefit fund of Sam Apted, the most famous of all groundsmen. The memorial of Apted's skill (or shall we say genius?) in his craft is the condition of the Oval today. Apted came into the heritage of a great post 23 years ago; he has been a great steward. If there was room for improvement, he has improved; if there was not then his unswerving loyalty to the Surrey Committee is shewn in the continued splendour of the Oval turf. When Apted came to the Oval the Surrey County Cricket Club was approaching perhaps the zenith of its fortunes. Its greatest achievements were accomplished on wickets prepared by Apted.'

When war broke out in 1914, although Apted had by then retired, *Sporting Life* thought of him as the War Office requisitioned the Oval:

> One Samuel Apted, I fancy, must have suffered a very real shock when he heard of the plan which broke cricket off with a jerk on the Surrey ground – the first open space to be selected by the War Office of all London's many open spaces. For he reverenced that stretch of velvet grass which under his care came to produce the best wickets in England. 'Were Apted grounds-man still,' someone said, half seriously, half playfully, when the news was heard that necessity was to bring a regiment to the Oval, 'he would have stood at the gate and declared that the soldiers should only take possession over his dead body.'

It was perhaps lucky for the military that Apted had retired – the *'ils ne passeront pas'* notion is not too fanciful – but in 1911, Apted had made way for Austen Martin, the boy whose wages had been 25 shillings a week in 1895. It cannot have been easy following the great Sam, and coping with the depredations of the war, and Martin must at some point have got on the wrong side of the Committee. In 1924, the Committee ruled that he was to go at the end of the season, and that his wages were to be paid up to 18th October 'subject to good behaviour on his part'.

Austen was succeeded by his brother, T.W. 'Bosser' Martin, who stayed until the middle of the next war, having started at the Oval as a 16 year old in 1889. Bosser was another great groundsman, 'a specialist,' wrote Louis Palgrave, 'who was always being called here, there and everywhere to put things right that had been going wrong.' The proudest moment of his life, said Bosser, was when the MCC asked him to go to Lords to see if he could rid Headquarters of the 'leather-jackets' that were turning their ground into a wasteland.

Bosser was a firm believer in the 'prepared' or, to some, artificial wicket, which he called 'a first-class wicket for first-class cricketers'. He was adamant that a natural wicket, given modern bowlers, of whom he had a low opinion, would mean half the batsmen in the land would be knocked out or maimed before the season had been in progress very long. He claimed that liquid dope was used on wickets as early as the 1890s, by one of his brothers at Southampton, and that the great Sam himself experimented with 'dope' at the Oval in 1898. He was proud of the fact that in one season Surrey never once failed to pass the 300 mark in an innings at the Oval – they made 600 twice, 500 three times, 400 four times and 300 four times.

While Bosser was in charge at the Oval, the ground gained its reputation as a bowler's graveyard. Batsmen from all over the country looked forward to coming to Kennington, seeking great improvement in their averages. In his autobiography, Wally Hammond referred to Bosser's 'perfect turf', though the Oval was not one of his most successful grounds – he made only nine centuries there.

Over the years the Oval became too perfect, too easy, too dead. It took all

Percy Fender's ingenuity to conjure results there in the 1920s and 1930s –
constantly switching his bowlers, mixing his own bowling, and forcing some
kind of point into games with a series of provocative declarations. It was hard
work, and few Surrey bowlers had sufficient success to become famous. Draw
after draw was mechanically materialised at the Oval – 15 in 1926, 15 in 1927,
20 in 1928, 20 in 1930, 17 in 1931, 16 in 1932, in Championship games alone.
The 1938 Test was final proof that something needed to be done, and, had the
war not intervened, Martin might have taken more drastic action.

A square does not last forever. After twenty years of filling and dressing and
rolling, the top becomes compacted and lifeless, and the hard table below,
which brings life, pace and bounce to the wicket, ceases to be accessible. When
Bert Lock succeeded Martin in 1943, he made plans for remedial surgery as
soon as the war ended. From 1946 onwards, Lock worked on the square,
experimenting with two approaches – digging down and replacing the subsoil,
or grafting a new top. Eventually, the Oval had an entirely new square, and
pitches that produced results. But it was Bert Lock's misfortune to be groundsman at the Oval at a time when Surrey did almost too well. Lay opinion in pubs
and railway carriages throughout the rest of the land, and in some Quisling
clubs in Surrey itself, believed that the amazing analyses of Loader, Bedser,
Laker and Lock owed more than a little to the preparation of wickets that
would suit them. How this was done, nobody would explain, and, as a mere
schoolboy member, I certainly wasn't party to any such conspiracy. At least the
drawn game became a thing almost unknown. In their whole fixture list, Surrey
played only 5 draws in 1952, 7 in 1956, and none in 1955.

I remember watching Bert Lock at work during those years. The umpires
would remove the bails for lunch or tea or between innings, and Bert and his
staff would bustle out, moving to the strip with besom and roller, brush and
whitewash. I saw no special phials of elixir (Essence of Off-Break, Syrup of Leg
Cutter, Eau de Vie de Topspin) poured on the pitch, no heels dug in on a length.
I munched my tomato sandwiches and saw nothing untoward – and in those
days my eyes never left was was happening in the middle.

Sadly, Lock's health deteriorated in the 1960s, and by 1965 he could work
only a few hours a day. He accepted the Committee's suggestion that he retire at
the end of the season, and his place was taken by Ted Warn, who had worked as
Lock's assistant for many years and was a long serving member of the Oval staff.

Warn's occupation of crease, pitch, outfield, terraces, stands, buildings and
hereditaments as Head Groundsman at the Oval was comparatively brief, but he
accomplished much while he was in charge. For some time, people had
regarded the Oval square as being too far from the Vauxhall stand – it is nothing
like centre on a north-south divide of the ground. In 1973, Ted Warn and his
team began work on an attempt to move the square away from the pavilion. A
90 yard section of the middle was moved thirty yards back towards the Vauxhall
end. The scheme was never completed, however, and to those in the Vauxhall
stand, the square and the action are as remote as ever.

13th February 1970. Early precautions against Anti-Apartheid demonstrators. The Oval Test v South Africa was not due for another six months. Ultimately the entire tour was cancelled.
© *Hulton-Deutsch Collection*

Warn was a Londoner, but with very much a countryman's way of working. He kept old baths full of cow dung and horse manure behind the Vauxhall stand, the smells from which vied with those from the Marmite factory. He built a rockery and a rose garden by the perimeter wall, both of which fell into neglect after being given a bad time by vandals. Warn was regarded as a good teacher, and a man who knew the Oval as thoroughly as Apted had done. He knew where every drain and every pipe lay, he knew the grass and how it should be dressed and treated. He knew the scorebox – he had worked in it in the 1930s.

27th August 1968. Oval groundstaff heroically ensuring England (and Underwood) get a chance to bowl out Australia. Ted Warn's expert knowledge of how the Oval drained was invaluable.
© *Hulton-Deutsch Collection*

And he knew how the ground worked. During the 1968 Test against Australia, when the field had been flooded by a thunderstorm, Ted Warn assured Cowdrey that play would be possible in a couple of hours. The surface was baked hard, but, once the top had been spiked, the water ran quickly away. Without Ted Warn's assurance, the probability is that the match would have been called off, and Underwood and England would have missed a golden opportunity.

Warn retired in 1976, and his place was taken by the present Head Groundsman, Harry Brind. Like Newton back in the 1880s, Harry came from Essex, wanting a Test match ground. The square he came to was slow, with a low bounce that promised little for bowler or strokemaker. Once again, the layer upon layer of top soil, added year after year, match after match, to repair damage, was producing its fatal 'cushion' effect. So Harry Brind spent the next three years relaying the square. At first he experimented, digging out one pitch to the depth of a foot. Into this he put an eight inch foundation of Ongar clay, and on top of that four inches of a mixture of loams, two parts Essex to one part Surrey, for Surrey loam is heavy and makes grass growing difficult. Twenty tons of this mixture are still used every year at the Oval.

Prepared for rain, whichever direction it comes from, Harry Brind and the groundstaff in 1976. *From the Oval Collection*

For the experiment was a success. In 1978, five pitches were similarly relaid, and gradually Harry and his team moved across the entire centre. The result is a wicket which many reckon to be the best in the country, and recognition for the man who created it. Harry is Pitches Consultant for the Test and County Cricket Board, so that, at the drop of a hatful of seed, he may have to leave the Oval he loves every bit as much as Sam did, and visit any pitch in the country that the TCCB has doubts about. In such a position, there is considerable pressure on him to keep the Oval wicket at the highest possible level. *Quis custodiet . . .*

The Oval has a large square, 108 yards by 28 yards. It holds twenty first-class pitches and seven others for what Harry describes as 'smaller games'. At the beginning of the season, he plans where the pitch for each match will be sited. The Test Match pitch has pride of place. It is always the same – dead centre, smack in front of the pavilion – and it is used only for the Test. Every other pitch will have two first-class games played on it each season, including one-day games. Even the 'odds and sods' (commercial companies, industrial firms, the Brixton Police, etc.), who hire the Oval for a day are allowed a pitch on the square.

For Harry, looking after the Oval is 'a piece of cake'. At the end of a match, you simply flood down the wicket, repair the ends with a mixture of soil and grass seed, and generally tidy the battlefield. The outfield is checked. And, as fast as one pitch is exhausted, another is ready. On the morning of the first day of a match, while Oval regulars and 'three bobbers' (who are now 'five pounders') are clutching sandwiches and thermos (thermoi?) in bus, tube or train, on their way to the ground, Harry and the groundstaff remove the covers, cut and roll, and officially hand over responsibility for the pitch to the umpires. And, if it's a Test match, well, the pitch simply requires more rolling, so that it lasts longer. And the advertising boards that fringe the ground have to be checked continuously, to make sure no macs or T shirts are masking clients' names, or that no ardent fan is seeking to sit on the grass in front of them, as ardent fans were able to do in the days before television. And to make sure that the cushions, still hired from the British Cushion Company, are not being abused in any way. Otherwise, there are no problems. Fuserium, almost the last disease prevalent on sports grounds, is easily dealt with – it is all 'a piece of cake'.

Nevertheless, he is proud of the praise given his wickets in the umpires' post-match reports to the TCCB. He is proud that he is the first Groundsman to be elected to the Pitches Committee at Lords – another sign that HQ is pulling itself, a little late, into the 20th century – the sarcasm is mine, not Harry's. And he is proud of the whole blooming Oval.

By the end of the season, Harry has a list, as Sam did before him, of the many things that need to be done round the Oval. In late October, when the Australian Rules Football game has finished trampling all over the square, the outfield is scarified, and the ground is put to bed. Then the groundstaff start on Harry's list: painting, mending, greasing, tidying, checking, and leaving their summer schedule behind. For Steve and Andrew Howes, it may well come as a welcome relief from working the scoreboard on the east terraces. They have a reputation for speed and accuracy second to none: Michael Henderson, writing in *The Guardian* (14th June 1989), paid tribute to 'The Oval's superb score-board – far and away the best in the country. The Howes brothers are also

Harry Brind: The Oval is 'the best place in the world'. © *Patrick Eagar*

Lucy, the Oval cat, with New Zealand friend. © *Reg Lancaster, Daily Express*

probably the best judges of a run at the Oval. If Mike Gatting is batting there, and he hits the ball into the deep, it is said that he looks to the scoreboard to see how many they have anticipated he should get from the shot.'

The scorebox, inhabited by Steve and Andrew for four and a half months of the year is bigger inside than might be expected, but there is very much a feel of below decks in one of Nelson's 'wooden walls'. There are periods of calm and stillness, and then all is action, and the number plate for the 'overs bowled' is thrust out of one gun port, while the giant wheels whirl to register the new total and the batsman's score. They work in silence, never speaking to each other, but moving like synchronised swimmers, in parallel, to left and right, according to which batsman has scored. The moment a scoring shot is made, before the batsman has finished his follow through, they are up from their battered old chairs, and the scoreboard is again slightly ahead of the action. The giant wheels spin. The Howes brothers sit down again, but their gaze never leaves the field. They stare out, over extra cover or long leg, depending on which end is bowling, with concentration as deep as any of the players. Like all the members of the groundstaff, they are very unassuming about how good they are, dismissing any suggestion that they are efficient – it's simply 'the layout of the box', 'everything is to hand'.

The Oval scoreboard: the fastest in the land. © *Patrick Eagar*

For all this, the terraces, the stands, the chalet development, the workshop, the equipment, the pipes, drains, seed, soil, nets, markers, brushes, ropes, boards – everything – the budget is some £70,000, a large slice of which goes to pay gas, electricity, phone and water bills. There is a mountain of paper work, with which Sam Apted's pencil would have found it hard to cope. There are phone calls, visits, meetings, committees, requests from sports clubs and local schools, earnest seekers after information. Harry deals with them all. He is happy and so is his team: some of whom have spent their entire working life at the Oval, and some of whom say they 'worship' the place. Harry wouldn't go anywhere else now. The Oval, in his words, is 'marvellous', more than that – it is 'the best place in the world'. You look around his domain – at the Clayton Street urinals, and the dimly visible Vauxhall stand, and the concrete terraces,

22nd August 1934. A massive crowd invasion after Australia beat England by 562 runs. Note the litter in the background: perhaps standards have not declined. © *Central Press Photos Ltd.*

the 'unspeakable' Press-box, the 'nice' pavilion, the gas-holders, the LCC flats, the condition of the passage between the pavilion and the Tavern – and you think of the Taj Mahal, or Chartres Cathedral, or the Tsar's Winter Palace, or the Parthenon . . . and of course, he's right.

Chapter Seventeen

Foster Parenting

Since 1845, there have been several occasions when the survival of the Oval has seemed unlikely. As recently as 1971, the Oval came within £15,000 of financial disaster. An appeal to the members raised the necessary money, and those members who contributed may never know just how crucial their contribution was. Towards the end of the 1980s, the Oval faced another crisis. The appalling fire at the Bradford City Football Ground had alerted every sports club in the land to the potential dangers of old structures with wooden flooring, and that included the upper level of the West Stand at the Oval. In the words of the Surrey Committee, this was 'old and sub-standard'. It needed an enormous amount of money to make it acceptable to safety inspectors, and Surrey did not have such money. Something had to be done for the Oval to keep its status as a Test Match ground, and the 'Save The Oval Appeal' was launched in May 1988 with Sir Leonard Hutton as Patron.

The aim was to raise at least £1 million through the Appeal to add to the existing £4.8 million for the Ken Barrington Centre. This had been planned for some time as part of a west development, giving facilities for a wide range of indoor sports. When it is completed, the Ken Barrington Centre will have a Sports Hall, with provision for hockey pitches, cricket nets and other indoor team games, as well as changing and lecture rooms, coaching facilities, a shop, a refreshment area, treatment rooms for injuries sustained on the cricket ground and a viewing gallery with access by lift for the disabled.

A Test Match ground has to be maintained for 365 days a year, though it may only be used as such for half a dozen. Merely knocking down the old West Stand and building a new one would not bring in any substantial extra revenue, nor would it reduce running costs. What was required was a major new development that would do for the west side of the ground at least what had been done for the east side. A lot more money was needed. The Government was not in a helpful mood and Surrey did not have the political connections of Lord Dalmeny some eighty years earlier. For an ugly period, it seemed that the Oval might not be saved.

The Oval was rescued by Foster's with a major and unique sponsorship deal under a fifteen year agreement. This has safeguarded the ground for the foreseeable future and it may well have been as dramatic a turn around as the ground has seen. It is not the function of a history to evaluate the events it records, but the deal between Foster's and Surrey is one that does credit to both parties. Foster's financial investment is large and comes with few, if any, strings attached. At the same time, Surrey would not have been on the receiving end of such generosity if Foster's had not, in the words of Derek Newton, presumably 'liked the flavour of the Oval'.

The Foster's Oval. A new wall and a new façade, but the Hobbs gates remain. © *Patrick Eagar*

There are a few who shake their heads at the way in which these changes are taking place. The knight in shining armour isn't always loved by those he rescues. The Oval is now The Foster's Oval. To some, the chocolate of Surrey lacks lustre beside the gleaming blue and gold of Foster's. A tradition appears broken. There is, however, another tradition that has been maintained. Without the help of Foster's, top-class cricket would not have lasted at the Oval. For many, including those now shaking their heads, this would have been the ultimate cricketing tragedy, and this book would end by recording the demise of the Oval rather than celebrating its regeneration. As it is, Ian Greig, the present Surrey captain, stresses how much brighter the ground is, how much Foster's are doing for the Club and the players, how members and the general cricket-loving public will benefit. 'And,' he says, 'the chocolate will never disappear.'

Alec Bedser's straight drive: demolishing the old boundary wall. *From the Oval Collection*

What happens on the cricket field is the end product of a great and unseen process. The thirteen flannelled players, and the Lords of Appeal in white coats, are placed there by a host of committees, caterers, secretaries, bar and restaurant staff and stewards. A crucial dynamic is the relationship between administrators, groundstaff and players. Players usually receive due recognition, groundstaff occasionally, administrators seldom. The vast majority of us would rather watch batting and bowling than cutting and rolling, but even scattering grass-seed is a more exciting spectator sport than witnessing a committee at work. The Foster's Oval, however, has been the home of some of the greatest administrators in the history of cricket. A hundred years ago, Alcock and

Alverstone guarded and guided the Oval through a period of major development. Today it isn't the lack of historical perspective that makes it difficult to draw a modern parallel at another time of enormous growth. A visitor to the Foster's Oval will hear administrators praising marketing folk, players praising administrators, marketing folk praising players and administrators, almost everyone praising Foster's. The atmosphere isn't smug, but one of reciprocal respect. This is an exciting time for the Foster's Oval. When completed, the west development will extend from the pavilion as far as the site occupied by the old scorebox. The old West Stand has already gone. At the end of the 1988 season Alec Bedser took a sledgehammer to the seats from which I watched him run in to bowl hundreds of times during the 1950s, but it doesn't do to get sentimental over corrugated iron and old concrete. The old stand had to go. In its place there is, at present, a deep hole. Over this hovers a slim crane, higher than Bonner's mighty skier that G. F. Grace gratefully clutched in the first Test ever played in England. Eventually, there will be a six-floor stand, with new seating for a 1000 spectators, twenty hospitality suites, new changing rooms for both teams, an umpires' room, a workshop for Harry Brind's squad, and, hopefully to the delight of Matthew Engel, a new press-box.

The old Nets Bar in 1983, subsequently a victim of the West side development. *From the Oval Collection*

Some cricket grounds thrive on never changing. They are part of a pastoral England that many rightly wish to preserve. The Foster's Oval is not such a ground. There are no longer meadows in Kennington, or idle brooks, or leafy glades. The Foster's Oval is surrounded by traffic and houses and office blocks and shops and gas-holders, and hustle and bustle and noise and fumes. It has always had to come to terms with this, and these days it has to come to terms with new market forces. To attract crowds, the Foster's Oval has to be an attractive place. A 125 year lease has recently been signed with the Duchy of Cornwall. This affords Surrey the opportunity to take a deep breath and a long look at what may be possible. The excitement is all the greater because all these changes and more *must* take place.

There is talk of mammoth developments at the Vauxhall end, of a hotel overlooking the ground, of a car park beneath the playing area, of artificial turf, of pitches grown in greenhouses. Already Harry Brind is experimenting with a

Rebuilding, June 1989, and the west terraces are out of bounds. © *Patrick Eagar*

reinforced pitch that could be used for some matches in 1990. A carpet has been placed just below a section of the square, through which grass grows. This will save wear and tear, allowing more cricket per square yard. To some all this is disturbing. To others it is exciting. The likelihood is that the Foster's Oval will see more changes before the century is out. In the end, only the shingle on which the Foster's Oval dried, as the Thames narrowed and receded, will remain the same: that, and the fact that members still complain because a corned beef sandwich is more expensive at the Foster's Oval than, say, Grace Road.

Survival is as much a matter of enthusiasm and hard work as it is of money. Derek Newton, Chair of the Surrey Club for the last twelve years, regards the Head Groundsman as *primus inter pares*, with the team captain a close *secundus*. He is, however, most forceful in his appreciation of Bernie Coleman, whose entrepreneurial skills he considers have done more for cricket at both parochial and national levels than anyone else's over the last twenty years. As befits a Club that occupies the Foster's Oval, Surrey is conscious of a responsibility to the national side. The Chair, the Secretary (David Seward), the Chair of the Executive Committee (Raman Subba Row) and the Captain agree that Surrey's primary objective is not to win the Championship or other trophies, but to produce and support cricketers who will play for England. David Seward says that 'the cornerstone of our Club is English cricket, and the success of English cricket decides how far the ground is filled'. Derek Newton describes Surrey's aim as being to 'improve and enlarge the cake (English cricket) rather than take a larger slice of the existing one'.

Supporters of other counties may raise their eyebrows and upper lips, cynically suggesting that this is a noble way of explaining away Surrey's recent comparative lack of success. But success comes in many forms. The Foster's Oval has yet again produced the Groundsman of the Year; it is second only to Lords in the revenue it generates from Test matches, revenue that ultimately benefits every cricketing county; and it is still possible at the Foster's Oval, on any summer's day, to see local born and bred cricketers playing attractive cricket. The personalities at the Oval do not seek the limelight. Ian Greig will be happy if his captaincy brings on a team that eventually wins the Championship, even if he is no longer in charge.

The Foster's Oval won't be the same. It wasn't the same when sheep ceased to crop the grass, or when the Effra was driven underground, or the first pavilion built, or the terraces banked. It wasn't the same when the underarm lobs of Martingell gave way to Caffyn's round arm, or when Willsher raised his arm higher yet and took on John Lillywhite and the Laws of Marylebone. It wasn't the same when Sam Apted had finished with it, or Bosser Martin, or Bert Lock. It wasn't the same when they stopped printing 'up to date' scorecards on the ground, or when Eldorado ice creams disappeared. It wasn't the same when the military occupied it and left a 100 concrete posts sunk deep into the earth.

England v Australia,
1989, from a
balloon.
© *Patrick Eagar*

The personnel of the Foster's Oval crowd changes, though it forever preserves its personality. It is still knowledgeable – it knows when and why and how to applaud the right thing at the right time. There is still not a dilettante among it. It is still happy to abuse and curse those whom it regards as boring or unenterprising or unsporting.

Even memories change. Did I really see Laurie Fishlock hit fifty odd in twenty minutes against Worcestershire forty years ago? It was the start of the Surrey innings, and he went for the opening bowlers as though he had some awful grudge against them. One blow landed in the Harleyford Road. The 'three bobbers' faced a fusillade of hooks and pulls. Straight drives threatened the members. It was an awesome display. That's how the memory is now, but it may have altered across the years. Cricket lovers live on memories for seven months in every year, and some memories tend to get damaged by over-use. It doesn't matter. What matters is that something like that happened at the Foster's Oval, just as something like that happened forty years before that and forty years earlier still, yes, and even forty years before that. In 1932 Kingsley Amis saw Surrey beat Middlesex off the last ball of the match, when Jardine hit ten off the last three balls. In 1987 I saw Surrey beat Middlesex off the last ball of the match. Middlesex had declared, leaving Surrey 60 overs or so to score 344 runs. With two balls remaining, Surrey had two wickets left, and Martin Bicknell, batting at number 10, needed to hit 7 runs. He settled at the crease, looking slim and very young and rather pink in the face, as though embarrassed by the excitement around him. But he swung hard and straight, and the penultimate ball thumped, full toss, into the pavilion. One to win – one ball to come. Bicknell and Tony Gray, the other Surrey batsman, met in the middle, while Downton, who was the Middlesex skipper that day, waved his gloves in all directions and the fielders took up positions as though for the beginning of a ballet. Bicknell went back to his crease, and prepared himself for death, glory or anticlimax. Over came the bowler's arm, Bicknell lunged, Gray ran, Bicknell ran, the bowler ran, Downton ran, Surrey won. We stood. We cheered. That day, that moment, I forgave Middlesex for what Edrich and Compton had done to my heroes in 1947. It had been a beautifully judged declaration by Downton that had set up the finish, and Middlesex had themselves gone full out for victory.

The ground cleared. I didn't stay for a celebratory drink, as I was going through one of my pathetic attempts at total abstinence at the time. I clattered down the steps and out into the car park. At the side of the Tavern, I undid the padlock on my bicycle, and then slowly cycled out through the Hobbs Gates. Pedalling was easy until I reached the hills of Camberwell.

Sources

C.W. Alcock – FAMOUS CRICKETERS AND CRICKET GROUNDS – Hudson and Kearns: News of the World – 1895

J. Allen – HISTORY OF LAMBETH – J. Allen, 23 Prince's Road, Kennington 1826

Viscount Alverstone and C.W. Alcock – SURREY CRICKET: HISTORY OF THE ASSOCIATIONS – 1901

Frederic Boase – MODERN ENGLISH BIOGRAPHY – Frank Cass and Co 1965

Sir Neville Cardus – CARDUS ON CRICKET – Souvenir Press 1977

Sir Neville Cardus – FULL SCORE – Cassell and Co. 1970

Leslie Duckworth – S.F. BARNES. MASTER BOWLER – Hutchinson/The Cricketer 1967

Sir Robert Ensor – ENGLAND 1870–1914 – Oxford University Press 1936

David Frith – ARCHIE JACKSON – Pavilion Books 1987

Frank E. Huggett – VICTORIAN ENGLAND AS SEEN BY PUNCH – Book Club Associates 1978

Michael Manley – A HISTORY OF WEST INDIES CRICKET – Andre Deutsch 1988

Ronald Mason – JACK HOBBS – Pavilion Books 1988

Michael Meyer (ed) - SUMMER DAYS – Methuen Ltd 1981

Louis Palgrave – THE STORY OF THE OVAL – Cornish 1949
(Story of the SCCC from the turn of the century)

Gordon Ross – THE SURREY STORY – Stanley Paul 1957

Richard Streeton – P.G.H. FENDER – Pavilion Books 1987

E.W. Swanton – BACK PAGE CRICKET – Queen Anne Press 1987

E.W. Swanton – AS I SAID AT THE TIME – William Collins 1983

A.J.P. Taylor – ENGLISH HISTORY 1914–1945 – Oxford University Press 1965

Sir Pelham Warner – LORDS 1787–1945 – Pavilion Books Ltd 1987

WHO WAS WHO 1897–1915 – A & C Black, London 1920

G.M. Young – VICTORIAN ENGLAND, PORTRAIT OF AN AGE – Oxford University Press 1953

SURVEY OF LONDON XXVI: Parish of St Mary Lambeth Pt II: Southern Area – Athlone Press, London 1956 pp 22–24

Wherever possible I have tried to use eye witnesses as sources of information, and have therefore drawn heavily on contemporary newspaper reports in *The Times, The Manchester Guardian, Morning Post, Daily Telegraph, The Cricketer, The Sportsman, Daily Mail, Evening News, Evening Standard,* and others.

The facts and figures come mainly from *Wisden*, various years, editions and editors. Some of the statistics relating to Surrey players come from the Surrey County Cricket Club Yearbooks.

The backbone of this book comes from the records of the Surrey County Cricket Club.

Wherever possible, the author and the publishers have credited the copyright owners of the illustrations reproduced in this book. We apologise for any omissions.

Index

References in italics indicate illustrations